YANKEES 1936-39, BASEBALL'S GREATEST DYNASTY

Also by Stanley Cohen

The Game They Played (1977, 2001)

The Man in the Crowd: Confessions of a Sports Addict (1981)

A Magic Summer: The '69 Mets (1988, 2003)

Dodgers! The First 100 Years (1990)

Willie's Game (with Willie Mosconi, 1993)

Tough Talk (with Martin Garbus, 1998)

The Wrong Men: America's Epidemic of Wrongful Death Row Convictions (2003)

The Execution of Officer Becker (2006)

Beating the Odds (with Brandon Lang, 2009)

The Man in the Crowd: A Fan's Notes on Four Generations of New York Baseball (2012)

Convicting the Innocent: Death Row and America's Broken System of Justice (2016)

YANKEES 1936-39, BASEBALL'S GREATEST DYNASTY

LOU GEHRIG, JOE DIMAGGIO, AND THE BIRTH OF A NEW ERA

STANLEY COHEN

Skyhorse Publishing

A Herman Graf Book

Skyhorse Publishing books may be purchased in bulk at special discounts for sales promotion, corporate gifts, fund-raising, or educational purposes. Special editions can also be created to specifications. For details, contact the Special Sales Department, Skyhorse Publishing, 307 West 36th Street, 11th Floor, New York, NY 10018 or info@skyhorsepublishing.com.

Skyhorse® and Skyhorse Publishing® are registered trademarks of Skyhorse Publishing, Inc.®, a Delaware corporation.

Visit our website at www.skyhorsepublishing.com.

10 9 8 7 6 5 4 3 2 1

Library of Congress Cataloging-in-Publication Data is available on file.

Cover design by Brian Peterson
Cover photo credit: AP Images

Print ISBN: 978-1-5107-2063-3
Ebook ISBN: 978-1-5107-2064-0

Printed in the United States of America

To the Entire Cast

Linda and Greg
Steve and Monique
Michael and Jessica
Sammi and Matt
and, as always,
my co-producer and life's partner, Betty

Contents

"Baseball isn't statistics; it's Joe DiMaggio rounding second."

—Jimmy Breslin

1936

With Joe DiMaggio in the lineup, the Yankees win their first
World Series since 1932, the start of baseball's first true dynasty.

1

A Savior Arrives from Out of the West

Back in the day, when baseball was truly the national pas-time, the game seemed to reflect the shifts in style and mood that defined its era. It was as if the texture of the sport was sewn into the fabric of its time, its pulse measured beat-for-beat by the events taking place around it.

The Yankees of the 1920s embodied that decade in its every aspect. It was, after all, the Roaring Twenties—the Jazz Age, when the country bounced to its own tune, full of the snap and sizzle of champagne pop, flappers strutting to the frenzied rhythms of the Charleston, speakeasies humming with a wink and a nod. True to their time, the Yankees of the twenties won with flair and flourish, with an air of superiority that would soon become the logo of the franchise. The dead-ball era was over, and just in time for Babe Ruth to explode upon the scene in a spanking new Yankee Stadium, with its short right-field porch tucked into a cavernous depth that gave it the intimidat-ing aura of a Roman coliseum. The Bambino, who dwarfed ev-erything around him, was the incarnation of the 1920s in both size and performance, a boisterous, fearless Caravaggio who did what he did better than anyone had done it before him.

The Yankees won six pennants during the twenties, the last in 1928, but their reign ended a year later, the year the New York Stock Market crashed and the Great Depression descended upon the nation. The early thirties belonged to the St. Louis Cardinals, a team that became known, appropriately enough, as the Gas House Gang. The Cards were a perfect fit for their time, tough and relentless and without the slightest suggestion of grandeur or majesty. They were a hardscrabble, grind-it-out band that featured the likes of Frankie Frisch, Pepper Martin, Ripper Collins, Joe Medwick, and Leo Durocher who, it was said, gave the team its sobriquet. The Cards, who won pennants in 1930, '31, and '34, often took the field in scruffy, unwashed uniforms, forging an identity with fans who understood the need to make do. They had a ball club that shared the deprivations of the times.

By mid-decade, the times had begun to change. The nation was still in the grip of the depression, but the tide seemed about to turn. Unemployment, as high as 25 percent in 1933, had dipped to 17 percent by 1936. Attendance at Yankee Stadium, which had dropped precipitously in 1934 and '35, rose sharply by almost one-third. It was a time of measured optimism, hopeful but cautious. There was the growing sense that things would eventually right themselves if attention was paid and the work that had to be done was done with dispatch and efficiency. Production rather than style was the key to recovery.

It was a mood that was nutrient for the Yankees of 1936, the rookie year of the incomparable Joe DiMaggio, the start of baseball's greatest dynasty. The Yankees would go on to win four consecutive World Series, and they did it with room to spare. They finished an average of nearly fifteen games ahead of the second-place team. They won their four World Series by an overall margin of 16–3, sweeping the last two. The 1936 team featured six future Hall of Fame players and a manager that would bring the total to seven. And that was just the beginning. They seemed to improve every year. The '39 team, the last of the dynasty, was, by any measure, the best of them all.

But 1936 was the transformative year; it represented an awakening of sorts. The Yankees had dominated the twenties in devastating fashion. Driven by the power tandem of Ruth and Lou Gehrig, they had won six pennants between 1921 and '28. The 1927 team, considered by many as the best of all time, was known as Murderers' Row and for good reason. They won 110 games, finishing nineteen games ahead of the second-place Athletics, and then swept the Pittsburgh Pirates in the World Series. They squeaked through by a narrower margin the following year, their third league championship in a row, and then it all stopped.

In 1929, the Yankees crashed, along with the stock market. They fell into their own depression, albeit briefly, finishing behind Connie Mack's Athletics by margins of nineteen, sixteen, and thirteen-and-a-half games from 1929 to '31. They made a brief recovery in 1932, defeating the Chicago Cubs in the World Series, but it was the last of the Ruthian years. His numbers sagged the following season and fell off the charts in 1934, his final year as a Yankee. The Yanks finished second that year, as they had the year before, and began the 1935 season without Ruth in the lineup for the first time since 1919. The power burden fell squarely upon the shoulders of Lou Gehrig, but without Ruth hitting ahead of him, he found himself exposed as the team's only home run threat. He had won the Triple Crown (leading the league in batting average, home runs, and runs batted in) in 1934 but saw his figures tail off a bit a year later. Although a batting average of .329 with 30 homers and 119 RBIs would have been an outstanding season for most players, it was a significant drop from his .363, 49, and 165 the previous year.

Still, the Yankees made a respectable show of it in 1935. The pitching staff, led by Red Ruffing and Lefty Gomez and buttressed by Johnny Allen and Johnny Broaca, compensated somewhat for the power shortage, and the team was in the hunt well into September. They had started the season in good form and led the league in late July, but then the Detroit Tigers, defending league champions, got hot. They put together winning streaks of ten and nine games and slipped past the Yankees into first place on July 26. Detroit stayed hot right on through Labor Day and, on September 8, led the league by ten games. But the Yankees had one last burst left in them. They closed the season winning eight of their last nine games and finished just three lengths off the pace. It was a significant improvement over the previous season when they had ended up seven games in back of Detroit.

There seemed to be reason for hope as 1936 dawned, but the Tigers were a formidable outfit. After clinching the pennant, they polished off the Chicago Cubs, four games to two. Remarkably enough, they had never won a World Series before, not even during the glory years of Ty Cobb when they lost three in a row, from 1907 to '09. In the first two, they had fallen victim to the Cubs of "Tinker to Evers to Chance" fame by margins of 4–0 and 4–1. A year later, they lost to Honus Wagner's Pittsburgh Pirates in seven games. It took twenty-five years for them to get another shot at it, but in 1934, they were beaten 4–3 by the St. Louis Cardinals Gas House Gang, losing all four games to the brothers Dean—two each to Dizzy and Paul. Now, champions at last, they were looking ahead to a future that offered the promise of fame and glory.

Their pitching staff featured Tommy Bridges and Schoolboy Rowe, who between them had accounted for eighty-six wins in the two previous seasons. Mickey Cochrane, voted the league's Most Valuable Player in 1934, was behind the plate, and a sound infield had Charlie Gehringer at second base and the 1935 MVP, Hank Greenberg, at first. Greenberg was to the Tigers what Ruth had been to the Yankees. At age twenty-four, he already had taken his place among baseball's power elite. In 1935, while batting .328, he led the league in RBIs with 170; total bases, 389; extra base hits, 98; and tied Jimmy Foxx for the lead in home runs with 36. At the All-Star break Greenberg had driven in 103 runs, a record that still stands, but was not selected to the All-Star team. He was, however, the unanimous choice for MVP at season's end.

The Yankees, for their part, certainly had the credentials of a worthy adversary. Gehrig, still in his prime, was ready to return to form in 1936. Named the first Yankee captain since

Everett Scott eleven years earlier, he would continue to bat cleanup and produce runs in a lineup studded with .300 hitters and enough power to give a pitcher cause for concern. At second base, Tony Lazzeri was a charter member of Murderers' Row, having debuted in 1926 with 18 home runs and 114 runs batted in while hitting .275. Frank Crosetti was in the early stages of a long career—twenty-seven years—with the Yankees at shortstop and later as third-base coach. Three players—Red Rolfe, the slick-fielding third baseman; outfielder George Selkirk; and relief pitcher Johnny Murphy—were all brought up from their Triple-A Newark farm team in 1934 and went on to play prominent roles in the dynasty that would follow. The pitching staff was anchored by Red Ruffing and Lefty Gomez. Ruffing was another gift (Ruth, of course, was the first) from the Boston Red Sox. Having compiled a record of 39–93 with the Sox, he turned into the ace of the Yankees' staff, winning at least twenty games each season during the dynasty years from 1936–39. At the other end of the battery was Bill Dickey, destined for the Hall of Fame along with Ruffing, Gomez, Gehrig, and Lazzeri. It was already an imposing cast that was headed toward the 1936 season, but the pulse of anticipation was quickened by the prospect of the long-awaited appearance of a rookie from the San Francisco Seals by the name of Joe DiMaggio.

The Seals played in the Pacific Coast League, which occupied a special status in those pre-flight days. It was viewed as a shade better than the Triple-A minor league, though not quite on a par with the majors. And everyone who was paid to keep an eye on fresh talent knew that a twenty-one-year-old kid named Joe DiMaggio, the middle of three baseball-playing brothers, was tearing the league apart. In 1933, his rookie season, he batted .340 with 28 home runs and 169 RBIs. Along the way, he hit safely in sixty-one consecutive games, still a record for professional baseball. From that point on, his every movement was tracked closely by every major-league team.

In those years, long before players were drafted in an orderly sequence and decades before computer technology had put its hand to the wheel, it was left to a special birddog breed to find major-league talent wherever it was. They were called scouts, and if they were really good they could earn a place in baseball legend that would memorialize their names alongside those they had discovered. Paul Krichell, who signed Lou Gehrig to a Yankee contract in 1923 after seeing him hit two home runs in a game at Columbia University, fills an Internet site more than ninety years later. Two West Coast scouts for the Yankees, Joe Devine and Bill Essick, enjoyed an equally enlightening experience ten years later when they saw the eighteen-year-old DiMaggio in his rookie season. But they were not alone in their discovery. The entire baseball world would soon know that he was as close to a sure thing as one was likely to find— Ty Cobb and Babe Ruth rolled into one.

However, some reservations surfaced the following season. DiMaggio tore cartilage in his knee while stepping out of a taxi cab at Fisherman's Wharf, and, in a shortened season, his numbers fell off drastically. Scouts grew tentative and major-league owners became wary of paying too high a price for damaged goods. Devine had an orthopedist examine the knee, and the verdict was that he would recover fully. The Yankees decided to make their move while the market price was depressed. When the 1934 season ended, they sent five minor-league players and $25,000 to San Francisco for the rights to DiMaggio and waited anxiously to see how he fared with the injured knee in one more season with the Seals. The results were more than gratifying. DiMaggio led the league in almost every department while being voted Most Valuable Player. He batted .398 with 34 homers and 154 RBIs. Also among his phenomenal total of 270 hits were 48 doubles and 18 triples. He was one of baseball's rarest commodities—a power hitter who seldom struck out. And yet, his batting achievements were only part of the story. Beyond statistical measure was the fact that DiMaggio was at least as good in the field and on the bases as he was at the plate.

Rarely had expectations been so high for a player who had yet to put on a major-league uniform. It was not just on-field performance that DiMaggio was expected to contribute; it was his unspoken mission to replace Babe Ruth, to become the face of the team and embrace its destiny. It was the equal of asking someone to fit a mold that had already been cast and broken. Ruth was a figure around whom legends were woven. It was said that a boy who was paralyzed rose from his bed and walked when Ruth delivered on a promise to hit a home run for him. In the 1932 World Series against the Cubs, Ruth stepped into the batter's box and pointed his bat in the direction of the center field fence, then dispatched Charlie Root's next pitch precisely to that part of the ballpark. The question, never directly answered, was whether Ruth had engaged in prophesy or was merely pointing at the pitcher as if to give warning. But it didn't really matter. No one asks for a replay of the race between the tortoise and the hare, and no one cares whether Icarus actually flew too close to the sun. Mythology survives on its own terms, and no mythological figure on the planet had the stature of Babe Ruth.

DiMaggio, whose very name suggested the presence of magic, had begun to inhabit his own myth even before he set foot in the Bronx. Ruth was now retired but Gehrig was still in his prime and the presumptive heir to the unofficial title of team leader. He was arguably as good as any player in the game and was in fact named team captain in 1934, a post that had remained vacant for more than forty years after his departure. But Gehrig, though a favorite of both teammates and fans, never seemed to endow the team with a personality that was all its own. He was uniquely himself, a man to be admired for what he was but whose style was not suited for export. It did not infiltrate the mood of those around him. And it did not help that, despite his league-leading achievements, the Yankees had not won a pennant in the past three years; they had never won a championship without Ruth in the lineup.

DiMaggio, by contrast, carried himself with a style that seemed to alter the shape of whatever landscape he inhabited. It was a subliminal message that was sent silently, without ostentation or the slightest suggestion of bravado. A bit shy and somewhat formal of manner, DiMaggio would stride upon the New York stage with the aplomb of Olivier about to deliver *Hamlet* to the waiting audience once the curtain rose. It was as if he had just stepped down from Mount Olympus but saw nothing special about his address. He was not arrogant or given to the bluster that would define great athletes of a future generation. While others stood in awe of his magisterial presence, DiMaggio seemed entirely unaware of the magic he turned loose simply by entering the field. There was no plan or road map that he followed. Those who appropriate the mystique of the gods do so by instinct only.

So it appeared from the moment he arrived on the scene, when he put on the pinstripes with the No. 9 on the back of the jersey (he did not wear No. 5, which put him in sequence with Ruth's 3 and Gehrig's 4, until the following season), the New York Yankees were DiMaggio's team. Now discarded was the image of 1920s sparkle and flash, the overwhelming sense of transcendence that Ruth brought to the team. DiMaggio's Yankees would be sober and businesslike. They won with a mechanical efficiency that would define them for decades. One needed to get the job done as quickly and efficiently as possible. No points were given for style.

Prior to the 1936 season, DiMaggio, Lazzeri, and Crosetti, all from the Bay Area in San Francisco, drove east together to the Yankees' spring training site in St. Petersburg, Florida. None of the three was much given to conversation, and it was said that during the five- or six-day drive the only sound in the car came when Lazzeri cleared his throat. Crosetti asked, "Did you say something?" and Lazzeri said, "No."

DiMaggio's arrival was awaited with the breathless anticipation of the Second Coming. The New York papers were filled with news from training camp. There, surrounded by palm trees and a landscape that instilled a sense of serenity and quiet purpose, were photographs of the Yankees in their pinstripe uniforms getting ready for the start of the season. There were many photos of DiMaggio—close-up head shots, his nostrils flared like those of a thoroughbred racehorse; others showed him in his spread-eagle batting stance, bat held high, motionless, awaiting a pitch he was certain to propel into the far reaches of the ballpark. John Thorn, the official historian of major league baseball, offered this description of DiMaggio's stance: "He was like the Colossus of Rhodes, with ships sailing between his legs." Even up north in New York, one could almost smell the warmth of the sunlit afternoon, the air light and sweet; time, moving slowly, now frozen in a moment of expectation. Spring training had finally arrived; the start of the season was just weeks away.

2

An Auspicious Beginning Ends with a Setback

Spring training was a more serious endeavor back then, before the advent of television, before the Internet, before technology had made its presence felt. There was at the time no overlap among the sports seasons. The NFL and college bowl games had closed shop in December, so football was a distant memory. There were no professional basketball leagues of any consequence in the thirties, the NCAA and NIT college basketball tournaments were still on the horizon, and ice hockey's Stanley Cup playoffs ended in early spring, before the start of the baseball season.

In any event, baseball was the only professional sport that really mattered at the time. Fans counted down the days until training camps opened and the pre-season games were played with earnest intent. With only sixteen teams divided neatly into two leagues and a reserve clause that tied players to a team in perpetuity, there tended to be little change in most lineups from season to season. The games, especially those between contending teams, were considered a prelude to what lay ahead, and most teams used their starting players right from the start of what was glibly called the Grapefruit League season. That's as it was when the Yankees opened their spring training season against the St. Louis Cardinals on Tuesday, March 17.

The Cards, still composed mostly of the old Gas House Gang, had won the world championship in 1934 and finished second by four games to the Chicago Cubs a year later. Their starting lineup included, among the regulars, Terry Moore in center field flanked by Pepper Martin and Joe Medwick; Johnny Mize at first base; Frankie Frisch at second; and Leo Durocher at shortstop. The Yankees played their regular infield: Lou Gehrig at first, Tony Lazzeri at second, Frank Crosetti at shortstop, and Red Rolfe at third. The outfield featured Joe DiMaggio, batting third in the order, playing center field.

The brutal winter-like weather on this St. Patrick's Day was likely the reason that a crowd of only about two thousand turned up at Waterfront Park in St. Petersburg, Florida. According to James P. Dawson, writing in the *New York Times*, spectators wore overcoats to protect them from "a blustery wind that blew out of the north with gale-like force." The start of the game was delayed while "the infield was rendered presentable by burning gasoline."

It did not seem to be a matter of concern that the Cardinals won the game 8–7. DiMaggio owned the headlines. In his first game in pinstripes, he went four-for-five, including a triple, drove in two runs, and scored two others and, wrote Dawson, he made "a glittering catch of Charley Gelbert's long fly in deep center starting the seventh . . . If there was any doubt about this newcomer, he dispelled it today." The Cards had 14 hits, four of them by Frisch, and capitalized on six Yankee errors. They beat the Yanks again the following day 6–5 but DiMaggio once more captured the headlines, going two-for-four, with another triple.

The return of baseball and the dazzling audition of DiMaggio were a welcome distraction from other events that had begun to intrude on a wider scale. Just ten days before the Yanks and Cardinals played their first game, Adolf Hitler sent German troops to reoccupy the Rhineland in defiance of the Treaty of Versailles, which had been drafted at the end of World War I. It was just the first step in a series of brazen moves that would eventually plunge the world into war. Storm clouds were drifting across the European continent, but most of the world seemed to be looking the other way. There were troubles at home, too. Dust Bowl problems continued to plague the Midwest and prairie states. Many miles of crops and pasturelands were ruined. Farmers and their families suffered severe health problems and began a trek west, mostly to California. With these issues tugging at the heart of a nation still in the throes of the Depression, baseball was a balm that helped ease the tension, and DiMaggio provided the focus. It was an unlikely role for the twenty-one-year-old son of an Italian immigrant.

Joseph Paul DiMaggio was born on November 25, 1914, in Martinez, California, just northeast of San Francisco. He was the eighth of nine children, one of five sons. A year after Joe was born, the family moved to The City, as San Francisco was called, where his father, Giuseppe, resumed his work as a fisherman. The plan was for his five sons to take up the fishing trade as had generations of DiMaggios before him. But just two of the boys were interested. The other three, despite their father's protestations, moved in an entirely different direction—they became major-league baseball players.

Baseball was more than a pastime in San Francisco. It was played on all levels. Joe played shortstop for several amateur and semipro teams while his older brother, nineteen-year-old Vince, was an outfielder for the San Francisco Seals, the cream of the Pacific Coast League. The Seals found themselves in need of a shortstop near the end of the 1932 season, and Vince persuaded manager Ike Caveney to give his seventeen-year-old brother a chance. Joe played the final three games of the season and was signed to a contract in 1933 for $225 a month. He was moved to the outfield because his strong but erratic arm was deemed too much of a risk at shortstop. The outfield was exactly right for Joe. He covered vast swaths of ground with his long, loping strides and seemed to have a radar-like sense of exactly where the ball was headed and where it would descend—and, more often than not, he was in precisely the right spot for the ball to drop harmlessly into his glove. Years later, when he was playing for the Yankees, a reporter suggested that in order to get to the ball in time, he had to leave with the crack of the bat. No, said DiMaggio, the crack of the bat would be much too late; you have to get going as soon as the batter starts his swing.

Joe wasted little time in putting his batting skills on display. It was in his rookie season that he hit safely in sixty-one consecutive games, and curiously enough it was the hitting streak that turned him into a baseball aficionado. "Baseball really didn't get into my blood until I knocked off that hitting streak," he said. "Getting a daily hit became more important to me than eating, drinking, or sleeping. Overnight, I became a personality." His future stardom seemed assured, and he got to the major leagues a season ahead of his older brother. Vince, a sound but unspectacular player, left San Diego of the Pacific Coast League for the Boston Bees (soon to be renamed the Braves) at the end of the 1936 season. He batted .256 as a rookie, but he clearly had nowhere near the promise of his brother. The following year, although he led his team in home runs with the rather paltry total of fourteen, he batted only .228 and set a National League record for strikeouts with 134, almost 100 more than Joe. The third DiMaggio, Dom, would have a long and distinguished career with the Boston Red Sox from 1940 to 1953. Joe, of course, was at the threshold of a storied career that would earn him a place among baseball's immortals.

Recognized as the team leader even before he played his first game as a Yankee, he was the driving force that spearheaded the team to its record four straight championships. He is probably best remembered for his fifty-six-game hitting streak in 1941, a year he led the league in RBIs with 125 while batting .357 and hitting 30 home runs. That season, he won his second of three Most Valuable Player awards, beating out Boston's Ted Williams who batted .406 and remains the last player to reach the .400 mark. The hitting streak, a record that still stands and is unlikely ever to be matched, appears even more remarkable when it is noted that in his 223 times at bat during its course he struck out only five times. In fact, he struck out only thirteen times in his 541 at-bats during the season.

After spending three prime seasons—from 1943 to 1945—in the service during World War II, DiMaggio was never quite the same when he returned at the age of thirty-one. But he was still good enough. In 1946, he batted .290 with 25 home runs and 95 runs batted in, and he remained the unquestioned team leader. Though he continued to play through 1951, 1948 was his last great season in terms of statistics. Despite playing with a bone spur in this right heel, he led the league in home runs with 39 and RBIs with 155 while batting .320. In sum, his post-war batting average was .304, with an average of 24 home runs a year, compared with .339 and 31 homers a year between 1936 and 1942.

Over the course of his career, DiMaggio hit .325 with 361 home runs and 1,537 RBIs. He was an All-Star in each of his thirteen seasons. He was named MVP three times and finished in the top nine of ballots cast seven other times. Perhaps most impressive was his strikeout record. In 6,821 times at bat, he struck out only 369 times, only eight more than his total of home runs—an average of once every 18.5 times at bat.

Statistics, however, are no way to define what DiMaggio was. To some degree, his stature was described by the sports columnist Jim Murray who wrote: "Joe DiMaggio played the game at least a couple of levels higher than the rest of baseball. A lot of guys, all you had to see to know they were great was a stat sheet. DiMaggio, you had to see. It wasn't only numbers on a page—although they were there too—it was a question of command, style, grace."

The spring training season moved right along with the Yankees showing their potential and DiMaggio displaying his. He batted .600 during the first week and tailed off just a bit throughout March and into April. But early in April, not long before opening day, DiMaggio suffered a freak mishap that caused him to miss the first seventeen games of the regular season. He had suffered a minor foot injury, and as part a new heat therapy technology, his foot was attached to a diathermy apparatus. The team doctor, Doc Painter, left the room for too long, and DiMaggio's foot was burned seriously enough to sideline him for a month.

Still, the team's pre-season performance had to be considered a solid success, and the outlook was promising. The Yankees had, after all, closed fast at the end of the 1935 season, and the core of that team, still in its prime, would be returning. The addition of DiMaggio was expected to offset the Tigers' acquisition of future Hall of Fame outfielder Al Simmons. With hopes high and the future beckoning, the team packed its bags and headed north. They would open the season on April 14 in the nation's capital against the Washington Senators.

The day came up overcast with a mid-April chill in the air, not unusual in Washington that time of year. President Franklin Delano Roosevelt, following a tradition that began with William Howard Taft in 1910, threw out the first ball before a crowd of 31,000. It was a cheerful FDR, clad in overcoat and fedora, who made the toss while cameras flashed and the crowd applauded. He was nearing the completion of his successful first term and on the way to a landslide victory over Kansas Governor Alf Landon.

The hometown team was looking ahead to what would be a far less sanguine future. The Senators, perennial contenders during the early thirties and league champions in 1933, had slipped badly. They finished sixth in 1934 and seventh, next to last place in the old eight-team leagues, the following year. But they would start the new season auspiciously. In a breathless pitchers' duel, Washington's Bobo Newsom got the better of Lefty Gomez. The game was scoreless going into the bottom of the ninth, but it ended quickly when Carl Reynolds opened the inning with a double and the next batter, Cecil Travis, drove him home for a 1–0 opening-day victory.

Manager Joe McCarthy had chosen Gomez over Red Ruffing to start the season despite his having a losing record, 12–15, in 1935. Gomez had been a twenty-game winner in three of the previous four seasons. In 1934, he had his best year, going 26–5. Ruffing, the Boston import, would have to wait a year before becoming the ace of the staff, winning twenty or more games in each season of the team's four-year dynasty.

Gomez was one of the most popular Yankees, a fan favorite and a prized teammate. His comedic antics became part of his legacy. They had earned him the nickname "Goofy," and he reveled in being called Goofy Gomez. In the years to come, he was one of a very small group of players who could coax a laugh from an innately serious, if not solemn, Joe DiMaggio. His most celebrated gesture of comic relief would occur during the 1936 World Series against the New York Giants. With runners on base and Mel Ott, who had already tagged Gomez for a homer, at the plate representing the potential tying run,

Gomez casually stepped off the mound and gazed skyward at a plane that had just taken flight from nearby LaGuardia Airport. Lefty did not think there was anything particularly remarkable about taking such a pause in the midst of a World Series game. How is it any different, he asked, from stepping off the mound to tie your shoelace?

Named Vernon Louis at birth in Rodeo, California, Gomez was the son of a father whose roots were Spanish and a mother of Welsh-Irish descent. He often was referred to as Mexican American and earned another nickname, the Gay Castilian, when the term "gay" had an entirely different meaning from what it has today. He came of age in Oakland, part of the same San Francisco Bay Area that produced the Italian trio of DiMaggio, Lazzeri, and Crosetti. After playing on the local sandlots, he signed with the San Francisco Seals and was purchased by the Yankees for $39,000, a bit more than they paid for DiMaggio.

His first appearance for the Yanks came in 1930 in a relief role, and he finished the season with a 2–5 mark. He hit his stride the following year, winning twenty-one games, then twenty-four the next season, and twenty-six in 1934. As effective as he was on the mound, he was just so inept at bat. His lifetime batting average was an anemic .147. In 904 at-bats, he never hit a home run or a triple and very few doubles. After one of his two-base hits, he was immediately picked off second base. When he returned to the dugout, McCarthy asked him what happened. "How should I know?" Gomez said, "I've never been there before."

In a classic exchange with an umpire, Gomez came to bat on a foggy afternoon with the hard-throwing Bob Feller on the mound. Just before stepping into the batter's box, Gomez struck a match. "What's the big idea?" the umpire asked. "Do you think that match will help you see Feller's fast one?" "No," Gomez replied, "I'm not concerned about that. I just want to make sure he can see me."

Gomez and the rest of the staff enjoyed the luxury of excellent defense up the middle of the diamond, covered as it was by three players of Italian descent—Lazzeri at second, Crosetti at shortstop, and DiMaggio in center field. In those less sensitive times, it was not always considered an insult to use ethnic terms, such as "dago" for an Italian, which would be verboten in the years ahead. So it was that during a game in 1936, with men on base and less than two out, Gomez fielded a sharp one-hop drive and threw the ball to Lazzeri at second, ignoring Crosetti who was covering third. When Gomez returned to the dugout, McCarthy demanded an explanation. Gomez explained: "When I got the ball, I heard someone shout 'throw it to the dago,' but he didn't say which dago." "Maybe I should be thankful," McCarthy replied, "that you didn't throw it to DiMaggio."

DiMaggio also played a role in another tale of Gomez's flippancy. In a game at Yankee Stadium, the Detroit slugger Hank Greenberg hit a drive to the deepest reaches of center field. DiMaggio turned his back to the plate and took off in the direction of the center-field flagpole, more than 450 feet from home plate. When he reached its base, he turned just in time to meet the ball's descent. Walking off the field at the end of the inning, Gomez crossed paths with Greenberg and said, "Got you to go for a bad one, didn't I?" The remark was appropriate enough. Over the years, Gomez often joked that the secret of his success was "clean living and a fast outfield."

One of Gomez's favorite lines, often repeated when events spun in his favor, was "I'd rather be lucky than good." He was, of course, both. He won twenty-plus games four times and was an All-Star every year from 1933 to 1939. He led the league twice each in wins, winning percentage, and ERA. He had his best season in 1934 when he posted a record of 26–5. In both 1934 and 1937, he won pitching's Triple Crown, leading the league in wins, ERA, and strikeouts. He won six World Series games without a loss, a career record.

Gomez's narrow loss in the opener foretold the early part of the season for the Yankees. They got off to an indifferent start, losing three of their first four games. Still, there was little cause for concern. By any standard, the Yankees' lineup was solid from top to bottom, and McCarthy went with much the same cast game-for-game: Red Rolfe, 3B; Roy Johnson, LF; George Selkirk, RF; Lou Gehrig, 1B; Bill Dickey, C; Ben Chapman, CF (until DiMaggio was ready); Tony Lazzeri, 2B; Frank Crosetti, SS; and the pitcher.

There was, of course, no designated hitter in the thirties, and there would be none for nearly forty years. Nor had the concept of platooning—matching right-hand batters against left-hand pitchers and vice versa—yet manifested itself. Lineups by and large remained stable; pitchers took the mound with only three days' rest and were expected to pitch a complete game. The ritual of the pitch count lay far in the future; relief pitchers were a relatively new commodity and were brought into the game only when the starting pitcher had begun to falter. Games were played in the afternoon beneath the sun of summer, and they moved along quickly. Rare was the game that dragged on for three hours, and it was not unusual to complete a game in less than two. The season opener had taken just two hours and thirteen minutes.

The next day's game took a few minutes longer as a lot more runs were scored, but the result was the same. The Yanks suffered a second straight one-run loss. They seemed to have the game under control with a 5–0 lead after five innings, but Monte Pearson, who had been obtained from Cleveland in a trade for Johnny Allen in the off-season, gave up a pair of runs in the sixth, and when the leadoff batter opened the seventh with a single, McCarthy called for Johnny Murphy, the Yankees' prime reliever. Murphy was not at his best that day. He yielded a double to the leadoff batter, and after an error by Rolfe at third loaded the bases, Murphy gave up a single, a double, and two walks, which accounted for a total of four runs and a 6–5 Senators lead, and that was how the game ended.

It was a rare unsuccessful effort for Murphy, who was one of the first relief specialists of his time. Relief pitching was an entirely different proposition in those days. The bullpen was not the critical factor that it became decades later. For the most part, teams had only one relief specialist; some had none. A pitching staff consisted of a four-man starting rotation and a cluster of spot starters who filled in when the schedule grew crowded, most often with doubleheaders, which were a regular practice at the time. They also were hailed from the bullpen when the starting pitcher needed help or when the game was out of reach one way or the other. Johnny Murphy was an exception.

A product of the Bronx, Murphy was a graduate of Fordham Prep and Fordham University. He came to the Yankees in 1934, started twenty games, and posted a record of 14–10. The following year, he started only eight times and began specializing in relief. He registered seven saves (a statistic that did not exist in the thirties) and had a 10–5 win-loss record. From that point on, he was used almost exclusively in relief, setting the standard for what was to come. There were no designated relievers at that time. Starters were expected to complete their games. Relief pitchers generally were those past their prime or those who had not yet reached theirs. Members of the starting rotation were often called upon in crucial situations.

Murphy, who sat quietly in the bullpen until peril called for his appearance, was the exception. But he was not what would later become known as a closer, a ninth-inning specialist who came in with a three-run lead and picked up a save by retiring the side before giving up three runs. He usually entered the game with men on base and the opposing team threatening. It was his job "to put out the fire," and for that reason, he was nicknamed "The Fireman."

Though Yankee starters still completed the vast majority of their games, Murphy, whose "out pitch" was a devastating curveball, was relied upon to bail them out when the need arose. Gomez was often the beneficiary of his efforts. When asked how many games he expected to win one season, Gomez responded, "Ask Murphy."

Although the save was not an official statistic in the thirties, applying the formula retroactively, Murphy led the league four times in five seasons. His 19 saves in 1939 were second in history only to Firpo Marberry's 22 for the 1926 Washington Senators. Murphy made the All-Star team three years in a row, from 1937 to 1939. He pitched in six winning World Series and posted a 2–0 record while compiling an ERA of 1.10, along with four saves in eight games.

Having lost twice to open the season, the Yankees righted the ship and entered the win column by turning around the previous day's score and winning the last of the three-game series 6–5. Now, they were headed home to the Bronx. Awaiting them were the Boston Red Sox who were undefeated in their first three games. The Yankee–Red Sox rivalry was not yet as intense as it would become in the post–World War II years. It had begun in 1920, not with a game, ironically enough, but with a business venture. Boston owner Harry Frazee sold Babe Ruth to the Yankees for $125,000, presumably to fund a Broadway show. From that point on, the Red Sox, a formidable outfit in the teens, fell on hard times. In the eleven-year period from 1922 to 1932, they finished last nine times. In 1932, they lost 111 games and finished 69½ games behind the first-place Yankees. The difference in performance between the two teams since the purchase of Ruth became known as the Curse of the Bambino, and it would persist to one degree or another until 2004 when the Sox finally defeated their rivals in the American League playoffs.

But Boston had every reason to be optimistic when they helped the Yankees open their home season in 1936 before

22,256 spectators. Their starting pitcher was Lefty Grove, perhaps the best left-hander ever to take the mound. Beginning in 1925 with the Philadelphia Athletics, Grove had won twenty or more games seven years in a row, including thirty-one in 1931. In 1935, with the Red Sox, he posted a mark of 20–12. Ruffing started for the Yankees on a dismal, dreary day. Clouds filled the sky and a cold wind swept through the stands. So far as the Yankees were concerned, the weather fit the mood of the day. The game was no contest. The Sox opened a five-run lead after four innings and won the game by an 8–0 margin. Grove did not disappoint. He pitched a two-hitter, both singles by Lou Gehrig.

The Yankees recovered quickly. Gomez defeated the Red Sox 3–2 the following day. They then won four of their next five and, after another loss to Boston, they won five straight, putting them into second place, a half-game behind the Red Sox with a record of 11–6. Everyone in the lineup had been playing well. Crosetti, moved into the leadoff spot, was hitting around .400. Outfielder Ben Chapman was well above that mark; Gehrig and Dickey were not that far behind. The eleven victories were distributed among six pitchers, Gomez leading the way with three. And now, on Sunday, May 3, the Yanks were about to go into high gear. The second largest crowd of the season, upwards of 25,000, turned out to see the Yankees take on the lowly St. Louis Browns. The visiting team was not the attraction. Joe DiMaggio, batting third and playing left field, was about to play his first game as a Yankee.

3

The Yanks Take Charge, and New York Embraces DiMaggio

America was in need of a hero. The country had flexed its muscles during World War I, and then, in the twenties, it flourished in a manner that suggested a coronation. Suddenly, it seemed, the relatively young nation had become a world leader. Its economy thrived; its military might could no longer be questioned; its production lines moved swiftly; and technologically, it was breaking new ground. But when the decade ended, the bottom fell out. The Depression hit with a crash in the fall of 1929. The economy was in free fall, and with Europe increasingly under siege, the mood of the country had turned somber. The upbeat rhythms of the Jazz Age now, in the early thirties, were being played in a minor key.

By mid-decade, however, the outlook had begun to brighten. FDR's New Deal offered hope in place of resignation, but a piece of the puzzle was still missing. The country yearned for a symbol of transcendence, a presence that carried with it the promise of a destiny beyond measure, one that was capable of appropriating the magic of the gods. In times of stress, heroes come in many forms, but rarely are they accorded heroic status on the basis of potential yet unfulfilled. DiMaggio had gained such recognition on the West Coast but here, nearly three thousand miles and a five-day journey away, New York was ready to install him on the mountaintop, and the rest of the nation was looking on expectantly.

It was a bright May afternoon in the Bronx when DiMaggio debuted in left field. Lefty Gomez was on the mound for the Yankees, but it was not to be a good day for pitchers. The feeble St. Louis Browns battered the Yankee ace, scoring three runs in the first inning, another in the third, and one more at the start of the fifth when he was replaced by Johnny Murphy. But the Yankee bats were hardly silent. They drove the Browns' starter, Jack Knott, from the game after a third of an inning as they scored four runs to take a 4–3 lead. Earl Caldwell, in relief, fared not much better. He yielded five more runs in just over four innings, and the Yankees concluded matters with a 14–5 victory.

As for DiMaggio, batting third, he had a day that any rookie would relish in his introduction to the big leagues. He went three-for-six, including a triple, drove in one run and scored three more. In his first at-bat, he hit a ground ball to the pitcher that should have been a routine out. But Crosetti, who was on third after leading off with a triple, broke for the plate. Knott threw the ball away, and Crosetti scored. DiMaggio, who had reached on the error, scored the first run of his career when Gehrig walked and Ben Chapman doubled. His first hit came an inning later when he blooped a soft popup into center field, and he scored again on a sacrifice fly by Bill Dickey. He struck out in the fourth, something he would do only thirty-nine times during the entire season, but hit a triple to deep center field in the sixth, flied out in the seventh, and closed out his day with a single in the eighth. His overall performance set the tone for his rookie season and for the Yankees', as well.

They moved into first place, a half-game ahead of Boston, on May 10 with a 17–7 win over the Athletics, and it was a lead they never relinquished. It also was the occasion of DiMaggio's first home run, a drive to the opposite field with one on and one out in the first inning. From that point on, the Yankees gradually pulled away from the field. By Memorial Day, they led the Red Sox by 4½ games. By July 4, the lead was eleven games, with defending world champion Detroit now in second place. In effect, Detroit's season had ended months earlier. On April 24, Hank Greenberg broke his wrist in a collision with Washington's Jake Powell and was lost for the year. Twelve games into the season, Greenberg was batting .348 and giving every indication of putting together another season to match his 1935 Most Valuable Player exploits.

Greenberg, who grew up in the Bronx, was the first Jewish baseball player to achieve superstar status. At age twenty-four, he had already taken his place among the power elite, compiling numbers that put him in company with Ruth, Gehrig, and Jimmie Foxx. In 1935, while batting .328, he led the league in RBIs with 170; total bases, 389; extra base hits, 98; and tied with Foxx for the lead in home runs with 36. At the All-Star break, he had driven in 103 runs, a record that still stands, but he was not selected to the All-Star team. Now, with Greenberg out of the lineup, the Red Sox would provide the main competition for the Yankees the rest of the way, but at no time after mid-season did the Yanks have cause for concern.

For the most part, they were winning with power. Their pitching, with Ruffing and Monte Pearson joining Gomez in the rotation, was respectable but not dominating. It was at the plate that the team prospered. Six of the eight starters would finish the season with batting averages higher than .300, and five would drive in more than 100 runs. Gehrig was on his way to leading the league with 49 homers, while DiMaggio hit 29 and Dickey had 22. DiMaggio had 44 hits in May, a record for a rookie in his first month in the big leagues. It was at around this time that the nickname Murderers' Row began to morph into the Bronx Bombers.

Perhaps the most awesome display of raw power came in a three-game series at Philadelphia's Shibe Park on May 23 and 24. (A doubleheader was played on May 23.) The Yanks beat the Athletics by scores of 12–6, 15–1, and 25–2, adding up to 52 runs on 49 hits. They also set a record with a total of 11 home runs in two consecutive games. Second baseman Tony Lazzeri had the day of a lifetime in the final game of the series. He set a record of 11 RBIs in a single game, hitting three home runs, two of them grand slams. The grand slams came in the second and fifth innings, and his third, a solo, in the seventh. He nearly added a fourth an inning later but had to settle for a triple with two men on, bringing his RBI total for the day to 11, eclipsing Jimmie Foxx's mark of nine. Tony also hit three homers in the previous day's doubleheader, giving him a record total of six in two days. At the age of thirty-three, Lazzeri was having one of the best seasons of his fourteen-year career.

Anthony Michael "Tony" Lazzeri was the eldest of the Italian trio to come to the Yankees from the San Francisco Bay Area. He had dropped out of school to work with his father as a boiler-maker, but in 1921, at the age of eighteen, he began playing base-ball with the Salt Lake City Bees of the Pacific Coast League. He was one of scout Paul Krichell's earliest discoveries. The Yankees purchased him after the 1925 season for the bargain price of $5,000 and two marginal players. As was the case with DiMaggio ten years later, Lazzeri came cheap due to questions about his health. He was known to suffer from epilepsy, and teams that might have entered the bidding were reluctant to take a chance on him. Krichell, characteristically, was ready to roll the dice.

Lazzeri had played shortstop in the minors, but manager Miller Huggins moved him to second base, pairing him with Mark Koenig, also a rookie, as the team's double-play combi-nation. He immediately took his place in the 1926 Murder-ers' Row lineup, batting sixth behind the triumvirate of Ruth, Gehrig, and Bob Meusel. In his rookie year, he played in all 155 games, hitting .275 with 18 home runs and 114 RBIs. His home run total was third in the American League behind Ruth and Al Simmons, and he was second to Ruth in RBIs. He was a member of the original 1933 All-Star team and was given the colorful nickname of "Poosh 'Em Up," meaning "hit it out," by his Italian-speaking fans.

Lazzeri, who, early on, had become known for being averse to conversation, especially among sports writers, nonetheless had a reputation as being especially savvy on the ballfield. Reporters who groused about his reluctance to respond to their questions often celebrated his on-the-field smarts, making him a perfect foil for the antics of Lefty Gomez. Lew Freedman, in his entertaining book *DiMaggio's Yankees*, offers an illustration which, as history sometimes merges with mythology, might be a somewhat different version of the "throw it to the dago" story:

> Once, during a game, with a runner on first, Lefty Gomez fielded a grounder hit back to him. Instead of throwing the ball to Crosetti coming in to cover second as he should have, Gomez threw the ball to a nonplussed Lazzeri. As soon as the play ended, Lazzeri called time and trotted over to the mound to ask Gomez what he was thinking. 'I keep reading about how smart you are,' Gomez said. 'I wanted to see what you would do with the ball.'

Despite a Hall of Fame career, Lazzeri is best remembered for an unfortunate incident that occurred in his rookie season. Trailing the St. Louis Cardinals 3–2 in the seventh game of the 1926 World Series, Grover Cleveland Alexander, way beyond his peak at age thirty-nine and, as word had it, laboring "under the influence," strode in from the bullpen with the bases loaded and two out in the seventh inning and struck Lazzeri out on four pitches to save the Series for the Cardinals.

Long after his retirement, Lazzeri occasionally expressed regret that he was identified with that strikeout more closely than with his many outstanding achievements. For example, in addition to his record-setting RBI display in May 1936, in that year's World Series he hit a grand slam into the right-center field seats at the Polo Grounds; it was only the second grand slam in World Series history. That year was Lazzeri's last outstanding season with the Yankees. He was released at the end of 1937 and signed with the Cubs as player-coach. He played sparingly in 1938, a year in which the Cubs won the National League pennant before losing to the Yankees in the World Series. The Cubs released him at season's end. He had a brief stay with the Brooklyn Dodgers in 1939 before retiring.

In his twelve-year career with the Yankees, Lazzeri averaged 14 home runs and 96 RBIs a year, including seven seasons with more than 100 RBIs and five in which he batted .300 or better, with a high of .354 in 1929. During that period, the Yankees won six pennants and five world championships.

As an Italian American, Lazzeri was obliged to endure a bit of ethnic abuse, which was not uncommon at that time. He heard more than a few unflattering terms for "Italian," and even in print some writers deemed it helpful to note his ethnic roots, sometimes referring to him as "the lanky Italian." Such questionable practices were routine at a time when European immigrants—mostly Irish, Italian, and Jewish—were making their way to the United States. A degree of bigotry was tolerated in those days before political correctness, occasionally offered as an attempt at humor and more often grounded in prejudice and ignorance. Anti-Semitism tended to be exceptionally virulent, given the centuries-old pattern of physical and emotional abuse that had been taking place in parts of Europe. In the thirties, of course, Germany was in the midst of an inhuman attempt to exterminate the entire Jewish population. As for racism, it was taken for granted in many areas of the United States that blacks were to be treated as less than human, deprived of basic civil rights, and lynched whenever the mood struck. Racism and bigotry, it must be concluded, are buried deep in America's psyche, part of its DNA, and poised to surface whenever circumstances seem to suit. The world of sports is hardly immune to such feelings, and one episode came to light during the summer of 1936.

On June 24, the Yankees traded Ben Chapman to the Senators for Jake Powell. On the surface, it was just a straight-up swap of outfielders. Chapman had played left field in 1932 on the Yankees' last championship team with Ruth in right and Earl Combs in center. As Combs edged towards retirement, Chapman was moved to center, and he was first-rate in the field as well as at the plate, batting over .300 for four straight years between 1930 and 1933 and twice driving in more than 100 runs. He also led the league in stolen bases three years in a row, from 1931 to '33 and was selected for the first three American League All-Star teams beginning in 1933. But as good as he was, Chapman came with some heavy baggage. A citizen of Alabama, he was a world-class bigot, most notably an anti-Semite. The early thirties was not a good time and New York not a good place to openly practice anti-Semitism, but Chapman was not deterred. He taunted Jewish fans seated nearby in left field with Nazi salutes and anti-Semitic epithets.

In 1933, he touched off one of baseball's biggest on-field brawls when he charged into second base spikes high and buried them in the thigh of second baseman Buddy Myer whom Chapman incorrectly believed to be Jewish. Myer responded with his fists, and the brawl quickly spread with more than three hundred fans taking part. It lasted for twenty minutes and resulted in five-game suspensions and one-hundred-dollar fines for each of the players involved.

The Yankees, playing in the Bronx, where Jews accounted for a substantial part of the population, were no doubt unhappy with Chapman's behavior but not sufficiently so to rid themselves of a talented player—winning, or trying to, came first. But in 1936, with DiMaggio on board, they felt they could get by with a lesser player who would play left field while DiMaggio took Chapman's place in center. So they settled on Powell. Though not as talented as Chapman, Powell pulled his own weight. He was more than ample in left field and not an easy out at the plate, hitting in the .270s throughout his career. Somewhat of a daredevil both on and off the field, he was dubbed "The Wild Man of the Base Paths" by a Washington sports scribe. There was a reckless dimension in the way he carried himself. It did not take much to provoke him, and he had more than his share of fistfights during games. Through it all, there was a degree of irony in his being traded for Chapman, for it gradually became clear that Powell might have been more of a bigot than the man he was traded for.

Whatever suspicions might have prevailed in that regard were eventually erased three years later, on July 29, 1938, in Chicago's Comiskey Park. In a dugout interview with WGN radio announcer Bob Elson, Powell was asked what he did in the off-season in order to stay in shape. His response resonated for many years and in fact played at least a small part in shining the light on segregation in the major leagues.

"I'm a policeman in Dayton, Ohio," Powell said (although his application for the position was still pending, and he never did become a policeman), "and I keep in shape by cracking niggers over the head with my nightstick."

All hell broke loose. According to Chris Lamb, writing in *The New York Times,* "Hundreds of outraged listeners called the station. Others called the Chicago office of the baseball commissioner, Kenesaw Mountain Landis. Before the next day's game, a delegation of black leaders presented a petition to umpires demanding that Powell be barred from baseball for life." Landis, himself a racist who for years blocked efforts to integrate baseball, suspended Powell for ten days for making "an uncomplimentary reference to a portion of the population." In addition, the Yankees ordered him to walk through Harlem as a gesture of apology, accompanied by Hubert Julian, a noted black aviator.

Powell was not new to trouble, either on the field or off. Many believed that his collision with Greenberg, which ended Hank's season, was no accident. His private life was also lived on the edge. While he was with Washington, his creditors had threatened to sue the Senators to settle his gambling debts.

Lamb, a professor of communications at the College of Charleston in South Carolina and the author of a book about Jackie Robinson's first spring training with the Dodgers, noted that sportswriters were divided on what had become known as

L'affaire Jake Powell. Which side they took was often decided according to race. Most white writers tended to dismiss or trivialize Powell's remark. Dan Daniel, a New York writer and longtime president of the Baseball Writers' Association of America, wrote that Powell should have been more careful but stressed that "he is a hustling player, aggressive, and always getting into a jam."

A notable exception was Westbrook Pegler, a prominent and often controversial columnist for Hearst newspapers. Pegler called Landis hypocritical for suspending Powell while condoning the de facto ban on black players. He referred to baseball as "the national game (that) has always treated Negroes as Adolf Hitler treats the Jews. If all American employers did the same, the entire Negro population of this country would starve, become public charges, or go back to slavery."

Black journalists spoke for the most part with one voice. According to Lamb, they urged their readers to boycott Yankee games and the corporate sponsors of the team's radio broadcasts. They also demanded, unsuccessfully, that the Yankees trade or release Powell. The Yankees responded with a public apology and an offer to help improve relations with the black community. However, Powell remained with the team for two more seasons, though he was used sparingly, before being released. He played his last big-league game for the Philadelphia Phillies in 1945. His manager on the Phillies, as fate would have it, was none other than Ben Chapman. Powell attempted a comeback in 1948 with a Class D minor-league team but managed to hit only .220 and was released.

Later that year, he was arrested in Washington with a woman for passing three hundred dollars' worth of bad checks. They said they planned to marry later that day after taking a train to New York. It would have been an unorthodox ceremony since it was later discovered that Powell already had a wife. In any event, they never made it to New York. While in police custody, Powell asked to speak to his companion. After a short visit, the story goes, Powell shouted, "Hell, I'm going to end it all." He then reached into his pocket and pulled out a .25-caliber handgun. He shot himself in the chest and then put the gun to his head and fired again. He was thirty-nine years old.

Ben Chapman, by contrast, lived out his post-baseball years in a less turbulent fashion, although it never was clear to what degree his bigotry might have been tempered. He was named manager of the Phillies in 1945 but earned prominence in that role chiefly as one of the most vicious antagonists of Jackie Robinson when Jackie broke the color line with the Dodgers in 1947. Not only did he lead the chorus of verbal attacks from the bench, but it was also widely bruited that he instructed his pitchers to throw at Robinson's head rather than walk him any time the count ran to 3–0. The Phillies, displeased with the negative publicity Chapman attracted, fired him in 1948.

About a year before Chapman died in 1993, the sports biographer Ray Robinson, while working on a book about Lou Gehrig, caught up with him by telephone at his home in Alabama. Robinson was eager to discover whether his views on race might have softened over the years. Chapman was eighty-four years old. Recounting their conversation in the *Times* in 2013, Robinson said that Chapman was not reluctant to discuss his treatment of Jackie or his anti-Semitic behavior. Speaking slowly and with a slight drawl, Chapman explained:

A man learns about things and mellows as he grows older. I think that maybe I've changed a bit. Maybe I went too far in those days. But I always went along with the bench jockeying, which has always been part of the game. Maybe I was rougher at it than some other players. I thought that you could use it to upset and weaken the other team. It might give you an advantage. The world changes. Maybe I've changed too.

"Look," he continued, "I'm real proud that I raised my son different." He noted that his son was coaching a local football team that had a number of black players. "And he gets along well with them," Chapman said. "They like him. That's a nice thing, don't you think?"

Although racism continued to haunt America, it was now at least called by its name. The Chapman-Powell incidents had helped to make it part of the country's dialogue. The ban on black players in major league baseball was finally being called to question. Still, a decade would pass since the Powell-Chapman incidents of the thirties before the color line would be broken. In the meantime, America's Pastime was preparing to put on one of its biggest shows. The fourth annual All-Star Game was soon to be played at Boston's Braves Field.

4

*The Yankees Dominate,
and Pennant Drought Ends*

The All-Star Game was still something of a novelty, just three years old, in 1936. The first game was played on July 6, 1933, in Chicago's Comiskey Park as part of the city's World's Fair. The brainchild of Arch Ward, the sports editor of the *Chicago Tribune*, it was intended to be a onetime event, part of the city's Century of Progress Exposition. The idea of putting the best ballplayers in the country on the field at the same time for a single baseball game indeed seemed appropriate for a celebration of the future. It was in fact too good an idea to let it slip away after just one game; with unanimous approval, it became an annual rite of summer.

The managers of the two teams were both legends long before the game was played. The American League team was managed by Philadelphia's Connie Mack and the National League by John McGraw, manager of the defending champion New York Giants. A near-capacity crowd of 47,595 filled the park and saw the American League team prevail 4–2. Fittingly enough, Babe Ruth hit the game's first home run, a two-run shot, into the right-field stands to provide the difference in the final score. Four Yankees—Ruth, Gehrig, Gomez, and Chapman—made it to the starting lineup; Lazzeri and Dickey brought the total to six, one-third of the eighteen-man roster. The number of players on each team was increased to twenty in 1934, twenty-five in 1939, and finally to thirty-four in 2009.

The following year's game, played at New York's Polo Grounds, provided what many consider to be the most memorable performance in All-Star Game history. Playing in his home park, Giant pitcher Carl Hubbell chalked up one for the ages. The game's first batter, Detroit second-baseman Charlie Gehringer, led off with a single and Heinie Manush, Washington outfielder, followed with a walk. With two on and nobody out, Hubbell was obliged to deal with Ruth, Gehrig, and Foxx, the three most prolific home run hitters in baseball. Using a pitch that was then called a screwball—a curve that broke in the opposite direction—Hubbell struck out all three batters. But he was not yet finished. He opened the second inning by striking out Al Simmons, White Sox outfielder, and Joe Cronin, Senators shortstop. Bill Dickey broke the string with a single, and Lefty Gomez followed and, not surprisingly, struck out.

The zany Gomez later complained that if Dickey had not screwed things up, he, Gomez, would have had his name in the record books alongside six of the best hitters in baseball. Lefty had no illusions about his prowess at the plate. "I was the worst hitter ever," he boasted. "I never even broke a bat until last year when I was backing out of the garage." Given the attention attracted by Hubbell's performance, it is sometimes forgotten that the American League won the game 9–7 with a six-run flurry in the fifth inning that erased a four-run deficit. Gomez fared no better on the mound than he did in the batter's box, giving up four runs in the third inning. Ruffing, his right-handed counterpart, also had an off-day, yielding three in the fourth.

The American League made it three in a row the following year with a 4–1 victory at Cleveland's Municipal Stadium. Nearly 70,000 spectators were in attendance, a crowd that stood as a record until 1981 when it was eclipsed by more than 72,000 at the same ballpark. In 1935, three seasons away from their last pennant, the Yanks placed only three players—Gehrig, Gomez, and Chapman—on the team. But it was Gomez who played the starring role. Improving vastly on his performance of the previous year, he gave up just one run on three hits in six innings. Foxx, playing third base in deference to Gehrig's starting at first, hit a two-run homer in the bottom of the first, giving the American League a lead it never surrendered.

Now, heading into the 1936 game, the Yankees were having things their own way. They led both Boston and Detroit by ten games and, by all appearances, they were ready to increase their lead. On June 24, the same day as the Chapman-Powell trade and two weeks before the All-Star Game, the Yanks and White Sox had put on a memorable show at Comiskey Park. Both teams seemed to be taking batting practice as the runs and hits piled up. The Yanks won the game 18–11; they doubled the Sox in hits 24–12. Trailing 7–5, they exploded for 10 runs in the fifth inning to put the game away. The heart of the

Yankee lineup—DiMaggio, Gehrig, and Dickey, batting third, fourth, and fifth respectively—each had four hits. DiMaggio was a show all by himself. He hit two home runs in the run-filled fifth, matching his two doubles and bringing his total bases to 12. In addition to DiMaggio, Dickey, Powell, and the light-hitting Crosetti also homered. The White Sox attack was hardly anemic. They chased Gomez in the fourth inning, scoring three runs, to make for a total of seven against the Yankee ace. Pat Malone was the winner although he yielded four runs while closing out the game.

One of the little-noted but distinctive aspects of the game was that it took only two hours and twenty-nine minutes for the teams to score 29 runs. A total of six pitchers were used—two by the Yanks and four by the Sox. Such a game would likely have taken at least twice as long in the modern era, as batters stepped out of the batter's box after each pitch to practice their swings and make adjustments to their wardrobes, while pitchers moseyed about the mound and managers made pitching changes on the vaguest of whims.

But of greater significance was the fact that the game marked the beginning of a winning streak that in effect put the pennant under lock and key by the Fourth of July. On June 24, the Yankees led the second-place Red Sox by five-and-a-half games. In the next two weeks, they won ten of eleven to double their lead to eleven.

Reflecting the team's success, seven Yankees were selected for the All-Star team as part of a twenty-man roster. Only DiMaggio and Gehrig were chosen to start, DiMaggio became the first rookie ever to start an All-Star Game. Somewhat of a surprise was that Bill Dickey, with his .369 batting average, placed behind Boston's Rick Ferrell as the starting catcher. Gomez, Chapman, and George Selkirk also made the team, as did Frank Crosetti, a first-time choice, who was having the season of his life, batting .319 and, even more remarkable, showing some home run power.

Crosetti's teammates called him "The Crow." It was a nickname that had dual derivations. On the one hand, it was an abbreviation of sorts, the first syllable if his name. It also mimicked a sound he made, letting out a cry like that of a crow to signal teammates in the field or on the bases in situations where other players would have whistled. It was a distinctive feature that seemed consistent with his background and nature.

Crosetti was born in 1910 in San Francisco and grew up in the North Beach section, a largely Italian American sector of the city. At age seventeen, Crosetti began his baseball career playing the infield for the San Francisco Seals in the Pacific Coast League, the same incubator that produced his two Italian compatriots. He came up to the Yankees four years later, in 1932, four years before DiMaggio and long after Lazzeri, with whom, playing shortstop, he formed an agile double-play combination. Unlike the other two, Crosetti was slight of build, 165 pounds on a 5-foot-10 frame. Also distinguished from them, he earned his keep with his glove rather than his bat. His lifetime batting average was only .245, but he knew how to bunt and was adept at getting on base by other means. He drew more than his share of walks and was never reluctant to take one for the team. He led the league in being hit by pitches in eight seasons. In 1938, he was hit fifteen times, a Yankee record that stood for forty-six years. Also in 1938, he delivered what probably was the most significant home run of his seventeen-year career.

It was in the second game of the 1938 World Series. The Cubs were leading the Yanks 3–2 going into the eighth inning at Wrigley Field, and Dizzy Dean had yielded only five hits to the Yankees' power-laden lineup. A future Hall-of-Famer who had won thirty games in 1934, Dean was now at the tail end of his career. His arm was shot, and his once-overpowering fastball was just a memory. Crosetti stepped to the plate with a man on base and promptly put his team ahead with a drive that barely made it over the left-field fence. Dean, never very shy, recalled shouting at Crosetti as he rounded the bases, "Hey, Frankie, betcha wouldn't have gotten a loud foul off me two years ago." Then, according to Dean, Crosetti responded, "You're damn right, Diz." Years later, when asked about the exchange, Crosetti said, "If Diz yelled something at me, I didn't hear it, and I didn't say anything back to him."

Not saying anything was a Crosetti trademark. The silence that muted the air over him, DiMaggio, and Lazzeri was legendary and illustrated in a variety of stories. The tale regarding their cross-country ride in 1936 was the one cited most often. But the one told by Jack Mahon, a sportswriter for International News Service (INS), was the most credible. It took place during the summer of 1936 in the lobby of the Hotel Chase in St. Louis. Mahon noticed that the trio was seated together nearby and had not spoken a word to each other for quite a while. "Just for fun," Mahon related, "I timed them to see how long they would maintain their silence. They didn't speak for an hour and twenty minutes. At the end of that time, DiMaggio cleared his throat. Crosetti looked at Lazzeri and said, 'What did he say?' And Lazzeri said, 'Shut up. He didn't say nothing.' They lapsed into silence and at the end of ten more minutes I got up and left. I couldn't stand it anymore."

Crosetti was more than modest; he was self-effacing and hard-nosed, some said to the point of being mean-spirited. He rarely made public appearances and never understood the attraction of celebrity. He expressed it this way: "Why does everybody insist about making such a fuss over baseball people? We're just doing a job, like the butcher, baker, or plumber. Doctors, scientists, and people who really do important work aren't bothered this way. I can't see it at all."

When it comes to longevity, Crosetti's career statistics are imposing. In a seventeen-year playing career, he won eight World Series rings and was twice an All-Star. As a third-base coach, from 1946 to 1968, he won an additional nine Series rings. By every measure, he had his best year as a player in 1936. He batted .288, more than forty points above his lifetime average; he also hit 15 home runs and drove in 78 runs, both career highs. He was selected for the All-Star Game as a bench player and struck out in his one at-bat, pinch-hitting for pitcher Mel Harder.

The game itself was a thriller. The National League, loser in the first two games, took an early lead with two runs in the second and two more in the fifth. Dizzy Dean and Carl Hubbell each threw three shutout innings, but the American League began to stir in the seventh when Curt Davis took over. Gehrig led off with his first All-Star home run, a drive that landed halfway up the stands in right field. Earl Averill and Bill Dickey grounded out, but the American Leaguers managed to load the bases with two out, and Luke Appling, the White Sox shortstop, singled and brought in two more runs to close the gap to 4–3. Lon Warneke replaced Davis and walked George Selkirk to load the bases again. DiMaggio, who was having a bad game all around, ended the rally when he lined out to Leo Durocher. Still needing one run to tie the game, the American League went down meekly in the ninth with three harmless ground balls, the last, once again, off the bat of DiMaggio.

All told, DiMaggio, who was hitting .358 going into the game, went hitless in five turns at bat. Batting third, he hit into a double play in the first inning and never got the ball out of the infield. To add to his woes, he made an error in the fifth inning which allowed a critical run to score. After Cubs shortstop Augie Galan had opened the inning with a home run, Billy Herman, Cubs second baseman, lined a single to right. DiMaggio bobbled it, allowing Herman to go to second from where he scored the National League's fourth and deciding run on a single by Cardinals outfielder Joe Medwick.

However, DiMaggio's poor showing did nothing to mar his image. On July 13, one week after the game, the Yankees' heralded rookie graced the cover of *Time* magazine. Making *Time*'s cover was, and remains to this day, a bow to relevance. It is not bestowed as a tribute for some honorable achievement; it is, rather, a sign that one has made a difference—and not always for the better. Rarely has it been awarded to an athlete, and hardly ever to a first-year player. Others who were on the magazine's cover in 1936 were Adolf Hitler, Benito Mussolini, and Chiang Kai-shek, leader of the Republic of China.

The sequential appearance of the three heads of state was not coincidental. Step-by-step, the world was drifting toward the most devastating war in history. Hitler had already repudiated the Treaty of Versailles, which had ended World War I and reoccupied the Rhineland. Italy, under the direction of Benito Mussolini, invaded Ethiopia, giving him a foothold in Africa. It was not long before the two nations formed the Rome-Berlin Axis. Hitler was also moving on another front. The Nazis enacted the Nuremberg Laws, which essentially deprived Jews of the rights of citizenship. Under Heinrich Himmler, a breeding program was initiated to prevent racial pollution and produce an "Aryan super race." In Asia, the Empire of Japan was preparing to invade Chiang Kai-shek's China and begin the second Sino-Japanese war. With a wider conflict appearing inevitable, the United States, wanting no part of it, passed a series of Neutrality Acts designed to deny aid to either party engaged in warfare. It would prove to be a futile attempt to remain a spectator while the world was teetering at the edge of the abyss.

The tense global scene was reflected in every aspect of life, and the world of sports was no exception. A few months earlier, on June 12, Joe Louis, the undefeated heavyweight title contender and the distillation of the fondest hopes of Black America, was knocked out by Max Schmeling, Germany's embodiment of Nazi supremacy, at Yankee Stadium. Joseph Goebbels, German minister of propaganda, proclaimed Schmeling's victory "a triumph for Germany and Hitlerism." Hitler had come to power just a few years earlier, and now, flushed with an air of conquest, he was ready to showcase Aryan preeminence on a worldwide stage at the 1936 summer Olympic Games, which were being held in Berlin. With Nazi military forces stationed about the stadium in full array, he watched incredulously as a black American athlete, Jesse Owens, ran away with four gold medals in track-and-field events that Hitler expected to be dominated by German athletes.

By all rights, Owens's medal in the four-man, 100-meter relay should not have been his. It came at the expense of another American track star, Marty Glickman, whose place on the relay team was taken by Owens when the Germans requested that no Jews be allowed to participate in the games. Also deprived of a place on the team was another Jew, Sam Stoller. Glickman, who later became a pioneer in the radio broadcast of football and basketball games, was outspoken in denouncing the apparent indifference of Avery Brundage, president of the US Olympic Committee, and his coach, Dean Cromwell, who quite respectfully succumbed to Hitler's wishes. Brundage, in the process, went a long way toward establishing his reputation as a racist and anti-Semite. In 1998, Glickman was given the Douglas MacArthur Award for lifetime achievement in the field of sports by the United States Olympic Committee.

By the time the Olympics ended in late August, the Yankees were leading the defending champion Detroit Tigers by eleven games and were on cruise control. On September 9, they clinched the pennant with doubleheader wins over Cleveland that stretched their league-leading margin to eighteen games in front of Detroit. It was the earliest pennant clinching in history. They finished the season with a record of 102–51, a winning percentage of .667, 19½ games ahead of the second-place Tigers.

There was no secret to their success; they did it with muscle. They scored a total of 1,065 runs, an average of almost seven runs a game and just two runs short of the all-time record held by the 1931 Yankees. By contrast, the 1927 Murderers' Row team scored a measly 975. While Gehrig once again led the way, he had no shortage of help up and down the lineup. Six of the starting players hit .300 or more. DiMaggio batted .323, with 29 homers and 125 RBIs. He also scored 132 runs while his 206 hits included 15 triples and 44 doubles. Dickey set a record for catchers with a .362 batting average while driving in 107 runs and scoring 99 others. Red Rolfe, in his role as leadoff hitter, batted .319. Right fielder Selkirk accounted for 18 home runs while batting in 107. Playing little more than half a season for the Yankees, Jake Powell hit .302. Lazzeri, nearing the end of his career, hit .287 with 14 homers and 109 RBIs. But it was Gehrig, batting cleanup, who was the powerhouse. While batting .354 and driving home 152 runs, he led the league with 49 home runs, 167 runs scored, 130 walks, a .478 on-base percentage, and a .696 slugging percentage. He was also among the leaders with 205 hits and 403 total bases. At season's end, he was named Most Valuable Player for the second time.

Their eighth pennant now safely in hand, preparations were being made to face the New York Giants in the World Series. Measured against their cross-city rivals, the Giants were the opposite side of the coin. With just slightly better than average hitting, they relied on pitching to carry the day. Led by "King" Carl Hubbell, who posted a record of 26–6, the Giants closed the season at 92–62, finishing five games ahead of the Cardinals and Cubs. On the offensive end, right fielder Mel Ott carried the team almost single-handedly. Ott batted .328 with 33 homers and 135 runs batted in. Only two other regulars, Jo-Jo Moore and Gus Mancuso, hit better than .300, and no other Giant had more than nine home runs. Outfielder Hank Lieber was second to Ott in RBIs with 67. As a team, the Giants scored only 4.7 runs a game, more than two runs fewer than the Yankees. On paper, they appeared to be woefully overmatched. They did, however, have home field advantage. The Series was to open on September 30 at the Polo Grounds in Upper Manhattan.

5

The Dynasty Starts with World Series Victory

The Yankees and Giants had some history between them. They faced each other in three consecutive World Series, from 1921 to 1923, with the Giants winning the first two and the Yankees taking the third. But the contention between the two teams went back much further, to the very beginnings of the Yankees franchise, to the start, actually, of the American League itself.

The Yankees had begun life in Baltimore as the Baltimore Orioles in the late nineteenth century. They were part of the fledgling American League that found itself in heated, often hostile, competition with the long-established National League. Ban Johnson, American League president, was convinced that the upstart league needed a team in a big-city market like New York. Both the Giants and the Dodgers, whose home was across the East River in Brooklyn, employed every device, including the use of as much political influence as they could muster, to keep a new team from coming to New York. But they failed.

The New York Highlanders became part of the American League in 1903. Their nickname came from their home field, Hilltop Park, located on a high-elevation peak between 165th and 168th Streets on Broadway in Manhattan.

The Yankees played there for ten years with indifferent results. In 1913, they moved into the Polo Grounds as tenants of the Giants. With the change in venue, the name Highlanders no longer applied and the team was officially christened "The New York Yankees." They also introduced their new white uniforms with pinstripes and the interlocking NY on the jersey for home games. Their road uniforms were gray with "New York" printed across the chest. Unlike other teams, the Yankees never changed the design of their uniforms nor did they print the player's name on the back. The pinstripes became part of Yankee tradition.

Their new but temporary home, the Polo Grounds, was located on Coogan's Bluff in Harlem. It had just been rebuilt in 1913 after being severely damaged the year before in a fire. At the time, it was considered to be a state-of-the-art ballpark, although its configuration was more suited to polo, for which it was originally designed, than baseball. Shaped in the form of a horseshoe, the distances to the left- and right-field stands were temptingly short—279 feet to left and 258 to right. Dead center was a prohibitive 483 feet from home plate, and the clubhouse was 32 feet deeper and 60 feet high. *Baseball* magazine called it "the greatest ballpark in the world." It was a park wonderfully suited to a left-hand pull hitter, a hitter, for example, like Babe Ruth.

Ruth came to the Yankees from the Red Sox in 1920, and in his first season at the Polo Grounds he hit a record-setting

54 home runs, following it with 59 the next season. With Ruth putting on a home-run show and the Yankees winning pennants, the tenant team was growing in popularity and outdrawing their intra-city rivals. Until the arrival of Ruth, the Giants had owned the heart of the city. But after Ruth's home run display in 1920 and '21, the die was cast. John McGraw, the Giants' combustible manager, felt his team's popularity slipping; they were falling behind a team of intruders, and they did not welcome the competition. McGraw persuaded management that it would be best if the Yankees found a new home. At the end of the 1921 season, the Yanks were informed that they had just one more year at the Polo Grounds. They would have to start the 1923 season elsewhere.

As it was, Yankee ownership had been considering such a move for some time. The team had been purchased in 1915 by the brewery magnate Colonel Jacob Ruppert, Jr., and former US Army engineer Tillinghast L'Hommedieu "Cap" Huston. Ruppert in particular was a proud and aggressive owner. Shortly after buying the team, he complained indignantly that it was "an orphan ball club, without a home of its own, without players of outstanding ability, without prestige." He began to remedy the situation by spending lavishly to stock the team with new talent. When told that they were no longer welcome in the Polo Grounds, he seized the opportunity to build his own ballpark, and he moved swiftly; he had to. The new stadium had to be ready for opening day in 1923.

The site chosen was a lumberyard in the South Bronx between 158th and 161st Streets on River Avenue. Ruppert and Huston purchased it from William Waldorf Astor for $600,000, equal to $8.48 million in 2016 currency. It was just across the Harlem River from the Polo Grounds, perhaps a ten-minute walk over the Macombs Dam Bridge. The location could not have been more accessible. An elevated subway, with a station at 161st Street, ran along River Avenue before it ducked underground on its way into Manhattan. About ten years later, another subway line, the Independent, would be opened with a station just across River Avenue from the elevated line.

Construction of the stadium began on May 5, 1922, and it opened a year later on April 18. It was built in 284 working days at the cost of $2.5 million. The new ballpark, officially christened Yankee Stadium, was often referred to as "The House that Ruth Built." Some years later it became known as "The Home of Champions." It was the first baseball structure not to be called either a park or a field; it was named a stadium and with good reason. It was a towering structure, eventually framed by two full tiers with a mezzanine tucked between them. The entire field was capped by a sweeping roof that was adorned by a frieze of white battlements. It had the awe-inspiring look and feel of a medieval coliseum in which primitive combatants might have fought to the death. *Baseball* magazine said, "It looms up like the great Pyramid of Cheops from the sands of Egypt."

Its magisterial exterior was consistent with the cavernous field that was inside. The dimensions of the field were adjusted slightly over the first few years, but from the very start, its shape was unconventional with an outfield that seemed to sprawl into the next county. It finally settled in at 296 feet down the right-field line and 301 to left, but those relatively short distances

were deceiving. In left field, the fence fell away in a slight arc to
402 feet in straightaway left and 457 in left center, a yawning
expanse that was, for obvious reasons, dubbed Death Valley.
Right field, perhaps designed with Ruth in mind, turned more
sharply toward center—367 feet to straightaway right and 407
to right center. Dead center was an intimidating 461 feet. The
capacity was a flexible 60,000; flexible because opening day attendance was announced as 74,217, with 25,000 turned away.
Those estimates, of course, owed more to promotion than to
accuracy. But even at 60,000, the crowd was far more than the
previous major-league record of 42,000 set at Braves Field for
game five of the 1916 World Series.

The Stadium, as it was often referred to, became a focal
point and a tourist attraction in the Bronx, which, together
with the borough of Brooklyn, was growing rapidly in the
twenties. It was located just a few blocks west of the Grand
Concourse, a magnificent thoroughfare that was modeled on
the Champs-Élysées in Paris but is considerably larger. Stretching four miles in length and 180 feet across, it is separated into
three roadways by tree-lined dividers so that only major cross-
town streets can cross it. The Concourse Plaza hotel opened at
the same time as the 1923 World Series on the southeast corner
of the Grand Concourse and 161st Street. As lavish and distinctive as the Concourse itself, it became the temporary home of
Yankee players for the better part of fifty years. In addition to
hotel rooms, it offered apartments and efficiencies for full-time
residents and eventually a synagogue that held High Holiday
services for the countless number of Jewish residents who had
been moving up to the Bronx from the Lower East Side.

Baseball was a means of assimilation for tens of thousands of European immigrants—Italian and Irish as well as an increasingly large flow of Jews, who within a few years would begin fleeing the oppression of Hitler's Germany and Russia's pogroms. They filled the apartment buildings, some of them of art deco design, that lined both sides of the Concourse and filled the streets around it. Baseball was as American as one could be, and many of the Bronx residents boasted about living in the shadow of Yankee Stadium. Some of the buildings offered a free, albeit distant, view of the Stadium playing field from their roofs, and the No. 4 Woodlawn elevated train, running along River Avenue and into the bustling streets of Jerome Avenue, provided a quick glance into the outfield through a brief space in the bleachers. Another landmark, the Bronx County Courthouse, was built just across the street from the Concourse Plaza in 1933 and was clearly visible from the Stadium over the right-field fence.

It was in these environs that the Yankees took on and defeated the Giants four games to two in the 1923 World Series after having lost to them the two previous years. It was a fitting initiation for the new stadium, but in a touch of irony, the Yanks won only one of the games in their new ballpark. In the first subway series, the teams alternated playing fields from day to day. The Giants won the first World Series game played in Yankee Stadium and then went to the Polo Grounds where they lost game two. The visiting team won the next two games before the Yankees won game five at home; they clinched the Series the following day at the Polo Grounds. The two teams would not meet again until 1936, thirteen years later.

It was the first World Series the Yankees would play without Babe Ruth in the lineup. Batting in Ruth's third spot in the order was the rookie sensation Joe DiMaggio. Despite his exceptional first year, DiMaggio did not offer the sense of intimidation that Ruth provided, especially with Gehrig waiting on deck. The Babe's place in right field was filled by George Selkirk, a more than adequate presence, who hit better than .300 in his three seasons with the Yankees, though with nothing resembling the Bambino's home run production. Selkirk also inherited Ruth's No. 3 uniform number, which was not retired until 1948, just months before he died; the practice of retiring uniform numbers did not become routine until years later. The only number that had been retired by the Yankees at that time was Lou Gehrig's No. 4 on the memorable day in 1939 when, suffering from amyotrophic lateral sclerosis (ALS), he said goodbye at Yankee Stadium. In the outfield, Selkirk left little to be desired. He moved swiftly with an unusual gait, running on the balls of his feet and earning the nickname of "Twinkletoes," given to him by his teammates.

Selkirk was born in 1908 in Ontario, Canada. He spent nearly eight seasons in the minor leagues before being brought up to the Yankees from their Newark Triple-A farm team in 1934. He saw limited service during his rookie year, which was Ruth's last season in pinstripes. Playing in only forty-six games, he batted .313 with five home runs and 38 RBIs. In 1935, with Ruth gone, Selkirk slipped into his right-field position where he remained through 1940. His batting average over those years was remarkably consistent. He hit .312, .308, and .328 over the next three years. His playing time became limited in 1940 with the addition of outfielders Charlie Keller and Tommy Henrich to the roster, who also came up from Newark. In 1942, despite his Canadian citizenship, Selkirk joined the US Navy and served as an aerial gunner during World War II. He never played another game in the major leagues.

Having concluded his nine-year career with a batting average of .290, Selkirk continued to work in baseball in managerial and administrative positions. He was the manager of several of the Yankees' minor-league teams and also managed in the farm system of the Milwaukee Braves. Moving up to front-office positions, he was player personnel director for the Kansas City Athletics and field coordinator of player development for the Baltimore Orioles. He later became the second general manager in the history of the new Washington Senator franchise, now the Texas Rangers. Upon retiring from baseball, he was elected to the Canadian Baseball Hall of Fame.

Selkirk died at age seventy-nine in Fort Lauderdale, Florida, but not before earning a brief notice in the world of the theater. His name is mentioned in August Wilson's 1987 Pulitzer Prize-winning play *Fences*. The protagonist, Troy, arguing that black ballplayers would prove to be better than whites if allowed to play in the majors, notes that Selkirk batted only .269 in 1940. It is cause for wonder why Wilson chose Selkirk to make his case. He certainly would not have used him in that regard at the end of the 1936 season in which he batted .308, with 18 home runs and 107 runs batted in as he helped propel the Yankees to the American League pennant.

The Series opened on Wednesday, September 30, on a dreary, rain-filled afternoon at the Polo Grounds with the Yanks facing Giants' ace Hubbell. It was Selkirk who started the scoring, putting his team ahead with a home run to open the third inning. With twenty-game winner Red Ruffing holding the Giants scoreless, the Yankees held a 1–0 lead after four innings. But that was the best of it for the Yanks. They would not see home plate again for the rest of the day. The Giants tied the game with a solo home run by shortstop Dick Bartell in the fifth and scored the go-ahead run in the next inning on a double by Mel Ott and a single by catcher Gus Mancuso. The Giants put the game out of reach in the eighth, piecing together four runs on three hits, two walks, a sacrifice bunt, and an error by Crosetti. Aside from Selkirk's homer, Hubbell was masterful. He allowed only seven hits while striking out eight and recording all other outs in the infield; his outfield, in effect, had the day off.

So the Giants took an early lead, but any thoughts that they might reclaim New York as their own were thwarted the very next day. The Yankees responded in game two as though summoned by the call for redemption. They set a Series record for the most runs scored in one game as they pummeled the Giants 18–4; the 14-run winning margin also set a Series record. Despite the offensive barrage, the most memorable play of the game was made on defense. With two out in the bottom of the ninth, the Giants' Hank Lieber sent a drive 490 feet into deep center field. DiMaggio turned his back to the plate and made haste for the clubhouse. He caught the ball over his shoulder and continued running up the clubhouse stairs. The catch was made at least forty feet deeper than Willie Mays's fabled catch of a Vic Wertz drive to dead center in the first game of the 1954 Series against the Indians. When the game was over, President Roosevelt, who had stayed until the end, saluted DiMaggio as he rode off in the presidential limousine.

The offensive onslaught had begun quietly with a pair of runs in the first inning. The Giants answered with a single score in the second on a wild pitch by Gomez, but the Yanks exploded for seven runs in the third. The first three batters in the order—Crosetti, Rolfe, and DiMaggio—each got on to load the bases, ending the day for Giants' starter Hal Schumacher. He was replaced by Al Smith, whose fortunes proved to be no better. He was greeted with singles by Gehrig and Dickey, and after walking Powell, he was succeeded to the mound by Dick Coffman. The first batter he saw was Tony Lazzeri who welcomed him with a home run, only the second grand slam in World Series history. (The first was hit by the Cleveland Indians' Elmer Smith in game five of the 1920 Series.)

Two more Giant pitchers were used to close out the last five innings, but they fared no better than their predecessors. Leading 12–4 going into to the ninth, the Yankees showed no mercy. It was as though they wished to end the game with an exclamation point, a notice that this was the true difference between the two teams. The inning included a home run by Dickey and, even more remarkably, an RBI single by the weak-hitting Gomez who went the distance for the win. The game was a demonstration of unbrokered dominance. Every Yankee in the lineup got at least one hit for a total of seventeen. Given their show of force, the Yanks were understandably confident and at their ease with the Series headed to the Bronx for the weekend.

It was Saturday, October 3, and the 64,842 fans that filled Yankee Stadium were treated to a game that was the diametric opposite of the one played the previous day; the outcome, however, was the same. The Yankees won the game 2–1 in a pitchers' duel in which the Giants' Freddie Fitzsimmons outpitched Bump Hadley but lost nonetheless. Gehrig opened the scoring leading off the second with a home run deep into the right-field stands. The Giants chipped away at Hadley throughout the game but scored only once, on a homer by center fielder Jimmie Ripple in the fifth inning. The game remained tied at 1–1 until the bottom of the eighth. Fitzsimmons was pitching an airtight two-hitter when Selkirk opened the inning with a single. Powell walked, and Lazzeri bunted both runners up a base. Ruffing, pinch-hitting for Hadley, bounced into a fielder's choice with Selkirk being thrown out at the plate. With two out and runners on first and third, Crosetti tapped an 0–2 pitch back at the pitcher. Fitzsimmons, normally an excellent fielder, tried to scoop up the ball but it squirted off his glove; Crosetti made it to first, and Powell came home with what proved to be the winning run. Pat Malone pitched a scoreless ninth and Hadley came away with the win.

Hadley, a ten-year veteran, was a welcome off-season acquisition for the Yankees. A journeyman pitcher who had compiled a marginally losing record with a variety of clubs, Hadley threw hard but his control was an issue and the principal cause of his bouncing around the league—five years with Washington, one with the White Sox, three with the St. Louis Browns, back with the Senators for a year, and finally to the Yankees at the start of 1936 where he put together a solid 14–4 record. It was only his fourth winning season since breaking in with a single game in relief in 1926.

A native of Lynn, Massachusetts, Hadley earned letters in baseball, basketball, track, rowing, and football at Lynn English High School. In 1923, he set an interscholastic shot-put record, threw a no-hitter against Chelsea High School, and was attracting the interest of college football scouts. All the same, he opted for baseball and was signed by Washington where he pitched reasonably well until being traded to Chicago in 1932. After his four-year odyssey of little note, he found himself back in Washington from where the Yankees traded for his services in January 1936.

Yankees manager Joe McCarthy had had his eye on Hadley for some time. He saw that Hadley had a world of stuff to go along with his sizzling fastball and believed his command of home plate could be improved. He was right. As it turned out, Hadley was equally effective in relief and as a starter. His 14–4 record included three wins and one loss out of the bullpen. He became an integral part of the dynasty, posting winning records in the next three seasons, but his victory in game three in 1936 might be considered his most notable contribution as it gave the Yanks a 2–1 Series lead with Hubbell due to pitch the next day.

Still, despite their slim edge, game four was critical because a loss would even the Series and assure that it would be decided at the Polo Grounds, with Hubbell ready for game seven if necessary. McCarthy countered the Giant ace with Monte Pearson. Like Hadley, Pearson was another recent acquisition. He was obtained before the start of the 1936 season from Cleveland, along with another pitcher, Steve Sundra, for Yankee starter Johnny Allen. Allen, who had had four winning seasons with the Yanks, including a 13–6 record in 1935, was a fan favorite and a reliable member of the starting rotation. Pearson, by contrast, was coming off an 8–13 season with the Indians and the trade drew considerable criticism at the time it was made. However, Pearson more than justified McCarthy's faith in him, going on to put together the best season of his career.

Born in Oakland, California, in 1908, Pearson later moved to Fresno and started his baseball career at Fresno High School playing third base and catching. After graduating, he attended the University of California, Berkeley, where he played for two seasons and converted to pitching. In addition to buttressing the starting rotation, Pearson was an asset in the clubhouse where he serenaded his teammates by singing while accompanying himself on the guitar.

But his true value was on the mound, and he wasted no time in putting it on display. He won eight of his first nine decisions and was selected for the All-Star team on the way to the best season of his career. All told, he compiled a 19–7 record which gave him the third-best winning percentage in the league. His ERA of 3.71 and his strikeout total of 118 were both fifth in the league. But it was his performance in the fourth game of the World Series that earned him the distinction of being labeled a big-game pitcher. There had in fact been some doubt about whether he would be able to pitch at all—he had fallen ill with pleurisy near the end of the season but insisted on remaining in the starting rotation. Now, he proved his case by facing down Carl Hubbell with a complete game, 5–2 win, allowing just seven hits and striking out seven in the process.

As for the offense, the Yankees seemed to have solved Hubbell the second time around, and they struck early, scoring the game's first run in the bottom of the second when Selkirk drove home Powell with a single to left. An inning later, with the top of the order coming up, they added three runs to put the game away. After Crosetti doubled and Rolfe singled him home, Gehrig hit his second homer of the Series deep into the right-field seats. The Giants squeezed out single runs in the fourth and the eighth, but Pearson held fast, and the Yanks won their third straight game to take a 3–1 Series lead.

With Ruffing trying to close things out against Hal Schumacher the next day at the Stadium, game five turned into a nip-and-tuck struggle that went to extra innings. The Giants got started early, scoring three first-inning runs on five hits, including doubles by Jo-Jo Moore and Dick Bartell. The Yanks countered with a Selkirk homer in the second and a run in the third without benefit of a hit, on two walks, a wild pitch, and an error by shortstop Bartell. The game evened up in the sixth. The Giants scored once in the top of the inning, and the Yankees came back in the bottom half with two unearned runs on a Travis Jackson throwing error. With Pat Malone replacing Ruffing, who had been pinch-hit for in the sixth, the game remained tied at 4–4 going into the tenth. Moore opened the inning with a double, Bartell moved him to third on a sacrifice bunt, and Bill Terry, a player-manager who was in his final year as a player, sent him home with the winning run on a fly ball to deep center field.

The victory kept the Giants alive as the Series moved back to the Polo Grounds, but the home field proved to be of little help. Freddie Fitzsimmons, who pitched brilliantly in game three but to no avail, was shelled early in game six and driven from the mound in the fourth inning after yielding five runs on nine hits. The Giants had taken an early lead on a double by Mel Ott, but the Yankees scored two in the second on a Powell homer, one in the third, and two more in the fourth to take a 5–2 lead. The Giants narrowed the margin against Gomez with single runs in the fifth and seventh. Each team scored once in the eighth, so the score stood at 6–5 going into the ninth, but that was when the roof fell in. The Yanks rallied for seven runs on five singles—two of them by DiMaggio—four walks, and an error to wrap up the game and the Series with a 13–5 decision.

The season ended as a year of triumph and domination for the Yankees. And, as time would tell, it was just the beginning. Among the starters, only Lazzeri was nearing the end of his career. The others were pretty much in their prime; DiMaggio had not yet approached his. And, to darken the dreams of the rest of the league, the Newark Bears farm team was stocked with talent that was ready to supplement or replace any players who faltered. For the Yankees, the future was now.

1937

The Yankees march easily to their second consecutive World
Series as DiMaggio and Gehrig form a potent one-two punch.

6

New Season Begins with an Aura of Inevitability

There are no true upsets in baseball. No single game brings with it the element of shock or disbelief. Over the course of a season, one can expect the worst team in the league to defeat the best team, often more than once. In baseball, as opposed to sports such as football or basketball, size and speed, though often relevant, are not the defining characteristics. Baseball is different. A baseball game begins with the defense in possession of the ball; it is the defense that initiates the action and controls the pace and movement of the game. The pitcher, the most critical component in any game, changes from day to day. So far as the rest of the lineup is concerned, a team cannot invest its hopes for victory in its leading player. It cannot continually feed the high scorer, as a basketball team can, or give the ball repeatedly to its best running back or pass to its top receiver, as occurs in football. Each player takes his turn at bat in accordance with the starting lineup; a team cannot send its top hitter to bat in a clutch situation if its weakest hitter is due at the plate.

Attempts to quantify the game with newly concocted statistics tend to be futile. Among the most ludicrous is a new stat called WAR (Wins Above Replacement) that calculates the success of a team when a key player is replaced by a substitute. Such a stat is relevant only in the case of the pitcher. For starters, one would need to factor into the equation which teams and which pitchers formed the opposition when the replacement player was in the lineup. And, the level of competition aside, it is hardly unusual for a team to post a winning record while its best player is missing in action. Baseball is a game of streaks; the leading hitter in the league will slump for four or five games somewhere during the course of the season and a lightweight batter is likely to catch fire somewhere along the way. Unlike other sports in which a player must rely on the cooperation of his teammates, baseball is a team sport that is played mano-a-mano, pitcher against batter, and no help is available when a 100-mile-an-hour fastball nips the outside corner of the plate.

Of course, what is true for a single baseball game is not true for a season. While baseball is independent of the clock, it is nonetheless a prisoner of the calendar. The season is long, and it is played out day after day, from spring through summer to fall, and the inexorable passing of the days, game for game, begins to determine which team is best. Rarely does a team win 70 percent of its games as is true in football or basketball. Attrition sets in during the dog days of August, and as the days fall away and the 162-game season ebbs, each team's hopes will finally be governed by the bane or benediction of time. As often as not, the winner is not decided until the last weekend of the six-month season.

Although the Yankee dynasty had just begun, the 1937 season approached with an aura of inevitability. So dominant was the team's performance the year before, so potent was its lineup from top to bottom, that the mantra of "Break up the Yankees" was already being heard. Detroit was the only team given a chance to derail the Yankee steamroller. Hank Greenberg was back in the lineup and due to have one of his best years. Second baseman Charlie Gehringer was at his peak, and a rookie catcher, Rudy York, would burst upon the scene displaying exceptional power. But the Yankees seemed to be a well-oiled, relentless machine.

Manager Joe McCarthy, luxuriant in his star-studded collection of talent, sat back in the middle of the dugout with the quiet assurance of a man who knew he held the winning hand and all he needed to do was play his cards right. His low-key, self-effacing manner, combined with his unprecedented success, was fuel for a number of critics to minimize the role he played in producing a series of championship teams. White Sox manager Jimmy Dykes described him as a "push-button manager," overlooking the truth that he had to know which button to push and when to push it.

Joseph Vincent McCarthy was born in 1887 in Philadelphia and grew up idolizing the Philadelphia Athletics and their incomparable manager, Connie Mack. He had an undistinguished, though lengthy, minor-league career, mostly as a second baseman with the Louisville Colonels of the American Association. He earned notice as a manager while at the helm of the Louisville team from 1919 to 1925, winning pennants in 1921 and '25.

The following year he was summoned to manage the Chicago Cubs, a team that had fallen on hard times since the early days of "Evers to Tinkers to Chance." McCarthy revived the moribund franchise, which had finished either at or near the bottom of the league through most of the decade. The Cubs climbed the ladder slowly and finally won the National League pennant in 1929. Oddly enough, his success was also the seed of his undoing. The Cubs faced Connie Mack's A's in the World Series and did not fare as well as owner William Wrigley, Jr., would have liked. They lost in five games, but it was game four that sealed McCarthy's fate. Trailing the Series two games to one, the Cubs led 8–0 going into the seventh inning. But, aided by a loose defense, chiefly Hack Wilson losing Mule Haas's fly ball in the sun, the A's exploded for ten runs, turning an eight-run deficit into a 10–8 victory. McCarthy, already skating on thin ice, was fired before the end of the 1930 season as the Cubs slid to third place. Nothing could have done more to enhance his career.

The Yankees' imperious owner, Colonel Jacob Ruppert, Jr., took immediate notice. Miller Huggins, who managed the Murderers' Row team, had died suddenly in 1929. Pitcher Bob Shawkey was chosen to replace him but just for a year. The 1930 Yankees finished third for the second year in a row, much to the owner's dissatisfaction. Ruppert moved quickly to hire McCarthy but not without a firmly expressed caveat. At the signing, Ruppert made his expectations clear. "I'll stand for finishing second this year, McCarthy," he said in his distinctive German drawl. "But remember, I do not like to finish second." McCarthy responded immediately: "Neither do I, Colonel." Indeed, the Yankees moved up to second place in 1931 but were far behind the A's, trailing at the end by 13½ games. The following year, as choreographed, they reversed the 1931 finish, winning the pennant by a margin of thirteen games over the A's. To McCarthy's revengeful delight, the Yanks proceeded to sweep the Cubs in the World Series.

Dealing with the flamboyant, hell-raising Bambino presented McCarthy with a challenge that he met by letting Babe be the Babe and paying little heed to Ruth's occasional show of distemper. Ruth was already riled at not being considered for the manager's job. His agitated rapport with the new manager chilled still further in 1934 when Ruth began openly campaigning for the manager's job. His persistent dissatisfaction with an outsider like McCarthy being put in charge contributed to Ruth's being traded to the Boston Braves at the end of the season.

After celebrating the 1932 championship, Ruppert could barely suppress his frustration when the Yankees finished in second place three years in a row, once to Washington and then twice to the powerhouse Detroit team. Some critics began to refer to McCarthy as "Second-Place Joe," which the manager resented, and it set Ruppert to re-examining the wisdom of his decision. All that changed, of course, with the arrival of Joe DiMaggio in 1936.

The union of McCarthy and DiMaggio was a marriage conceived by the gods. Both were entirely unassuming, mechanical in their approach to the game, and devoted not only to winning but to perfection. Together, they forged the image of the Yankees as innately predominant, a team not only better than the opposition but somehow other-worldly, as if being champions was a birthright ordained by a power greater than themselves. Both shunned the glow of publicity and shied at public acclaim. So under-stated was McCarthy that he declined to wear a uniform number, never went to the mound to remove a pitcher, and rarely challenged the decision of an umpire other than to dispute an interpretation of the rules. His relationship with his players was matter-of-fact—rather cool but unrelenting. A player who suggested that anything less than victory was acceptable was soon gone. Sportswriters assigned him the nickname of Marse Joe, "Marse" being a Southern English rendering of the word "master." His players treated him with professional respect but an indifferent personal detachment.

In a *New York Times* article by Joe Durso, relief pitcher Joe Page said, "I hated his guts, but there never was a better manager." DiMaggio echoed Page's high regard for McCarthy, saying, "Never a day went by that you didn't learn something from McCarthy."

McCarthy's taste for formality applied off the field as well as on. He insisted on courtly behavior in hotel lobbies and on trains and maintained a strict dress code that required his players to wear jackets and neckties when in public. He did, however, make rare exceptions. When, in 1948, he became manager of the Red Sox, there loomed the possibility of a collision between him and Boston outfielder Ted Williams, perhaps baseball's best hitter ever and, in 1941, the last to hit over .400. Williams was known to scorn the wearing of neckties even when dressed in formal wear. When a Boston sportswriter asked McCarthy whether he would allow Williams to break his dress code, McCarthy wasted no time in responding: "I've always had one exception to that rule," he said. "Anyone who can hit .400 does not need a necktie." The remark was offered casually, with the off-the-cuff ease of a man whose legendary status was already assured—the first manager to win pennants in both the National and American Leagues and the only one to win four straight world championships.

Now, in the spring of 1937, the Yankees cruised into the new season as heavy favorites. All the pieces were still in place. Gehrig was in his prime; DiMaggio was approaching his. The pitching corps remained intact. There was every reason to believe that the Yankee juggernaut had not yet reached its peak. A reconfiguration of Yankee Stadium was also expected to prove helpful. Concrete bleachers were built to replace the aging wooden structure and, most significantly and perhaps with DiMaggio in mind, the intimidating area of the outfield known as "Death Valley" was trimmed by as much as thirty feet, though it was still a daunting distance from home plate. It now measured 415 feet to left-center, gradually increasing to 457 and finally to 461 as the stands curled from left field to center.

After opening the season with a 3–2 loss to Washington, the Yanks won five straight before losing again to the Senators and finishing the month of April in first place with a record of 5–2. The first week of May began with indifferent results.

The Yankees took two straight games at Detroit, but on the following day, May 6, the Tigers bludgeoned them by a score of 12–6. They were still in first place although the race was crowded with Detroit, Boston, Cleveland, and Philadelphia all in the mix. In the clubhouse after the game, McCarthy expressed his displeasure with the team's performance, and he overheard outfielder Roy Johnson say, "What's the guy expect to do, win every day?" It was, for Johnson, an unfortunate remark. According to the account by Marty Appel in *Pinstripe Empire*, McCarthy wasted no time in reacting. When he returned to the team hotel, he phoned general manager Ed Barrow and told him to "get rid of Johnson": "I don't want him with us anymore. Get rid of him right away."

"Why the big rush?" Barrow asked.

"I won't play him again. Send me the kid who's at Newark."

The kid at Newark was Tommy Henrich who had recently become the property of the Yankees on the decree of Commissioner Kenesaw Mountain Landis. Henrich, who grew up on the sandlots of Massillon, Ohio, had signed with Cleveland in 1934 but was looking for a way out after two seasons with the Indians' New Orleans farm team. The rights to the promising young outfielder were at the time a matter of conjecture. There was a question whether he was the property of Cleveland, New Orleans, or the independently owned Milwaukee Brewers, to whom New Orleans claimed to have sold him. Henrich and his father wrote to the commissioner, and Landis, reputed to be no friend of Cleveland scout Cy Slapnicka, declared Henrich a free agent. The Yankees were quick to snap him up to take the place of Johnson who was summarily dispatched to the Red Sox for the price of waivers. It was an agreeable turn of events for the Yankees. Their new acquisition proceeded to hit .320 in 67 games that year and went on to become a staple presence both in the field and at bat for the duration of the dynasty and well into the post-war years. Along the way, his clutch hitting earned him the nickname of "Old Reliable."

After the loss to Detroit, the Yankees proceeded to drop their next three games, two to the Indians and one to the White Sox, and fall to fifth place, though just one game from the lead. As events played out, the May 6 loss to Detroit, which led to the acquisition of Henrich, proved to be a positive turn for the team's future.

On a larger scale, the date of May 6, 1937, became etched into history for another reason, a disastrous event that pushed all other news into the background. The German blimp Hindenburg, the pride of Germany's aviation enterprise, burst into flames two hundred feet above its intended landing spot at New Jersey's Lakehurst Naval Air Station. Of the 97 passengers and crew members on board, 35 were killed along with one crewman on the ground while 62 managed to survive. The spontaneous horror of the event was captured forever by Herbert Morrison's frenzied description, broadcast on radio station WLS, Chicago:

> It's practically standing still now, they've dropped ropes out of the nose of the ship and they've taken ahold of it down on the field by a number of men. It's starting to rain again; it's . . . the rain had slacked up a little

bit. The back motors of the ship are just holding, just enough to keep it from . . .

It's burst into flames! Get this, Charlie, get this, Charlie, it's fire . . . and it's crashing! It's crashing terrible! Oh, my, get out of the way please. It's burning and bursting into flames and the . . . and it's falling on the mooring mast. And all the folks agree that this is terrible; this is the worst of the worst catastrophes in the world. Oh, it's . . . it's flames . . . crashing, oh. Four- or five-hundred feet into the sky and it . . . it's a terrific crash, ladies and gentlemen. It's smoke, and it's in flames now, and the frame is crashing to the ground, not quite to the mooring mast.

Oh, the humanity; the humanity! And all the passengers screaming around here. I told you, it . . . I can't even talk to people, their friends are on there. Ah! It's . . . it's, ah . . . I . . . I can't talk, ladies and gentlemen, honest. It's just lying there, mass of smoking wreckage. Ah! And everybody can hardly breathe and talk and the screaming. I . . . I . . . I'm sorry, honest, I . . . I can hardly breathe. I . . . I'm going to step inside where I cannot see it. Charlie, that's terrible. Ah, ah . . . I can't . . . Listen, folks, I . . . I'm gonna have to stop for a minute because I've lost my voice. This is the worst thing I've ever witnessed.

While the crash of the Hindenburg was a catastrophe of worldwide scope, it was especially devastating in Germany as it marred the image of superior aviation that Hitler was eager to project. Days after the explosion, he banned the flight of all hydrogen-filled airships, effectively marking the end of passenger travel by dirigible. At the time, however, Hitler had other things on his mind. He was busy planning the *Anschluss* (annexation) of Austria, which would take place less than a year later.

While Hitler was working out the details of the Nazi march into Austria, other ominous events were taking place around the globe. On May 7, 1937, just one day after the Hindenburg tragedy, a Falangist group called the Nationalists, led by General Francisco Franco, launched its drive to overthrow the Second Spanish Republic, and the Spanish Civil War was underway. At around the same time, Italy withdrew from the League of Nations and Japan invaded China. A step at a time, the world was inching closer to war. But the United States was paying little attention.

The Depression was stubbornly hanging on. Unemployment, which had dropped sharply since 1932, showed signs of climbing back up. The ranks of the homeless were increasing. Given such parochial concerns, whatever mischief was taking place in Europe seemed of minor importance at the time. Europe, after all, was a far distance from our shores. The early indications of menace were hardly felt at all in the United States. While dealing with our own pressing issues, we were more interested in a degree of diversion, and it was found easily enough, particularly in New York. The Glenn Miller band had made its debut in the Big Apple, and the Benny Goodman orchestra would soon turn Carnegie Hall into a capital of jazz. The Broadway theater was thriving. Moss Hart and George S.

Kaufman had won the Pulitzer Prize for *You Can't Take It with You*, and, though it was still early in the season, those with a feel for such things could see that the Yankees and the Giants were headed for another World Series.

7

Inevitability Takes a While to Kick In

During the first few months of the season, the Yankees bore a resemblance to a primed heavyweight in defense of his title, moving deliberately but confidently, testing the opposition, looking to identify any possible source of danger. Following the May 6 incident in the clubhouse that led to the dispatch of Roy Johnson in favor of the rookie Tommy Henrich, the team continued to win a few and lose a few, never falling much behind but not yet ready to stake their claim as the league's dominant force. To all appearances, the race promised to be a free-for-all with as many as half the teams in the league vying for supremacy. The heart of the Yankee lineup was still not playing to form. Gehrig was hitting what was for him was an anemic .288; DiMaggio was also sub-par at .303. But help was on the way, and it came from across the river.

The Newark Bears, the Yankees' Triple-A farm team, was loaded with talent and seemed able to furnish whatever help was needed at the time. Within days of one another, Henrich and a right-handed pitcher by the name of Spud Chandler arrived on the scene, and both lost no time in giving promise of good things to come. Henrich debuted on May 11, playing left field and going one-for-four with a two-base hit. Chandler, after a brief, lackluster relief appearance in Detroit on May 6, made his first start three days later in Chicago's Comiskey Park, and it was an impressive audition. He yielded an unearned run in the first inning and then proceeded to hold the White Sox scoreless until the seventh. The Yanks had tied the game in the top of the inning on an unlikely sequence of events. Red Rolfe reached base on an infield single and moved to second when DiMaggio's fly ball was misplayed by left fielder Hank Steinbacher. In a move that would be unimaginable today, Gehrig, batting cleanup, attempted to bunt. The ball rolled out, just in front of the plate where catcher Luke Sewell picked it up and started a catcher-to-third-to-first double play. DiMaggio moved to third and scored on a Bill Dickey double, evening the score at 1–1. The game turned in the bottom of the seventh when Zeke Bonura hit a game-winning homer, giving the White Sox a 2–1 decision. But Chandler, who was reached for only five hits and did not walk a batter, served notice that, for the next decade, he would have to be reckoned with.

Born Spurgeon Ferdinand Chandler in 1907, Spud Chandler was among a handful of ballplayers who, despite some exceptional seasons, managed to slip beneath the radar and go largely unnoted once their careers were over. Few baseball aficionados would be able to tell you that Chandler's winning percentage of .717 is the highest of any pitcher in the history of the game. He never had a losing season and finished with a lifetime-earned run average of 2.84.

Baseball was not the only sport at which Chandler excelled. At the University of Georgia, he played halfback on the football team, competed on the track team, and, most notably, began his baseball career as a pitcher. He graduated with a degree in agriculture and immediately signed on with the Yankees organization. His tenure with the Yankees organization, though spanning ten years, was abbreviated. After spending five years in the team's farm system, he was brought up to the parent club at the somewhat advanced age of twenty-nine. In addition to serving two years in the army during World War II, much of the rest of his career was marred by a series of injuries, beginning in his rookie season.

Following his solid though losing debut in Chicago, Chandler won his next three starts, pitching shutouts against the White Sox and Indians and yielding just three runs against the Athletics over an eleven-day span at Yankee Stadium. But he was unable to finish the season. A lingering football injury to his right shoulder benched him for the last few months and kept him off the World Series roster. He finished with a record of 7–4 and an ERA of 2.84. The sore shoulder continued to plague him throughout his career and was aggravated by his pitching style: Chandler's out-pitch was a sinking fastball that worked best without a full follow-through, putting severe stress on his ailing shoulder.

All the same, by the time he closed out his career at the end of the 1947 season, he had established a solid reputation as a winner. Every one of his 109 victories was a complete game, and almost one-fourth of them—twenty-six—were shutouts. He was the All-Star Game's winning pitcher in 1942, a season in which he went 16–5. He was even better the following year, with a record of 20–4 and a league-leading ERA of 1.64. In 253 innings pitched, he gave up only 46 earned runs and just five home runs. He won two games in the World Series, including a 2–0 shutout in game five that was the clincher against the St. Louis Cardinals. He was named the league's Most Valuable Player, a rare achievement for a pitcher. After returning from the service in 1946, he went 20–8 with a 2.10 ERA and a career-high 138 strikeouts. He closed out his career in 1947 with a 9–5 record, finally surrendering to injuries at age forty.

Despite the glittering array of statistics he compiled over the course of his career, Chandler's very first win, a 4–0 shutout of the White Sox on May 18, had a special, if little noted, significance. It moved the Yankees into a first-place tie with the A's, and they did not relinquish the lead for the remainder of the season. They lost the next day to the Sox, but the A's also were defeated, and then, on May 21, the Yanks mounted a winning streak that solidified and then swelled their lead as they marched toward September. They won six in a row, lost one, and then proceeded to take another four straight. On Memorial Day, at the start of a doubleheader with Boston at Fenway Park, they led Cleveland by three-and-a-half games, Detroit by four, and they were five games ahead of Boston and Chicago. Their bats had come alive. DiMaggio was hitting .358, seven points higher than Gehrig; Selkirk was at .299; both Rolfe and

Myril Hoag, who was sharing left field with Henrich, were batting .286 and Henrich an impressive .321. The starting rotation of Gomez, Ruffing, Pearson, and Hadley was keeping the opposition in check, and Johnny Murphy was performing up to his reputation as the "Fireman" out of the bullpen while serving on occasion as a spot starter.

Hadley, just a year after his brilliant performance the previous season, was off to a sluggish start in 1937. He had won just one game and had an elevated ERA, well over 5, when he took the mound against Detroit on Tuesday, May 25, at Yankee Stadium. The Yankees were in the midst of their six-game winning streak and looking to open ground on the Tigers, still considered to be their chief opposition. They led the game 1–0 in the third inning when Detroit catcher Mickey Cochrane stepped to the plate. Cochrane, who was also serving as Tigers manager, was nearing the end of his Hall-of-Fame career. He was thirty-four years old, an age that was past a ballplayer's peak, particularly for a catcher, and he had suffered from emotional problems in 1936. With the stress of a losing season perhaps wearing on him, Cochrane succumbed to what then was referred to as a nervous breakdown. He appeared in just forty-four games and batted a lowly .270, some fifty points below his lifetime average.

But he seemed to be back in form in 1937; he was playing regularly and batting a shade over .300 when he faced Hadley with two out and Detroit trailing by a run. Cochrane proceeded to tie the game with a drive into the left-field stands. It was the prelude to an event that would cast a dark shadow over the rest of the season for Detroit. In the fifth inning, Cochrane was at bat with a man on first and two out. With the count at 3–1, Hadley unleashed a fastball that was sent streaking in the direction of Cochrane's head. Cochrane threw up his arm to protect himself, but it was too late; the pitch struck him flush in the head and, as reported at the time, Bill Dickey watched him fall to the ground and shouted "God almighty!" It was long before the advent of batting helmets, and it brought to memory the horrendous incident seventeen years earlier when Ray Chapman, Cleveland Indians shortstop, was fatally beaned by a pitch from the Yankees' Carl Mays in the Polo Grounds.

Cochrane was placed on a stretcher and taken by ambulance to St. Elizabeth's Hospital. He had suffered a triple fracture of the skull. He remained in critical condition for more than forty-eight hours and was not fully conscious for more than a week. He was attended by a leading brain specialist as well as the team physician, Dr. Emmett Walsh. Ten days after he was hospitalized, Cochrane was sent to Detroit on a special railroad car. His recovery was slow but complete. Hadley had tried to visit Cochrane while he was in the hospital but never got to his bedside. Hadley did not have a reputation as a head-hunter, and given that he was pitching to Cochrane with the go-ahead run on base, it was unlikely that he was seeking revenge for the earlier home run. "I don't know why the ball sailed," he said, "it just did." Hadley was relieved when, pitching in Detroit a little more than a week later, the fans greeted him with a standing ovation. As for Cochrane, his playing career ended the moment the pitch struck his head. He returned to the bench later in the year but retired from the sport entirely during the 1938 season when he was replaced as manager by

Del Baker. He died of a long illness at his home in Lake Forest, Illinois, in 1962 at the age of fifty-nine.

On June 27, with the race tightening a bit, the Yankees took on the Tigers at Yankee Stadium in what would prove to be one of the season's decisive turns. The Yanks opened an early 5–0 lead, but starter Pat Malone faltered in the fourth and ceded four runs back to Detroit. Johnny Murphy was summoned from the bullpen. Relief pitchers in those days were not assigned specific innings when they were called upon to perform, and no one counted the number of pitches they were permitted to throw before being replaced. Murphy yielded just one more run the rest of the way while the Yankees continued their offensive barrage and won the game 9–5. The victory gave them a three-game lead over the second-place White Sox and a four-game margin over Detroit and Boston. But what was most notable about the victory was it was the start of a winning streak that, over the next month, put the pennant under lock and key. Following the Detroit game, the Yanks took to the road, winning three straight in Philadelphia, taking two of three in Washington, and completing a two-game sweep in Boston before pausing for the All-Star Game on July 7. The All-Star break interrupted a home-run binge by DiMaggio during which he homered on five consecutive days, from July 1 to 5, bringing his season total to 20. When play resumed on July 9, he added two more. During that week, he lifted his batting average from .338 to .359. Batting cleanup behind DiMaggio, Gehrig was hitting .368 and Dickey .312.

It was small wonder then that all three, in addition to Red Rolfe at third and Lefty Gomez who started on the mound, accounted for more than half of the American League's opening lineup for the All-Star Game, which was played that year in the nation's capital. And, to no one's surprise, they all justified their selection as the American League won for the fourth time in five years, 8–3. Gomez pitched three shutout innings, yielding just one hit, to earn the win; Gehrig had a double, a home run, and four RBIs; Dickey also had a double and drove in a run; DiMaggio chipped in with a single; and Rolfe, in the lead-off spot, had two hits including a two-run triple. It was Rolfe's first appearance in an All-Star Game, but hardly his last. He made the team in each of the next three seasons.

Robert Abial "Red" Rolfe might well have had "Yankee" tattooed on his chest, so representative was he of the manner and style of the DiMaggio-era Yankees. Newspaper columnist Dan Daniel framed him perfectly, describing him as "well-behaved, the parson of the outfit. Never raises his voice, always showing a smile, always working hard, the baseball ideal, always studying things out there, always asking questions of McCarthy. A ballplayer in a couple hundred." His penchant for study was come by naturally. A native of Penacook, New Hampshire, Rolfe was a graduate of Phillips Exeter Academy and Dartmouth College. He kept detailed notes on opposing batters that included which field a player was likely to hit to depending on the type of pitch he was thrown.

Rolfe, who began his career as a shortstop, became the Yankees' regular third baseman in 1935. He fit perfectly into

McCarthy's scheme of things. As a left-hand hitter batting second behind Crosetti, he was naturally inclined to hit the ball
to the right side, making it easier for a runner to move up a
base. In his second season as a regular, he led the league with
15 triples and hit .319. He played in all 154 games in 1937 and
was a solid presence on defense. His best season came two years
later. While the 1939 Yankees were winning 106 games and
finishing seventeen games ahead of the second-place Red Sox,
Rolfe led the league with 213 hits, 46 doubles, and 139 runs
scored. He scored a run in 18 consecutive games, a record that
stood until 2000 when it was equaled by Cleveland's Kenny
Lofton. He also set personal career records batting .329 with
14 home runs and 80 runs batted in. He led the league in
doubles throughout the entire decade of the thirties.

Rolfe retired after the 1942 season and served as baseball and
basketball coach at Yale University. In 1949, he was named manager of the Detroit Tigers, a position he held with marginal success for four seasons. He then returned to Dartmouth where he
served as athletic director from 1943–46. He died in 1969 at the
age of sixty. His value to the Yankees during the team's greatest
dynasty was summed up by Connie Mack in an interview with
sportswriter Red Smith: "They talk about all the other fellas on
that team," Mack said, "but I notice the man who hurts us when
it counts is that third baseman. There is a real ballplayer."

The All-Star break, as it turned out, was nothing more than a
benign interlude in the Yankees' march toward another championship. When play resumed on Friday, July 9, the Yanks
poured it on in the first game of a four-game series with the

Washington Senators at Yankee Stadium. The score was 16–2. The attack was led by DiMaggio who went five-for-five while hitting for the cycle—a single, double, triple, and two home runs, his 21st and 22nd of the season—driving home seven runs and accounting for 15 total bases, having drawn a walk with the bases loaded. Gehrig followed with three hits in four times up, including his 14th home run and four RBIs. Monte Pearson, the beneficiary of the onslaught, added two hits and two RBIs of his own while picking up his sixth win of the season against no defeats. The New York barrage continued the next day with a 12–2 victory in the first game of a Sunday doubleheader. The nightcap ended in a 5–5 tie when the weather intervened after nine innings. The winning streak picked up two days later in Detroit with 10–2 and 13–6 routings of the Tigers, Ruffing winning his eleventh game of the season and Gomez his twelfth. By this time, the Yankees had won thirteen of their last fourteen games. They led Boston and Chicago by seven-and-a-half games, Detroit by eight, and by all measure they appeared to be running on cruise control.

The streak ended abruptly on Friday, July 16, with a 14–7 drubbing in Detroit. The Yankees led 5–0 going into the sixth inning, but then their pitching collapsed. Detroit rallied for seven runs off Pearson, Malone, and Frank Makosky in an inning that was unusual by any standard. Yankee pitchers struck out the side, but the damage was done between the strikeouts. The seven runs were scored on only one hit. The Tigers' cause was abetted by six bases on balls and consecutive errors by two sure-handed fielders, Rolfe and Crosetti. Johnny Broaca finally retired the side on a pair of fly balls, but the Detroit assault resumed when he returned to the mound in the bottom of the eighth. The Tigers lit into Broaca as if he were pitching batting practice. They scored five runs on six hits, including a double, a triple, and two home runs. In more than one respect, it spelled the finish for Broaca. The events that followed were woven into an enigmatic tapestry that defied explanation.

John Joseph Broaca was an all-around athlete and a bit of a scholar as well. Born in Lawrence, Massachusetts, he attended Lawrence High School before transferring to the more prestigious Phillips Academy from which he graduated two years later. From there, he went on to continue his studies at Yale University, where he was a tri-sport athlete, competing in baseball, boxing, and track. He signed with the Yankees in 1933 while still at Yale and made his major-league debut a year later. Manager Joe McCarthy, generally modest with praise of a young prospect, made an exception of Broaca, whom he described as "a promising youngster whom nothing can stop." In his rookie season, Broaca appeared to justify his manager's optimism. In his third start, he pitched a one-hit shutout against the St. Louis Browns, striking out ten batters. He finished the season with a record of 12–9 as a starter. He improved in the next two seasons, posting marks of 15–7 and then 12–7 in 1936. Shortly after the World Series, Broaca took himself a bride, and life seemed to be all sunshine and lollipops. But at the start of the 1937 season, quite suddenly and apparently without cause, it all went bad.

He started the season's fourth game at home on April 26 and picked up a 7–1 win in a complete game against the Philadelphia A's despite pitching indifferently, giving up six hits and seven bases on balls. His next outing, on May 2 against the Red Sox, also fell well below expectations. Although again going the distance, he suffered a 5–4 loss, yielding ten hits and four walks. He did not pitch again until May 20, but the rest seemed to be of little help. He was battered for 13 hits in a 3–1 defeat at the hands of the White Sox. His fortunes did not improve. In the second game of a Memorial Day doubleheader against Boston, he never made it out of the second inning. He gave up three runs in the first and one in the second after retiring only one batter. Eight days later, he took a 5–4 pastime at Chicago, and McCarthy decided he had seen enough for a while. Broaca did not pitch again until the July 16 game at Detroit when he was hailed in relief and was shelled for five runs in the bottom of the eighth. That game marked the end of the season for Broaca and, as circumstances unwound, his career was all but over. And that was the least of it. Later that day, his life began to fall apart, and he was never able to pick up the pieces.

After the game on July 16, Johnny Broaca disappeared. He left the team without notice and abandoned his wife who was eight months pregnant. For months, there was no trace of his whereabouts. He was not heard from again until September when his wife filed for divorce in Cape Cod. She accused him of physically abusing her, chasing her from the house in her underwear, and threatening to cut her throat or shoot her in the head. The divorce proceedings made for prominent tabloid news. The Yankees wanted no part of Broaca, and he seemed to have no place to turn.

In 1938, he tried his luck at professional boxing but quit the ring without having won a fight. In 1939, the Yankees traded his rights to the Cleveland Indians where he pitched mainly in relief and posted a 4–2 record. But his arm, which had given him trouble from time to time since his college days, finally gave out. He was traded to the New York Giants where he never pitched an inning, and in June of 1940, still only twenty-nine years old, he was returned to Cleveland and promptly released. After serving briefly on the home front during World War II, he returned to Lawrence and earned his living as a laborer on road construction crews. He lived alone in a small apartment. His co-workers knew never to ask him about his career in baseball.

In 1985, he was found dead of a heart attack on the floor of his apartment. He was seventy-five years old. He had had no contact with his son in almost half a century although they lived only twenty-five miles apart. On the twenty-fifth anniversary of his death, a niece of Broaca's—his brother's daughter—was interviewed by Bill Burt, a writer for the *Lawrence Eagle-Tribune.* "My dad said he just gave up," she told Burt. "My father spoke very little about Johnny. It's sad. Still, all these years later, it's very sad." And all these years later, there is still no clue about what went wrong in the sad saga of Johnny Broaca.

As for the Yankees, they picked up exactly where they had left off. They moved into Cleveland where they won three straight games and then on to St. Louis where they dispatched the Browns in a similar fashion. At that point in the season, on July 21, they had won nineteen of their last twenty-one games. Their lead was seven-and-a-half games over Chicago, eight-and-a-half over Detroit, and eleven-and-a-half over Boston. They had finally hit full stride.

8

Inevitability Looks More Like Destiny; Yanks Win Second Straight

Now, with the season more than half over, it often appeared that the Yankees were looking ahead, past the end of the regular season, to a possible rematch with the Giants in the World Series. Detroit and Chicago, particularly Detroit, were giving the Yanks all they could handle. Charlie Gehringer, who was on his way to winning the Most Valuable Player Award, for reasons few could fathom, was batting third and hitting .347. Hank Greenberg, batting behind him, was performing up to his customary excellence, with a .358 batting average and 24 home runs at the end of July. The White Sox also were making their presence felt, and the Yankees, though clinging to the lead, seemed unable to put any distance between themselves and the opposition.

On the other side of town, the Giants were having troubles of their own. They were in a pitched battle with the Chicago Cubs, and it appeared at times that it would be a losing one. They trailed the Cubs from late July through

August, and it would require a late-season surge to get them back on top.

As was much the case the previous year, the Giants were driven by the bat of right-fielder Mel Ott and carried on the strong left arm of Carl Hubbell. This season, though still clearly the ace, Hubbell had some help on the mound in the person of twenty-five-year-old rookie southpaw Cliff Melton who won twenty games, saved seven, and had an ERA of 2.61, more than half a run lower than Hubbell's. Ott, on his way to leading the league in homers with 31 while batting .294, also received more offensive support than he did the previous year. Three other regulars—shortstop Dick Bartell and outfielders Jo-Jo Moore and Jimmy Ripple—all hit above .300. Still, it was Ott who shouldered the load. In addition to his 31 homers, he drove in 95 runs, scored 99, and walked 102 times.

Nevertheless, the Giants were still mostly about pitching and defense, and Hubbell was the man, as he had been throughout the decade, winning twenty-plus games every season since 1933. He started 1937 by winning his first eight decisions. Added to the sixteen consecutive wins to close out the previous year, Hubbell won twenty-four consecutive games, a record that was still standing eighty years later. Not for nothing was he dubbed "King Carl" and referred to often as the "Meal Ticket."

Strange as it might seem, Hubbell's career had almost ended before it began. He was originally signed by the Detroit Tigers in 1926 at the age of twenty-three. But neither player-manager

Ty Cobb nor pitching coach George McBride was particularly impressed. What gave both men pause, ironically enough, was Hubbell's best pitch—the screwball. Mastered by very few pitchers, the screwball is thrown with the opposite arm action of a curveball. For a lefthander like Hubbell, the arm moves clockwise and the pitch breaks away from, rather than into, a right-hand batter. The issue was that the torque places a great deal of stress on the elbow, and Cobb and McBride expressed concerns about the effect this would have on the pitcher's durability. What seemed to go unnoticed was that Christy Mathewson, whom Cobb faced countless times during his career, threw a similar pitch—which was called a "fadeaway" rather than a screwball—without it appearing to shorten his career.

Hubbell's spring training performance in 1926 did little to improve his prospects. He was sent to the Toronto Maple Leafs of the International League where he went 7–7 on a championship club. In 1927, he was dropped two levels to the Decatur Commodores of the Illinois–Indiana–Iowa League (Three-I League). Despite his compiling a 14–7 record, Detroit did not invite him back to spring training in 1928. He was dispatched to the Beaumont Exporters of the Texas League, and he lost no time in telling Beaumont manager Claude Robinson that if he were not sold to another organization by the end of the year, he would retire from baseball and go into the oil business in his native Carthage, Missouri.

He did not have to wait until the end of the season. In June, Giant scout Dick Kinsella decided to take in a game between the Exporters and the Houston Buffs while in Houston for the Democratic National Convention that nominated Al Smith to oppose Herbert Hoover. Kinsella was impressed. He followed Hubbell for the next month and became convinced. He called Giant manager John McGraw and, without reservation, recommended that they sign Hubbell. The Giants had been playing on the margins for the past few seasons, finishing behind St. Louis and Pittsburgh, and the prospect of adding a strong left-hander to the staff proved to be inviting.

Hubbell didn't disappoint. He went 10–6 in his first season and followed with eighteen wins in 1929. He won in double digits over the next three seasons, but it wasn't until 1933 that he filed his claim to stardom. He won twenty-three games against twelve losses, the first of five consecutive years in which he won more than twenty games. His twenty-three victories included ten shutouts, and his earned run average was a remarkable 1.66. At one point, he compiled a streak of 46.1 scoreless innings, which included four consecutive shutouts. The 1933 season was further embellished by his winning the National League's Most Valuable Player Award, a feat he repeated three years later, becoming the first player to win the award unanimously, as he led the Giants to the World Series.

One of his most stunning accomplishments came on July 2, 1933, in the first game of a doubleheader against the Cardinals at the Polo Grounds. Hubbell pitched eighteen scoreless innings, allowing only six hits, as the Giants prevailed 1–0 when second baseman Hughie Critz drove in Jo-Jo Moore with the only run of the game. Tex Carlton was almost as impressive for the Cards, pitching sixteen shutout innings before being replaced by Jesse Haines who yielded the game's lone run. Making the day even more memorable, the second game was also a 1–0 affair with the Giants beating Dizzy Dean behind Roy Parmelee. The game was completed in a fleeting one hour and twenty-three minutes. The eighteen-inning opener occupied just over four hours. Spectators out for a leisurely Sunday afternoon saw the equivalent of three baseball games, featuring a total of five pitchers, in about four and a half hours, approximately the length of time it would take for the Yankees to complete a nine-inning game against the Red Sox decades later, with perhaps a dozen or more pitchers taking turns on the mound.

In the final analysis, there is no telling to what degree pitching as much as he did shortened Hubbell's career. Eighteen innings was of course a case in the extreme, but it was not altogether unusual. He pitched more than 300 innings every season between 1933 and 1936. When he didn't quite meet that mark, he was close, usually upward of 250 innings. What has been little noted is that he pitched in relief in addition to starting more than thirty games every year from 1929 through 1937. In 1933, long before the age of bullpen specialists, he led the league in saves with eight and completed thirteen of the twenty-two games he started. But in 1937 the wear on his arm had begun to show. He later confessed that the pain in his pitching arm was becoming unbearable. He completed only eighteen of thirty-three starts that season, but he was at his peak down the stretch, winning five games in September when the money was on the table. Although he pitched into 1944 before retiring, he never again won more than thirteen games in a season.

While the Giants were caught in the fever of a late-season pennant push, the Yankees were chugging along with their goal clearly in sight and the outcome assured. They moved into the latter part of the season performing with a mechanical precision that belied any sense of urgency. It was as if they were adhering to a choreography that had been carefully scripted well in advance. Win a few, lose a few; the days followed one another in a slow but certain march to a destiny that was foreordained.

Their 19–2 winning streak, which ended on July 21, was followed by a lackluster finish to July, but at the start of August, they put their foot to the pedal. They took off on a nine-game winning streak, drubbing the lowly St. Louis Browns 14–5 with a display of raw power featuring the one-two punch of DiMaggio and Gehrig. DiMaggio went three-for-three with his 31st homer and a double; Gehrig hit his 21st home run and a triple while going four-for-five. Both men were hitting over .370. The beneficiary of the attack that day was Spud Chandler, who improved his record to 6–3. Two days later, the Yanks swept the White Sox in a doubleheader, DiMaggio and Gehrig again hitting homers and Red Ruffing winning his fourteenth game against three losses. They kept the streak going in the nightcap when a Bill Dickey grand slam in the eighth erased a 3–1 deficit. Johnny Murphy, in relief of Gomez, won for the ninth time against just two defeats.

The five-game win streak was put on hold briefly on August 6 when a 7–6 decision over Cleveland was overturned by league officials and declared a tie.

Following an unwritten script in which they thrived on late-inning comebacks, the Yankees had tied the score at 5–5, scoring three times in the ninth to send the game into extra innings. In the top of the tenth, Hal Trosky, the Indians' first-baseman, homered to give Cleveland the edge, but as had become their custom, the Yankees answered in the bottom of the inning. With runners on second and third and two out, DiMaggio hit a line drive that caromed off the glove of third-baseman Odell Hale and continued down the left-field line. The tying and winning runs crossed the plate, giving DiMaggio a double and the Yankees what appeared to be a 7–6 victory. As it turned out, not all the pieces were in place. Since third-base umpire, George Moriarty, had called the ball foul when it hit Hale's glove, left-fielder Moose Solters failed to pursue it. Subsequently, umpires' crew-chief Charles Johnston reversed the call, saying that Hale was in fair territory when the ball hit his glove, thus allowing both runs to score and giving the Yanks their sixth straight win—or so it seemed. Cleveland filed a protest with the league office which ruled that the runs might not have scored had the ball not been called foul, and the game went into the books as a no-decision, or tie.

All told, it was little more than a pause in the Yankees' relentless drive toward October. They picked up the pace the next day, scoring three runs in the seventh for a 6–3 win, with Gehrig hitting his 27th home run and Ruffing picking up his fifteenth decision. The streak swelled to seven when an eighth-inning run produced a 6–5 win, and to nine on August 11 with a twin-bill sweep of the Red Sox at Fenway Park. The opener went fourteen innings, the nightcap seven as darkness descended across the streets of Boston. Each game was decided in the late innings. The Yankees seemed to have evolved a pattern of winning games with late-inning rallies that were being descriptively referred to as "five-o'clock lightning." As all games were played in the afternoon in those halcyon days of baseball, and with a customary starting time of three o'clock, it was often around five o'clock when Yankee lightning struck.

The early August streak stretched the lead to eleven games over a late-surging Boston team, eleven-and-a-half over Chicago, and twelve over Detroit. From that point on, there was no looking back. The Yanks clinched their second straight pennant on September 23, with more than a week left in the season. At season's end, their margin over runner-up Detroit was thirteen games. They had matched their total of 102 victories of the year before. The individual stats were staggering. DiMaggio hit .346, led the league in homers with 46, and drove in 167 runs. He also led the league in slugging percentage, runs scored, and total bases. To the surprise of most observers, he finished second in the MVP voting behind Tiger second baseman Charlie Gehringer. Gehringer had an impressive year himself with a league-best .371 batting average, but his home run total was only 14 while his RBIs numbered 96. Hank Greenberg came in third, leading the league in RBIs with 183 and adding a home run total of 40 and a batting average of .337. The balance of the MVP list belonged largely to the Yankees. Gehrig, with totals of .351, 37, and 159, was fourth in the balloting; Dickey, who had the best year of his career, was fifth; Ruffing, eighth; and Gomez, ninth, giving the Yankees five of the top nine candidates.

For the second straight year, New York was going to be treated to a Subway Series: the Yanks and the Giants, as they had been for three years in a row from 1921 to 1923 and a total of five times in the past decade and a half. As fate would have it, there would not be another between the two New York clubs until 1951, the year of Bobby Thomson's "Shot Heard 'Round the World."

The Giants had not had an easy time of it in 1937. On August 13, they trailed the Cubs by six-and-a-half games. But two days later they began a streak of five straight wins while the Cubs obliged by dropping the same number of decisions. On September 2, the Giants moved into first place with a 5–4 victory over the Cardinals, and they held it for the duration of the season.

The Yankees, for their part, were in the midst of flexing their muscles, learning season by season just how good they could be. They would go on to dominate the forties, fifties, and early sixties as they had the twenties and late-thirties. The Giants, by contrast, were nearing the end of their two-decade run. Bill Terry, now the manager of the team and to this day the last National Leaguer to hit over .400, had played his last game at first base. Hubbell would not again approach twenty wins. Time, as was its way, was about to set in. But as the Series approached, the Giants were relatively sanguine. They seemed to be somewhat better balanced than they were the year before; such potency as they had was distributed more evenly through the lineup. And, of course, there was still the prime-time Mr. Hubbell, ready to open at Yankee Stadium against Lefty Gomez.

Hubbell seemed to be in total command right from the start. He yielded a one-out single to DiMaggio in the first in-ning but retired the next two batters—Gehrig and Dickey—on fly balls to center field. Then, looking every bit like the King Carl still at his peak, he set down the next twelve batters in order in innings two through five. He had been staked to a one-run lead in the top of the fifth when catcher Gus Mancuso grounded into a double play with runners on first and third, and Hubbell appeared ready and able to protect it.

But the Yankees had ideas of their own. The sixth inning began with an ominous turn of events. Hubbell walked the leadoff batter, Lefty Gomez, perhaps the weakest hitter in all of baseball. It was an unlikely way to end his string of retiring fourteen consecutive batters, and it proved to be a foreboding of what lay ahead. Crosetti followed with a single. With Red Rolfe at the plate, Hubbell picked Gomez off at second but shortstop Dick Bartell dropped the ball, and when Rolfe walked the bases were loaded with nobody out. It was a situation made to order for the Yankees, and the roof was about to fall in on Hubbell and the Giants. DiMaggio singled, scoring two runs, and he moved to second on the throw home. Gehrig was walked intentionally to reload the bases. Dickey singled, bringing home another run. Selkirk singled home two more runs. That ended Hubbell's day. Harry Gumbert was summoned in relief, and he allowed two of the baserunners he inherited to score. The Yankee totals for the inning were seven runs on just five hits. Lazzeri rounded out the scoring in the eighth with a home run deep into the left-field seats. Gomez gave the Giants nothing further, and game one ended in an 8–1 Yankee victory.

Sadly for the Giants, game two was not much different from the opener. The Yankees won by the identical score of

8–1. Again trailing 1–0, they scored twice in the fifth on hits by Myril Hoag, Selkirk, Lazzeri, and pitcher Red Ruffing. And, as in game one, they exploded in the sixth with four runs coming home on singles by Gehrig and Dickey, a double by Selkirk, and a two-RBI single by Ruffing. Ruffing's two hits and three RBIs were a welcome complement to his one-run, seven-hit pitching.

So, hardly breaking a sweat, the Yankees had taken a 2–0 lead with the Series heading to the Polo Grounds where the Giants were hoping to stem the tide on their home turf. But it was to no avail. This time, the Yankees did not wait until the middle innings to get matters underway. They chipped away at Hal Schumacher with a run in the second, two in the third, and one each in the fourth and fifth while Monte Pearson held the Giants scoreless until surrendering a lone run in the sixth. With a 5–1 lead, Pearson received a bit of help from Johnny Murphy who came in with the bases loaded to get the final out in the ninth.

Now, trailing three games to none, the Giants found themselves looking to avert a sweep. No team had ever come back from three games down to win the Series, and no team would for at least the next eighty years. But the Giants managed to save face, stemming the tide for at least one day. Hubbell was ready this time. He went the distance, allowing the Yankees only six hits in a 7–3 win. The game was all but over in the second inning, when the Giants put together six runs on seven singles off starter Bump Hadley who lasted just an inning and a third.

However, the victory did no more than prolong the festivities for one more day. In game five, the Yankees went to work early, taking a 2–0 lead on solo homers by Hoag and DiMaggio in the second and third innings, but a two-run drive by the Giants' Mel Ott evened the score in the bottom of the third. Matters were decided in somewhat surprising fashion in the fifth when the Yanks scored twice. Lazzeri led off with a triple and came home on a single off the glove of second baseman Burgess Whitehead by none other than Gomez himself. An RBI double by Gehrig concluded the scoring with the Yankees in charge 4–2.

The Series was by every measure a mundane tournament with little suspense and few memorable moments. For one Yankee, however, it might have been cast in amber as the highlight of his career. Myril Hoag, who during his career played all three outfield positions, was one of those rare commodities whose greatest value was that of a utility player whose insertion in the lineup did not in any way weaken his team. His hitting, though not imposing, was respectable; he was sound in the field; and he had good speed on the bases. Hoag had been a member of the team since 1931 but was used sparingly, chiefly as a back-up for Earl Combs, Ben Chapman, and Jake Powell.

Until 1937, he was best remembered for an outfield collision he had with DiMaggio the previous season. The rookie DiMaggio was playing right field with Hoag in center, and the two tracked a line drive struck by Detroit's Goose Goslin and collided at top speed. While Goslin circled the bases for an inside-the-park home run, Hoag and DiMaggio lay flat on the outfield grass. Neither man appeared to be seriously injured when they got to their feet, and both continued to play. But two days later, Hoag was found unconscious in his hotel room.

He was rushed to the hospital and received immediate surgery to relieve a brain clot. The initial concern was that even if he survived he might never be able to play again. But Hoag managed to recuperate quickly.

He returned to action in 1937 and had his best year. Playing mostly left field in place of the erratic Powell, Hoag appeared in 106 games, the most of his career, and batted .301 with three home runs, also a personal high. In his two previous World Series—1932 and 1936—Hoag had made just one appearance. He scored a run in 1932 after coming off the bench to run for Ruffing in the seventh inning of the final game in the Yankees' sweep of the Cubs. But he played left field in every game of the 1937 Series, batted .300, and his second-inning home run gave the Yanks the lead in the deciding fifth game.

Although Hoag's achievement was noteworthy, the star of the Series was Tony Lazzeri who sparkled in the field and led all hitters with a batting average of .400. As it turned out, it would be a fitting coda to Lazzeri's twelve-year career as a Yankee. Along with Gehrig, Lazzeri was the only holdover from the Ruthian era, and at age thirty-three, his production had begun to flag. He hit only .244 during the season, the lowest batting average of his career, and drove in only seventy runs, also a career low. But of equal consideration for the Yankees was their awareness that a promising replacement, Joe Gordon, was ready to move up from Newark to the parent club. At the same time, Phil Wrigley, who had inherited ownership of the Chicago Cubs from his father, was aware of the situation and certain that Lazzeri still had some good baseball left in him. The transaction was completed at the end of October in a manner typical of the Yankee organization at the time, efficiently and with due consideration of the parties involved. Ed Barrow, the Yankees' general manager, discussed the situation with Lazzeri who said he was more than willing to make the move. Accordingly, he was given his unconditional release, and he signed on with Chicago for a healthy salary and a generous bonus. Wrigley was delighted. The Cubs seemed to need a bit of a charge. Having won the pennant in 1935, they finished second to the Giants in 1936 and 1937. Wrigley was openly forthright about his motives in acquiring Lazzeri.

"What I am really trying to do," he said, "is to capture some of that Yankee spirit I admire so much. It seems to me that for a long time Lazzeri has typified that spirit, and I am sure he can impart it to our players."

Wrigley's premonition was right on the mark. The Cubs won the pennant in 1938, finishing two games ahead of Pittsburgh and five up on the Giants. Coming off the bench to spell Billy Jurges, the regular second baseman, Lazzeri hit a respectable .267, with five home runs and 23 RBIs. But whatever fragment of Yankee spirit he brought with him, it was not quite equal to what remained at its source. The Cubs would be no match for the Yankees when they met in October.

1938

The Yankees set a major-league record, winning a third consecutive world championship with a late-season surge.

9

Where Have You Gone, Joe DiMaggio?

With two straight titles in the books, looking ahead seemed to be less a matter of speculation than an exercise in scientific certainty. The Yankees, by all appearance, had become more than a powerhouse baseball team; they had taken on the aspect of a force of nature. One did not, after all, speculate on whether gravity would assert itself on the next such occasion; it was merely a condition that was taken into account. So it was with the Yankees' quest for a record-breaking, third consecutive championship. The telling factor in their two-year run was not that the team had won, not even that it had won by convincing margins. What was most impressive was that the Yankees performed with a sense of self-assurance, which left one to contemplate that even when losing they were still in control, that whenever it was called for they could right all the wrongs and convert impending defeat into victory. What could one possibly muster as a counter-force? Any deterioration in style or performance, it seemed, would have to come from the inside. Something essential would have to be lost or forfeited.

The only team that could beat the Yankees was the Yankees. And if loss might be the great equalizer, its shadow was cast unexpectedly even before the 1938 season began. Spring training opened with Joe DiMaggio nowhere in sight.

Offered a contract of $25,000, DiMaggio told owner Jacob Ruppert that he thought he was worth at least $40,000. Given his first two seasons, which were nothing less than spectacular, it was not as though he was short of evidence. He had a combined batting average of .335, with 75 home runs and 292 runs batted in. The argument could be made that at the age of twenty-three DiMaggio was already at least as good as anyone in the game, and he seemed to be improving. He had been paid $8,500 in his rookie season, and his salary was twice that—$17,000—in 1937. Ruppert was quick to point out that not even Gehrig, with fifteen all-star seasons behind him, earned as much as he was asking (Gehrig's salary in 1938 was $36,000), to which DiMaggio responded that it was too bad Gehrig had been underpaid all those years. Ruppert wasted no time in rejecting DiMaggio's request. Just as emphatically, DiMaggio turned down Ruppert's offer. When April came and spring training dawned, the Yankees' young superstar was officially a holdout, a rare situation in those days of the Depression.

As time passed, conditions grew more intense, and the dueling parties did nothing to alleviate the raw feelings that drove both sides. As spring training proceeded and opening day of the regular season drew closer, DiMaggio appeared to be trying to dramatize his case by antagonizing Yankee management. He was often seen in public in the company of a friend, boxing promoter Joe Gould. Ruppert and general manager Ed Barrow believed that Gould, who knew something about financial negotiations, might be behind DiMaggio's unyielding position, in effect acting as his adviser or player agent. In turn, Ruppert and Barrow regularly pled their case in the New York press, which covered the story daily and in glaring headlines, despite what DiMaggio thought to be an agreed upon, self-imposed gag order regarding negotiations. In one instance, most of the daily papers (there were nearly a dozen of them in the thirties) carried a photo of DiMaggio wearing an apron and cooking spaghetti in his restaurant, DiMaggio's Grotto, on Fisherman's Wharf in San Francisco. There was also a report by the Associated Press that the perennial American League doormat St. Louis Browns had offered the Yankees $150,000, a princely sum at that time, for the rights to DiMaggio. Colonel Ruppert was quoted as telling Browns' ownership that DiMaggio "is not for sale at any price."

Although New York had welcomed him enthusiastically on his arrival and had already begun treating him as a deserving successor to the legacies of Ruth and Gehrig, his attitude did not play well with a public that was still dealing with a sinking economy. Unemployment had risen from 14.3 to 19 percent between 1937 and '38. Few fans earned as much as DiMaggio had scornfully rejected, and hardly any came close to earning the sum that he was demanding.

Feelings grew increasingly strained as opening day approached and reached a crescendo on Monday, April 18, when the Yankees dropped the season opener 8–4 to the Red Sox at Fenway Park. They bounced back the next day to win the opener of a doubleheader, but in the second game they were humiliated when a little-known pitcher by the name of Fritz Ostermueller, who had never had a winning season, shut them out with just two hits. With a 3–2 loss the following day, the Yanks had dropped three of four to the Red Sox, scoring a total of only 11 runs. The Bosox, as they were called, were looked upon as the prime contender to unseat the Yankees in 1938. They had an all-star infield, featuring Jimmie Foxx at first base; Bobby Doerr, in his sophomore year, at second; manager Joe Cronin at shortstop; and Pinky Higgins at third. An outfield consisting of Ben Chapman, Doc Cramer, and Joe Vosmik rounded out a lineup in which seven starters—all but Doerr and catcher Gene Desaultes— hit better than .300.

The Yankees' poor start increased the pressure on DiMaggio, and following the Boston debacle he finally relented and agreed to sign for the original offer of $25,000. After delivering some words of praise for Colonel Ruppert, DiMaggio went on to explain his position in an article under his own by-line in *Liberty* magazine:

What I say about the Colonel is not a lot of soft soap. He offered me $25,000. I believed I was worth as much as $40,000. At no time was there anything personal in our disagreement. If you offer $8,000 for a house and the seller insists it is worth $10,000, does that mean you are deadly enemies?

I kept holding out because I thought I was right. But as the season approached I began to weaken. Not because I had changed my mind about what I was entitled to, but because the game gets into your blood.

When the Yankees dropped two out of three in Boston, I decided that my place was with the club and that money no longer was the first consideration. So I called up the Colonel, and in five minutes everything was straightened out.

I accepted the contract for $25,000 but did so without giving up my idea that from the books—not only the American League records but the attendance figures of the New York club—I was worth $40,000 to the Yankees.

DiMaggio returned to the lineup on Saturday, April 30, and went one-for-three in an 8–4 Yankee victory. He made his first appearance at Yankee Stadium on Tuesday, May 3, and was greeted with a cascade of boos. The newspapers had not been kind to him during his holdout, and the resentment in New York ran deep. The fans continued to show their disapproval, booing his every move in the field, at bat, or on the bases. He was seen as greedy and selfish during a time when most of them were scratching and scraping to stay afloat.

It was a far different era from the attitude that evolved decades later when athletes had a union and were represented by agents who orchestrated their contract demands. It was long before players could become free agents and demand multi-year contracts. Throughout the early years of baseball and right on through the first few decades of the post–World War II era, players were viewed as heroes but not as celebrities. Their

skills inspired awe, but they were not revered as presences beyond one's reach. They were treated as if they were part of
the neighborhood in the cities in which their teams played.
With few exceptions, it was as if they were "one of us." They
did not earn salaries that exceeded the dreams of the average
worker; a bit more perhaps, but given the glory they brought
to their cities, they were deemed to be worth it. If you were a
teenager back then, it was not thought to be unusual that you
might meet Phil Rizzuto or Yogi Berra walking down River
Avenue, beneath the elevated subway line on the way to the
Stadium, and you might briefly exchange pleasantries and get
an autograph, a warm hello, and a slap on the back. And then
you might scrape together some change and pay your way in
to cheer wholeheartedly as the fellow you just met gave you his
best on the playing field.

As times changed, players were looked upon differently.
They were not at all like you or those you knew and spent
time with. They were deities in a culture that had become fix-
ated on celebrity. You saw them close-up on television. You
knew what they looked like and recognized the sound of their
voices. They were somehow beyond the reach of work-a-day
folks like us, and fans did not seem to resent a superstar switch-
ing teams so he could earn $20 million a year instead of a mere
$15 million. They occupied a different orbit, and you expected
them to be treated differently. It was not that way in DiMaggio's day. If you cared enough about the game and admired the
player's gifts, you might place him in a showcase apart from
you and your next-door neighbor—but he was still one of you,
like a friend who had achieved great things and merited your

goodwill and admiration. But you still met on par with one another. So when DiMaggio appeared to strut his way about and assert his uniqueness, it was viewed by many as an act of betrayal.

DiMaggio was clearly hurt by the treatment he was receiving from the fans as well as in the press. Years later, in recollection, he told Joe Durso of the *New York Times:* "I know I was wrong holding out as long as I did. I hear the boos and I read in the papers that the cheers offset them, but you can't prove that by me. All I ever hear is boos. And the mail. You would have thought I had kidnapped the Lindbergh baby, the way some of the letters read."

DiMaggio understood that no matter how earnest his explanations might sound, they would not be sufficient to turn the fans in his favor. He needed to bring them back by his performance on the playing field, and he wasted no time in getting started. When he resumed playing, the Yankees' record stood at 8–7. Starting on May 2, his third game back in action, the Yanks won seven in a row. DiMaggio was hitting an even .500 with four home runs in a total of nine games. He had climbed his way back into the fans' affection, and the press gave every indication of having forgiven him.

On the last day of the streak, May 11, the Yankees defeated Cleveland 4–1 and edged into a first-place tie with Washington. Their stay did not last long, and they would not see first place again until the season was nearly half over. With the streak ended, they slipped into a kind of funk and lost seven of their next ten games as they headed into the Memorial Day weekend. On May 29 their record stood at 17–14; they were in fourth place, three-and-a-half games behind the league-leading Indians and also trailing the Red Sox and Senators. Several of their big hitters had failed to get untracked. Gehrig was hitting only .264; Powell in left field was at an anemic .200; and, in Lazzeri's absence, the second-base position was producing very little.

The wildly heralded Joe Gordon, up from Newark, started the season tentatively. An acrobat in the field, he was having trouble hitting major-league curveballs. His batting average was down to .156 at the end of May, and McCarthy thought it best to sit him down for a while and try to restore his confidence. Taking his place at second base was a six-year veteran by the name of Bill Knickerbocker whom the Yankees obtained in an off-season trade with the St. Louis Browns. A shortstop by trade, Knickerbocker was a sound, everyday player who was reliable in the field and was hitting a respectable .267 while filling in at second base. But give or take a few months, the future would belong to Gordon, the Flash, as he was called, a bow to the comic-strip character Flash Gordon, but even more apropos, a name that was descriptive of the quick deftness he displayed around second base.

Joseph Lowell Gordon, a native of Los Angeles, was raised in Portland, Oregon, where his mother took him and his brother when their father died. Joe soon displayed multi-talents both on and off the playing fields. At the age of fourteen, he played the violin in the Portland Symphony Orchestra. At the University of Oregon, though weighing only 150 pounds, he shared the backfield with Tuffy Leemans, who later starred for the

New York Giants in the NFL and was elected to the Pro Football Hall of Fame in 1978. But it was on the baseball field that Gordon excelled. Playing shortstop, he batted .380 in 1934 and a lusty .415 the following year as Oregon won the Northwest Conference championship in both seasons. Yankees scout Bill Essick signed him to a contract in 1936, and he was sent to their Oakland Oaks farm team in the Pacific Coast League. Playing shortstop in 142 games, he hit .300 with six home runs and 33 doubles. But it was in the field that he shined.

Described right from the start as "acrobatic," Gordon was moved to second base during spring training in 1937 as McCarthy decided to groom him to take the place of the aging Lazzeri. Gordon was dispatched to the Newark Bears, who won the International League championship with a record of 109–43, 25½ games ahead of the second-place Montreal Royals. Often described as the second-best team in baseball, just behind the Yankees, the Bears went on to win what was known at the time as the Little World Series, defeating the Columbus club of the American Association. Gordon did not disappoint. He batted .280 with 26 home runs while displaying the same skills at second as he did at shortstop. Newark manager Oscar Vitt told McCarthy that Gordon would be the "greatest second baseman you ever saw." Vitt went on to say that Gordon was "better than anybody in the big leagues now, with the exception of Gehringer, and he'll catch him in a year."

Paired with Crosetti at shortstop, the Yankees now had a double-play combination that revived memories of the Cubs' legendary "Tinker to Evers to Chance" in the early years of the century. So the Yankees viewed the 1938 season with optimism

and high expectations for Gordon. But while he did not disappoint in the field, he was having nothing but trouble at the
plate. He appeared to have lost his confidence; McCarthy took
note and took whatever measures he thought necessary to
bring Gordon to his peak. "Gordon is overawed by the pitchers
in this league," McCarthy told Dan Daniel, a columnist for the
·*New York World-Telegram*. "He doesn't know that he has the
makings of a greater second baseman than we have seen in the
majors in twenty years."

Gordon spent the month of May and the first week of
June on the bench seated next to the manager, who generally
preferred to sit alone. But McCarthy was now on a mission.
He was trying to instill a degree of self-assurance in his new
second baseman. As Freeman recounts, "One day during a
game against Detroit, the Tigers' future Hall of Fame second
baseman Charlie Gehringer made an error. McCarthy turned
to Gordon and said, 'Don't they say that he's the best second baseman in the game? You'd have fielded that ball with a
catcher's mitt.'"

Gordon was slated to return to action at the start of June,
but perhaps as the final step in his psychological rehabilitation,
he was granted a brief leave to wed his high school sweetheart,
Dorothy Crum. They were married on June 4, and five days
later Gordon was back in the lineup with an RBI-triple in a
5–3 victory over the Chicago White Sox. He was batting only
.180, with just two home runs to his credit, but those stats
were about to spike. After a full week at work, his batting average was up to .234. It continued to rise. In a doubleheader on
June 29, Gordon went six-for-seven with a double; two home

runs, bringing his total to six; and four RBIs, giving him 27 on the year. His batting average was a lofty .322. As might be expected, he cooled off somewhat in the dog days of July and August but finished his rookie season hitting .255 with 25 home runs and 97 runs batted in. His numbers would improve in every department the following season as he moved toward an eleven-year Hall of Fame career. Gordon gave his manager due credit for his turn-around. When asked what he had learned sitting on the bench next to McCarthy for a month, he responded, "Everything . . . [I] never knew there was so much baseball in the world before."

But some of that baseball mystique seemed to be missing from the Yankees' repertoire from the very start of the 1938 season. Even the resurgence that had followed DiMaggio's return to the lineup did not seem to put them back on track. Still, the fans remained faithful. Despite a month of mediocre baseball during which the Yankees were just two games over .500, attendance was keeping pace with what it had been in their two championship seasons. The largest crowd in Stadium history—81,841—filled the park to more than capacity for a Memorial Day doubleheader with the Red Sox. And the fans got their money's worth, watching the Yanks sweep the Sox in two games that bore no resemblance to one another.

Game one held out the promise of a titillating pitchers' duel, matching Ruffing, with a record of 5–1, against Lefty Grove, a perfect 8–0. Even at the tail end of his career, Grove was a force to be reckoned with. Pitching for the Athletics, from 1927 to 1933, he won more than twenty games in seven consecutive seasons, highlighted by thirty-one victories in 1931. His ERA was below three in five of those seasons. But not today; the Yankees got to him early, with a run in the second on doubles by Dickey and Powell. Two more runs were added in the third, which opened with singles by Rolfe, DiMaggio, and Gehrig and, following an out, another single by Myril Hoag. It all fell apart for Grove in the fourth. Ruffing grounded out to open the inning but five runs would score before another out was registered, and it was not Grove who recorded it.

Manager and shortstop Joe Cronin, in what appeared to be as much an act of mercy as a strategic maneuver, lifted Grove and brought in Archie McKain, a mop-up reliever and occasional starter of little distinction. Hardly accustomed to playing a feature role, McKain was about to make news in questionable fashion. Entering the game with runners on first and second, he gave up run-scoring singles to Dickey and Hoag, which brought to the plate Jake Powell. Powell, who was being used mostly off the bench to spell Hoag or Henrich, was batting a less than impressive .212 when he stepped in with two on and one out. McKain, not renowned for his control, plunked Powell in the midsection to load the bases. Although it seemed unlikely that a pitcher would intentionally hit the light-hitting Powell to put yet another runner in scoring position, Powell took umbrage and headed for the mound with blood in his eye. Cronin charged in from his shortstop position to intercept him and the two engaged in an on-field brawl that, word had it, was a prelude to another fight that took place under the stands. Both players were ejected, Henrich running for Powell and Eric McNair replacing Cronin in the field. As for Powell, he would soon seal his fate with the Yankees when he engaged in his racist interview in late July. When play resumed, McKain managed to retire the side, allowing one more run to score on a fielder's choice. The final score was 10–0, Ruffing going all the way with a three-hit shutout.

The second game, by contrast, called for the Yankees to come from behind in a 5–4 struggle that was not decided until the bottom of the ninth. Gomez, who was not off to a good start with a 2–5 record going into the game, did not get off well in this game, either. He surrendered three runs in the first inning and another in the fifth to put the Yanks at a 4–0 disadvantage. But they answered with a run in the bottom of the fifth and scored twice more in the sixth to bring them within one run at 4–3 going into the eighth. Then they struck with five-o'clock lightning. Dickey doubled home Crosetti to tie the score, and they won it with a run in the ninth that came by way of the grace of Boston third baseman Pinky Higgins. With Knickerbocker on first with a single, Gomez, still in the game, bunted toward third; Higgins fielded the ball and threw wildly to first. Knickerbocker, whose speed was one of his assets, came around to score all the way from first.

The sweep of the twin bill was satisfying, but it earned New York nothing in the standings. Cleveland also swept a holiday doubleheader, so the Yankees remained in second place, still four games behind the Indians who gave every indication of being a serious threat. Boston, too, held out the possibility of making a run for it. If the Yanks were going to make it three in a row, it wasn't going to be easy.

10

Late Season Surge Puts Yanks in Control

The Memorial Day sweep had no lasting effect. The Yankees continued to play in lackluster fashion. Throughout the first three weeks of June, they compiled a record of 11–10 despite a six-game winning streak beginning on June 9. On that date, Gehrig was way below par, batting .266. DiMaggio, hitting a fairly robust .331, was about to fall into a rare slump. In the course of the next week, his batting average would drop to .307. He was also suffering from a power outage. He had only eight home runs by June 6 and would not hit his ninth until June 22. On the mound, only Ruffing, at 8–2, was performing as expected. Gomez carried a record of 4–6; Pearson was 3–5. Things appeared to hit bottom in Cleveland on June 21 when the Yankees dropped the first of three straight games before avoiding a sweep with an 8–6 win. They fell to four -and-a-half games behind the front-running Indians and also trailed the second-place Red Sox. Their record stood at a meager seven games above .500.

Of course, the competition had something to do with their third-place standing. Cleveland was playing exceptionally well with a record of 36–20 following their shellacking of the Yankees. They had a power-laden lineup, particularly in the heart of their batting order. Left fielder Jeff Heath was hitting .308; center fielder Earl Averill a stunning .389; Hal Trosky at first base was at .352; and third baseman Ken Keltner was batting .309. The pitching core was anchored by Bob Feller who, in his third season and just nineteen years old, was coming into his own with a record of 8–2. Johnny Allen, the former Yankee, was 9–1 and flourishing. The Indians had taken first place on May 18 and would not relinquish it until mid-July.

The Red Sox also were in the mix. In fact, they would pass Cleveland with a late summer surge and remain the Yankees' most potent challenger. Their lineup was already without weakness, and as the season progressed and they made their move, a number of observers believed it was time to call from the minors a young outfielder who was tearing apart the American Association. Although he was playing for the Minneapolis Millers, a Double-A league team, his hitting had already attracted the attention of the likes of Rogers Hornsby, as well it should have. From late May through mid-June, Ted Williams put together a twenty-two-game hitting streak. By the end of the season, with the Millers placing sixth in an eight-team race, Williams had won the American Association's Triple Crown, hitting .366 with 46 home runs and 142 RBIs. The following year, as a rookie, he would prove that those numbers were fairly typical of what the Red Sox might expect.

The Yankees' four-game series in Cleveland concluded a two-week road trip during which they went 7–6, and they were no doubt looking forward to returning home. While they were away, however, Yankee Stadium was not totally abandoned. On June 22, as the Yanks were dropping a doubleheader in Cleveland, the Stadium was host to a heavyweight championship fight that had captured the attention of the nation and, in fact, much of the world.

Joe Louis, known in those racially primitive days as the Brown Bomber, was about to defend his heavyweight title against the pride of Germany, Max Schmeling. Two years earlier, almost to the day, Schmeling had beaten the then-undefeated Louis with a twelfth-round knockout. Nazi Germany, already perceived as a threat to world peace, trumpeted Schmeling's victory as evidence of Aryan supremacy. Joseph Goebbels, German Minister of Propaganda, called it "a triumph for Germany and Hitlerism." Since then, Louis had won the heavyweight championship from James Braddock, and the Nazis had continued to flex their muscles. In March, Hitler's army had marched into Austria in what was called an *Anschluss,* an annexation in which Austria, Hitler's native country, became part of a Greater Germany. With World War II clearly on the not-too-distant horizon, the Louis-Schmeling rematch was looked upon as a test of strength between the Nazis and the West, as well as between the races. Louis, one of the first "Negroes" to achieve worldwide acclaim, was the distillation of the fondest hopes of Black America. On the eve of the fight, he was also the embodiment of America's defiance of fascist Germany. Just a few months earlier,

Louis had met President Roosevelt, who squeezed Joe's arm and said, "We're depending on those muscles for America." Louis noted that "the whole damned country was depending on me."

The fight drew more than 70,000 fans to the Stadium, accounting for gate receipts of $1,015,012, an extravagant sum for the thirties. Schmeling, reenacting his strategy from the first fight, came out of his corner standing erect with his left hand ready to begin jabbing. Louis was prepared for it; he had devised a strategy of his own, not at all like the cautious, methodical approach he had taken previously. He had told his trainer, Jack "Chappie" Blackburn, that he was going to begin full-tilt and try to end the fight within three rounds. He went even further in an interview with sportswriter Jimmy Cannon, predicting he would knock out Schmeling in the first round. And he came out smoking. Here's how sportscaster Clem McCarthy described it to his radio audience:

> Louis hooks a left to Max's head quickly, and shoots a hard right to Max's head. Louis, a left to Max's jaw, a right to his head. Louis with the old one-two, first the left and then the right! He's landed more blows in this one round than he landed in any five rounds of their other fight.

Referee Arthur Donovan halted the action briefly after Louis connected with a series of body blows that had Schmeling bent over and groaning loud enough to be heard by the radio audience. When the fight resumed, Louis immediately dropped Schmeling to the canvas with a right to the head. Schmeling got up at the count of three, but three devastating shots to the head sent him back down. This time, he arose at the count of two but did not remain upright for long. McCarthy describes the finish:

> Right and left to the head, a left to the jaw, a right to the head! And Donovan is watching carefully. Louis measures him. Right to the body, a left to the jaw, and Schmeling is down! The count is five, six, seven, eight . . . The men are in the ring. The fight is over on a technical knockout. Max Schmeling is beaten in one round.

The fight lasted two minutes and four seconds. Louis had thrown forty-one punches, thirty-one landing solidly. Schmeling, stunned from the outset, had thrown only two. He was sent to Polyclinic Hospital where he remained for ten days, being treated for cracked vertebrae in his back. Returning home, Schmeling rebounded from the defeat and won the European heavyweight title in 1939. However, Hitler was not ready to forgive the fighter whom he had elevated to hero status just two years earlier. For his part, Schmeling was not, and had never been, a Nazi believer. In fact, he actively opposed the regime. During Kristallnacht, the Night of Broken Glass, during which the windows of Jewish stores, buildings, and synagogues were smashed by rampaging Nazis, Schmeling had provided sanctuary for several Jewish boys to protect them from the Gestapo. Hitler retaliated by drafting Schmeling into paratrooper duty in the German Luftwaffe. After brief military service, he mounted an unsuccessful comeback in 1947–48, after which he retired from boxing.

When the Yankees returned home, their fortunes had brightened. Perhaps the debacle in Cleveland had served to awaken them, for three days later they embarked on a nine-game winning streak that eased them into a first-place tie with the Indians. The streak began on June 25 with a 9–3 victory over Detroit. It carried through a July 4 doubleheader with the Washington Senators, being fed by an outpouring of runs. Following the 9–3 win, the offense erupted, winning by scores of 10–3, 10–0, 13–1, 7–1, 8–0, 12–2, 9–3, and 10–5. During their nine-game run, the Yanks scored a total of ninety-six runs, an average of better than nine runs a game.

DiMaggio was beginning to approach his true form. In the July 4 doubleheader, which resulted in a 10–5 win in the opener and a thirteen-inning tie in the nightcap, DiMaggio went six-for-nine, including his thirteenth home run; his batting average rose to .328. The pitching also was coming to form. Ruffing won three decisions to give him eleven for the season. Gomez and Pearson, who had not been doing well, each won twice. With one win, Chandler upped his record to 7–1. So effective was the starting pitching that no relief help was called upon during the first seven games. The bullpen finally came into play in the first game of the July 4 doubleheader. Ruffing faltered in the seventh inning, and Murphy came in with two out to shut things down. Murphy again was summoned in the second game, relieving Hadley after eight innings and pitching five of his own until darkness set in.

So it was with a shared and, as it turned out, short-lived grip on first place that the Yankees headed into the All-Star break. The 1938 All-Star Game was played on Wednesday, July 6, at Cincinnati's Crosley Field. Despite their thus-far uninspiring season, the Yankees again dominated the American League roster with seven players—DiMaggio, Dickey, Gehrig, Gomez, Ruffing, Murphy, and Rolfe—among the cast of twenty-five. DiMaggio, Dickey, and Gomez were in the starting lineup, but what made news was that Gehrig, for the first time since the All-Star Game was played, was not. He was hitting a paltry .277 at the time of the break and had gone one-for-ten in the doubleheader that preceded it. In his sixteenth season and at age thirty-five, Gehrig, still of all-star caliber, was clearly not the same player he had been.

There were, however, other reasons for not starting Gehrig. The American League enjoyed a surfeit of talent at the first-base position. Hank Greenberg, batting .294 with 21 home runs and 47 RBIs, also was missing from the starting lineup. But the shunning of both Gehrig and Greenberg provoked no controversy, for few could quarrel with the choice of Jimmie Foxx to open at first. Foxx, while with the Athletics, had made a serious run at Ruth's record in 1932, finishing with a total of 58 home runs to Ruth's 60. Now with the Red Sox, he was hitting .347 with 23 homers and 89 runs batted in.

The most curious selection among starting players was the choice of pitcher Johnny Vander Meer to open for the National League. Vander Meer, a member of the host Cincinnati Reds, entered the game with only four wins against seven losses. What recommended him was that two of the wins were no-hitters, and they had come in successive starts, which no one else had done before or since. A rookie southpaw with a live arm but erratic control, Vander Meer no-hit the Boston Bees (subsequently called the Braves) on June 11 by a score of 3–0. Four days later, he did it again, shutting out the Brooklyn Dodgers 6–0 in the first night game played at Ebbets Field. A touch of drama had been provided in the ninth inning when he walked the bases full before retiring Leo Durocher on an infield popup.

In his three-inning All-Star stint, Vander Meer retired the side in order in the first two innings before yielding a lead-off single to Joe Cronin in the third. Gomez gave up an unearned run in the first, and the National League went on to squeeze out a 4–1 victory in an unexceptional game that was memorable only for Vander Meer's hometown start and a bizarre play that occurred in the bottom of the seventh with the National League ahead 2–0. First baseman Frank McCormick had opened the inning with a single off Lefty Grove. Ordered to sacrifice, Durocher bunted toward third base where Foxx, who had been moved to third to allow Greenberg some playing time at first, fielded the ball and threw it into right field. There, DiMaggio, having been relegated to right field in deference to Earl Averill playing center, scooped it up and tried to head off McCormick at the plate. The ball sailed far over the head of catcher Bill Dickey, and Durocher circled the bases to round out the National League's scoring.

The All-Star break ended just two days later, and the season resumed with the Yankees at Boston's Fenway Park for a three-game set. Their tenuous share of first place slipped away abruptly as they dropped a 9–8 decision to the Red Sox in the opener as prelude to losing two of three and falling two games behind Cleveland. Their fortunes turned the following day, July 12, when they returned home to the Stadium. Conveniently, the opposition was the St. Louis Browns who were buried in last place, twenty-three games off the lead and on an eight-game losing streak that was about to increase by four. After sweeping a doubleheader by decisive scores of 7–3 and 10–5, the Yanks were just a half-game off the lead, and on Wednesday, July 13, they snatched the top spot from the Indians and never surrendered it.

Fittingly enough, the game was a slugfest that required ten innings and almost three hours of playing time before the Yankees nailed it down. Chandler, who was having an otherwise outstanding year, was driven from the mound in the second inning by a six-run outburst that gave the Browns a 6–5 lead. The Yanks tied the score in the fourth, but the Browns responded immediately with four runs of their own in the top of the fifth, and they clung to the lead while the Yankees continued to chip away. Trailing 12–11 with two out in the bottom of the ninth, Selkirk doubled and came home on a single by Joe Gordon to send the game to extra innings. DiMaggio decided things in the tenth with a three-run homer, his second of the game and sixteenth of the season. DiMaggio appeared to have shaken off his early season lethargy, his batting average now up to .333. Gehrig, too, was on his way back. He had hit his fifteenth homer of the season in the fifth inning and lifted his batting average to .280.

As events developed, the Browns had served as a tune-up. Detroit followed and the Yankees again took three in a row; Gomez, Ruffing, and Chandler accounting for the wins. Ruffing was now 13–3; Chandler, 8–2. For Gomez, who had been largely ineffective during the first half of the season, it was only his seventh win against nine losses, but he seemed to be back on track now and would go 11–3 the rest of the way. Detroit, by contrast, was having its troubles. When the series ended, they were in fifth place, five games under .500, and 13½ games behind the Yanks. Greenberg, however, was undiminished and enjoying one of his best years. In games two and three of the series, he hit his 27th and 28th home runs of the season on his way to matching Foxx's earlier total of 58.

The sweep of the Tigers brought the Yankees' winning streak to nine and earned them sole possession of first place, though only one-and-a-half games ahead of the Indians who had been doing some winning of their own. Through the rest of the month, the Yanks went on an impressive 9–3 run but still led Cleveland by just two games. The Indians were a formidable opponent. While they did not have the star power to match the Yankees, they had a sound balance between timely hitting and solid pitching. Drawing the line between the two teams, Bob Feller was the only future Hall-of-Famer on Cleveland's roster, contrasted with the Yankees' six—Gehrig, DiMaggio, Dickey, Gordon, Ruffing, and Gomez. But the Indians were playing at a clip that would be good enough to win a pennant in most seasons. They were twenty-three games over .500 with a winning percentage of .639.

And Cleveland was not the only contender the Yanks would have to deal with in the last two months of the season. The

Red Sox were coming on strong and Detroit, led by Greenberg, Gehringer, and a young power-hitting catcher by the name of Rudy York, was stirring and about to come alive. They had climbed back to the .500 mark, and though still a distant fourth in the standings, the Tigers had become a force to be reckoned with.

With it all, the Yankees had reason to view the remainder of the season with a degree of assurance. They were producing runs at a prolific rate. Dickey had 79 runs batted in; DiMaggio, 71; and Gehrig, 60. The starting pitching, backed by the juggernaut that the offense had become, was humming. The Yankees had finally taken control. World order had been restored. And the best was yet to come. The Yankees would own the month of August.

Four Yankee sluggers—Bill Dickey, Lou Gehrig, Joe DiMaggio, and Tony Lazzeri—at Yankee Stadium on September 20, 1936, on the way to defeating the New York Giants in the World Series. *Credit: Associated Press*

Yankee players line up in the Stadium dugout in 1938. Left to right: Frank Crosetti, shortstop; Red Rolfe, third base; Tommy Henrich, right field; Joe DiMaggio, center field; Lou Gehrig, first base; Bill Dickey, catcher; George Selkirk, left field; Myril Hoag, substitute outfielder; and Joe Gordon, second base. *Credit: Associated Press*

Gehrig crosses home plate after hitting a home run in the 1936 All-Star Game at League Park in Boston, home of the then-Boston Bees. The National League won the game 4-3. *Credit: Associated Press*

DiMaggio hits a solo home run off the Giants' Cliff Melton in game five of the 1937 World Series at the Polo Grounds. *Credit: Associated Press*

Joe DiMaggio shakes hands with Yankee owner Colonel Jacob Ruppert after signing his 1938 contract. Joe agreed to accept the team's offer of $25,000 after holding out for $40,000. Yankees executive Ed Barrow looks on approvingly. *Credit: Associated Press*

Yankee manager Joe McCarthy giving some pointers to team owner Colonel Jacob Ruppert at spring training in St. Petersburg, Florida, in 1936. *Credit: Associated Press*

Manager McCarthy, center, talks things over with his starting battery before the opening game of the 1937 World Series, pitcher Lefty Gomez, left, and catcher Bill Dickey. *Credit: Associated Press*

Top: Charlie Keller scores in the tenth inning of the fourth and final game of the 1939 World Series against the Cincinnati Reds. Keller barreled into Reds' catcher Ernie Lombardi, jarring the ball loose and leaving Lombardi stunned and motionless as the ball lies just beyond his reach. *Credit: Associated Press*

Bottom: DiMaggio, who had singled home Crosetti to break a 4–4 tie and kept on running, follows Keller across the plate. It was the third run to score on the play, giving the Yankees a 7–4 victory and their fourth straight World Series title. *Credit: Associated Press*

Babe Ruth embraces Gehrig on Lou Gehrig Appreciation Day, July 4, 1939, at Yankee Stadium. Gehrig, who spent his entire career in Ruth's shadow, looks straight ahead, offering no gesture to reciprocate. *Credit: Associated Press*

Gehrig wipes away a tear during the ceremonies. *Credit: Associated Press*

Lou Gehrig, left, congratulates first-baseman Babe Dahlgren on hitting his first home run against the Detroit Tigers on May 2, 1939, the day Dahlgren replaced Gehrig, ending Lou's consecutive-game string of 2,130 games. *Credit: Associated Press*

Lefty Gomez warming up on the sidelines of Yankee Stadium on September 23, 1936, nine days before he took the mound in the second game of the 1936 World Series. Gomez won that game as well as the sixth and deciding game against the New York Giants. *Credit: Associated Press*

11

Yankees Cruise to the Finish, Setting Major-League Record

The dog days of August loomed on the horizon like a long, winding road that had no end. The schedule called for the Yankees to play thirty-six games starting on Friday, August 2, and stretching to the end of the month. Among the dates were a staggering total of nine doubleheaders. From August 21 to 27, they would play six doubleheaders in seven days. Throughout the month, stamina would be as critical a commodity as talent. The diciest question of all was where would the pitching come from? The big three—Ruffing, Gomez, and Pearson—would all do extra duty, and each would eventually compile more than two hundred innings for the season; Chandler and Hadley would come close to that mark. A few late-season acquisitions chipped in an inning or two here and there, but one made a significant contribution.

Wes Ferrell, a starting pitcher of the first rank, was released by Washington on August 12, and the Yankees wasted no time in signing him. Between 1927 and 1933, Ferrell had won more than twenty games four times while pitching for Cleveland and twenty-five and twenty with the Red Sox in 1935 and 1936. He was 13–8 with the Senators when he was turned loose due to differences he had with owner Clark Griffith. Although approaching the end of his career, he gave the Yankees exactly what they were looking for. During the late August compression, he ate up thirty innings, making four starts while going 2–2.

The Yankees began the month by dropping a 4–3 decision to Detroit, ending a four-game winning streak they had carried with them from July. But they came back with five straight road wins against Detroit and Cleveland, opening their first-place lead to five-and-a-half games. The first of the three straight wins over the Indians, on August 5, was played in Cleveland before a record Ladies' Day crowd of 62,753 and was most notable for the uncharacteristically dismal start turned in by the Indians' young phenom, Bob Feller. With a record of 11–5 going into the game, Feller, whose fastball was probably quicker to the plate than any other pitcher in the game, had trouble locating it. Although he yielded only three hits, one of them a two-run homer by Joe Gordon, he walked eleven batters and hit another.

The Yanks left Cleveland with a healthy lead and were just beginning to pull away. After splitting a doubleheader with the A's on August 12, they won eleven of their next twelve, including consecutive doubleheader sweeps against Philadelphia and Washington. On August 13, they led Cleveland by seven games; on the 16th, the lead was eight; two days later it was nine; it rose to ten on the 19th; eleven on the 21st; and on the 23rd they held an eleven-and-a-half game margin over the Red

Sox, who had moved into second place ahead of Cleveland. By the end of the month, they had stretched the margin to fourteen. All told, they won twenty-eight of the thirty-six games they played in a thirty-day span. In the process, they scored a total of 275 runs, a record for a single month.

The pitching, luxuriating in the support it was getting, was nearly flawless. During the game-crammed month of August, Gomez won six; Ruffing and Pearson, five each; and Chandler, three. One of Pearson's wins came in the form of a no-hitter against Cleveland on August 27, with Pearson pitching on two days' rest. It was only the third such game in Yankee history and the first ever at Yankee Stadium. At the close of the month, Ruffing was 19–4, Gomez 15–10, Chandler 13–4, and Pearson 13–5. The pitching was complemented by an awesome display of power. Gehrig, showing signs of rejuvenation, hit nine home runs in August, giving him a total of 26 at month's end; DiMaggio, also with 26, hit seven in August; and Dickey and Gordon each had six. Henrich, now playing regularly in right field, went on a home run tear beginning on August 27 when he hit two in a 13–0 rout of Cleveland. He followed those with homers on each of the next two days and, after a two-day break, he homered again on August 31 and on September 1 and 4. In all, he hit seven home runs in the nine-day period from August 27 to September 4, and he would finish with a total of 22 for the year. In just his first full season, Henrich was establishing himself as a critical piece of the Yankees' dynasty.

Thomas David Henrich was born on February 20, 1913, in Massillon, Ohio, a small town of some 32,000 about fifty miles south of Cleveland. Although Massillon and nearby Canton were basically in football country, Henrich's parents barred him from playing what they felt to be a violent sport. He turned his attention to baseball, but since there were no baseball teams in Massillon, Tommy found his niche playing softball. He switched to baseball after graduating from St. John's Catholic High School in Canton and played for the semipro Prince Horn and Acme Dairy teams. He soon attracted the attention of Billy Doyle, a scout for the Detroit Tigers. The Tigers offered him a contract, but Henrich chose to continue playing semipro ball while earning a living as a clerk in a steel mill.

Despite Cleveland being the closest he had to a hometown team, Tommy had been a Yankee fan since the early twenties, drawn to the team by the appearance of Babe Ruth. His contractual differences with Indians' management (described earlier) further freed him from any allegiance he might have been expected to have to the Cleveland organization. He was of undivided loyalty when he signed with the Yankees in 1937. On his first trip to New York, Henrich recalled years later, he had this exchange with the bellhop when he checked into the Hotel New Yorker:

> The bellhop took my bag and discovered who I was before we even reached the room. 'So you're the new Yankee outfielder,' he said, sneering at me. 'How can you break in ahead of—let's see who we've got—Joe DiMaggio, Jake Powell, Myril Hoag, George Selkirk, and Roy Johnson? Did you ever see them guys hit?'

'Not yet,' I said bravely, 'but they never saw me hit either.'

It would not be too long before "them guys" saw Henrich hit. He was dispatched to the Newark Bears at the start of the season but was called up early in May when manager McCarthy turned Johnson loose after hearing him question the urgency of winning every day. He auditioned on May 11. Batting seventh in the order, he doubled in four times at bat. For the most part, spelling Selkirk in right field, he played in sixty-seven games, hitting an impressive .320, with eight home runs and 42 RBIs.

Henrich, in his way, typified the Yankees of that era. He never quite basked in the same light as Gehrig, DiMaggio, Dickey, or Gordon. Yet he served as the spine of the team for parts of three decades. He was described by one observer as "rock solid." He was steady though unspectacular. He rarely made a mistake in the field or went into a prolonged batting slump. Noting what it took to play the outfield, Henrich famously said, "Catching a fly ball is a pleasure. But knowing what to do with it after you catch it is a business." It was just after the war that Yankee broadcaster Mel Allen dubbed him "Old Reliable," which was the name of a train that ran from Ohio to Allen's native Alabama and was celebrated for always being on time. Bobby Brown, Henrich's post-war teammate, said of him: "If we were ahead 10–1 or 10–2, he was just average. If we were behind 10–1 or 10–2, same thing. But get him in a big game and he was terrific." DiMaggio echoed Brown's appreciation of Henrich, calling him "the smartest player in the big leagues." Recognition of Henrich's special qualities even found its way into literature. In his 1959 novella *Good-bye, Columbus*, Philip Roth offered this exchange between two characters:

"What do [you] think of Tommy Henrich?"
"I don't know, he's dependable, I guess."

When August ended, the magic went with it. It was as if some of the fuel that had driven the engine had been siphoned off, and what remained was adequate but lacking full measure. It happened gradually. The Yankees opened September with a thirteen-game lead over Boston. The two teams split a two-game set at Yankee Stadium, and each played win-and-lose for the first part of the month. Of course, the lead, as it stood, appeared to be insurmountable, and in reality, it was—thirteen games was too big a deficit to make up in the course of one month. But as summer gave way to autumn and with the promise of another World Series just weeks away, there was cause for wonder, if not concern.

Beginning on September 16, the Yankees lost seven straight games and the lead began to wear away. The Red Sox, as hot as the Yankees were cold, began making up ground on an almost daily basis. The Boston lineup offered opposing pitchers little respite. Jimmie Foxx was on his way to leading the league in batting with an average of .349 and RBIs with a total of 175. Despite hitting 50 home runs, he fell short of the Triple Crown as Hank Greenberg hit 58 in pursuit of Babe Ruth's record. In all, six of Boston's starters hit over .300. The exceptions were second baseman Bobby Doerr at .289 and catcher Gene

Desautels at .291. With the Red Sox in hot pursuit, the Yankees limped to the finish line with a losing September record of 14–15.

All the same, they closed out with ninety-nine wins and a comfortable margin of nine-and-a-half games over the Sox and thirteen ahead of Cleveland. DiMaggio hit a sub-par .324, but he had 32 homers and led the team with 140 runs batted in. Even more notably, he had more home runs than strikeouts, having fanned only 21 times. It was a feat he achieved in each of the next five seasons; he ended his career with only eight more strikeouts than home runs. By contrast, Barry Bonds, while setting the career home run record in a new era, struck out more than twice as often as he homered.

The rest of the lineup also produced generous numbers. Gehrig, though clearly on the decline, still batted .295 and accounted for 29 home runs and 114 RBIs. Bill Dickey enjoyed one of his best years with marks of .313, 27, and 115. Joe Gordon set a record for second baseman with 25 home runs. The pitching remained as sound as one could hope for. Ruffing led the league with twenty-one wins against seven losses. Gomez, recovering from a poor start, went 18–12; Pearson, 16–7; and Chandler, 14–5. A pleasant late-season surprise was a rookie by the name of Steve Sundra.

A native of Luxor, Pennsylvania, Sundra was one of ten children born to Czech immigrants who came to the United States at the turn of the century. His father earned his living working in the coal mines of western Pennsylvania. Steve began playing sandlot ball in Cleveland at the age of sixteen. He was signed by the Indians in 1932, and after four seasons in their minor-league system, he came to the Yankees along with Monte Pearson in the trade that sent Johnny Allen to Cleveland. He arrived with high expectations. His fastball had earned him the nickname "Smokey," and his repertoire featured a sinker thrown from a three-quarter sidearm motion that made his fastball look even faster. He debuted with the Yankees in April 1936, with two innings of mop-up relief, and was sent to Newark where he led the league with an ERA of 2.84 despite posting a mediocre record of 12–9. A year later, his record improved to 15–4 with a still enviable ERA of 3.09 for a Newark Bears team that won the International League championship by nineteen-and-a-half games.

Sundra opened the 1938 season with the Yankees as a spot starter and put together a less than compelling record of 3–4 through the first five months of the season. But he seemed to hit his stride in September, winning all of his three decisions, two of them against Boston. It was the start of a remarkable run that carried into the following season. In 1939, he went on to chalk up eleven straight victories, three of them in relief, before losing his last start to Boston on the final day of the season. From May 24 through August, he was virtually unhittable, going 6–0 with a 1.01 ERA. Combined with the three victories with which he closed out the 1938 season, Sundra had put together fourteen consecutive wins, two shy of an American League record, and establishing a new team mark that, shared later with Whitey Ford, stood for more than half a century until eclipsed by Ron Guidry in 1978. His earned run average over the course of the 1939 season was a miserly 2.76. His record of 11–1 gave him a winning percentage of

.917, ranking him fifth among pitchers with ten or more decisions in a single season.

Strangely enough, he never regained the form he showed from late 1938 through '39. After finishing with a losing record in 1940, he was sent to Washington for cash at the start of the 1941 season and to St. Louis a year later. He put together a respectable 15–11 mark for the Browns, did some time in the service during the war years, won two games in 1944, and his career was effectively over. However, he had arrived on the scene at precisely the right time. With the pitching staff taxed in a cluttered schedule, Sundra gave the team what it needed when it was needed most. He ate up 93.2 innings in twenty-five games, winning six while losing four.

While the Yankees were coasting to their third straight pennant, the National League race was a dogfight. The Chicago Cubs and Pittsburgh Pirates had at it from opening day until the season ebbed into its final days. The defending champion Giants also were in the mix, having turned in an eleven-game winning streak in April that kept them afloat until they faded at the start of September. The Pirates, who had last seen World Series action in 1927 when they were swept by the Yankees of Murderers' Row, snatched first place from the Giants in mid-July and held it until the dying days of the season. Then, they succumbed to a recent pattern in National League pennant races in which the team that held the lead on Labor Day lost it to a runner-up that came on with a late rush as the season drew to a close. Earlier victims of such unhappy endings were the Cubs of 1930 and '37, the Giants in 1934, and the

Cardinals a year later. Pittsburgh would soon add its name to the list.

The Pirates were driven by an offense that featured the timely hitting of shortstop Arky Vaughan, future Hall of Fame outfielder Paul "Big Poison" Waner, and rookie left fielder Johnny Rizzo. Rizzo, who hit .301, provided most of the meager power Pittsburgh could muster with 23 home runs and 111 RBIs. No one else on the team hit more than seven homers or drove in as many as eighty runs. The Cubs did not offer much in the way of muscle, either. First baseman Ripper Collins led the team in home runs with 13 and catcher Gabby Hartnett hit 10. Augie Galan's 69 RBIs were the most on the club. The Cubs relied mainly on pitching. Bill Lee's twenty-two victories and 2.66 ERA led the league. Clay Bryant, having the best year of a brief, undistinguished career, was second with nineteen wins.

While neither team featured an imposing lineup, both had mastered the fine art of winning, of appropriating precisely the right touch that would turn the game in their favor. The Pirates, as low as fifth place at the end of May and into June, seemed to strike gold at the end of the month. They took off on a thirteen-game winning streak that carried them into mid-July when they ousted the Giants from first place and made it their own for the next two months.

The Cubs, on the other hand, looking to recapture the technique that had brought them pennants in 1932 and '35, had trouble getting untracked. They struggled through most of the season, following any brief success with a period of failure. In mid-season, manager Charlie Grimm, who had led the

team to their league championships in 1932 and '35, yielded
the reins to veteran catcher Gabby Hartnett. It did not help;
not immediately. The Cubs were in third place on August 3,
eight games off the lead, and no higher in the standings on
Labor Day. As late as September 22 with less than two weeks
left in the season, they trailed Pittsburgh by three-and-a-half
games. But at that point, they went on a tear, mounting a ten-
game win streak that brought them into direct confrontation
with first-place Pittsburgh for a three-game series at Chicago's
Wrigley Field.

Hartnett elected to open the series with the legendary Dizzy
Dean, who had been acquired from the Cardinals in the off-
season. Dean, who had won 102 games for the Cards between
1933 and '36, had blown out his arm following a bizarre injury
suffered in the 1937 All-Star Game. A low line-drive off the bat
of Earl Averill struck Dean in the left foot, fracturing his big
toe. Told that his toe was fractured, Dizzy responded typically,
"Fractured, hell, the damn thing's broken." Eager to return to
the rotation, Dean altered his pitching motion to avoid landing
hard on the injured foot. The change put more pressure on his
arm and took much of the life from his fastball.

He started just ten games for the Cubs in 1938 and appeared three times in relief. His once-blazing fastball was now
just a memory, and he often winced in pain while delivering a
pitch. All the same, he carried a record of 6–1 into the game
with an ERA under two. And his record was about to improve.
Dizzy throttled Pirate bats for eight-and-two-third innings.
Protecting a 2–0 lead in the ninth, Dean hit the leadoff batter and yielded a two-out double to catcher Al Todd. With

runners on second and third, Bill Lee entered the game and allowed a run on a wild pitch before striking out the final batter. The Pittsburgh lead was now down to a half-game and about to disappear entirely.

Game two of the series was literally one for the ages. With the teams tied 5–5 after eight innings, late afternoon shadows had begun to engulf Wrigley Field. Umpire Jocko Conlon considered calling the game due to darkness but decided to resume play for at least one more inning. Pittsburgh went down quietly in the top of the ninth, and the Cubs came to bat against relief pitcher Mace Brown whose fifteen wins, all in relief, led the Pirates' staff. Brown had no trouble retiring the first two batters, which brought Gabby Hartnett to the plate. Hartnett, now wearing his managerial hat as well as working behind the plate, was thirty-eight years old and in his seventeenth season. A lifetime .297 hitter with modest power, Hartnett was well past his prime, but he was about to take one swing that would carve his name forever in baseball legend. With two strikes on him, he drove Brown's next pitch high into the darkening sky on its route toward left field. The ball barely cleared the ivy-covered wall, bounced back onto the field, and would be remembered always as the "The Homer in the Gloamin'." It is recorded that the field was so dark that the Cubs players on the bench were unaware of where the ball landed until the umpire signaled a home run.

Charlie Root, who had his own niche in baseball legend as the pitcher who yielded Babe Ruth's "called home run" in the 1932 World Series, also at Wrigley Field, was the beneficiary of Hartnett's heroics. Root, the sixth pitcher of the day, had come in to start the ninth and picked up his seventh win of the season. With the 6–5 win, the Cubs took first place by a half-game. They added a game to the lead the next day with a bruising 10–1 decision that seemed to drain the Pirates of any hope that might have lingered. In the few days remaining in the season, the Cubs lost two of three to the Cardinals, but Pittsburgh did no better, dropping three of four to the Cincinnati Reds. The season ended with Chicago in front by two games. Whatever celebration might have broken out in the Windy City, it did not last very long. Three days later, the Yankees were coming to town.

The Cubs did not match up well against the Yankees; few teams did. A number of sportswriters covering the Series reported that some of the Chicago players had told them that they did not think they had much of a chance against the defending champions. An exception was the former Yankee, Tony Lazzeri. Seeing limited action, Tony had batted a respectable .267 in fifty-four games for the Cubs, including five home runs and 23 RBIs. According to the veteran baseball writer Frank Graham, when asked about his new team's chances, Lazzeri exhibited his old Yankee bravado, saying, "Well, I ain't on their side anymore, and I think we'll beat their brains out." It didn't quite turn out that way, but the Cubs put forth a praiseworthy effort; they did not allow themselves to be humiliated.

To no one's surprise, McCarthy tapped Ruffing to open the Series. Since coming to the Yankees, Ruffing had eclipsed Gomez as the ace of the staff. His success with the team had defined one of the greatest turnarounds in baseball history. And his acquisition from the Red Sox marked the second time in exactly a decade—getting Ruth was the first—that the Yanks had picked Boston's pocket, obtaining a world-class player for practically nothing.

Charles Herbert "Red" Ruffing was born in 1905 in coal country and raised in Coalton and Nokomis, Illinois, by German immigrant parents. His father was a coal miner until he suffered a broken back. He then became superintendent of the mine and also was elected mayor of Coalton. Red left school at age thirteen to work for his father, and he played the outfield and first base for the mine's company team. But it was not long before he learned the perils of the trade firsthand. While working between two coal cars, one of them inadvertently ran over his left foot. He lost all or part of four toes and was no longer able to run well enough to play the outfield or first base. Doc Bennett, the manager of a nearby semipro team, suggested that Ruffing try his hand at pitching where his disability would be less of a handicap.

At a strapping 6-foot-2 and 210 pounds, Red took to pitching right from the start. He was a workhorse with a sizzling fastball, and before long he was earning twenty-five dollars a game pitching semipro ball. In 1923, the eighteen-year-old right-hander turned pro, pitching for Class B Danville in the Illinois–Indiana–Iowa (Three-I) League. Unfazed by his 11–16 record, the Red Sox purchased his contract for $4,000 and assigned him to pitch for the Dover Senators of the Class D Shore League in 1924. In desperate need of help, the Sox, who had finished dead last in both 1922 and '23, brought him up to Boston, and he made his major-league debut early in the

1924 season. He was not very impressive. He pitched in only eight games, six in relief, and compiled an earned run average of 6.65. His performance did not improve with time. His record over the next five seasons was a dismal 39–93. He lost twenty-five games in 1928 and twenty-two the following year.

But Bob Shawkey, who had replaced Miller Huggins as Yankee manager in 1930, saw something he liked. Despite a 10–25 record in 1928, Ruffing's ERA was a respectable 3.89. Shawkey also noted that, despite his losing record, he was striking out more than one hundred batters a season and that it was usually not until the late innings that Ruffing would run into trouble. Shawkey, who was a winning pitcher for the Yankees from 1916 to 1927, saw what he believed to be a flaw in Ruffing's pitching delivery. He was throwing almost entirely with his arm, which explained why he tired late in the game. Shawkey believed that if he altered Ruffing's motion so that he pitched more with his body, he would have himself a winner. Early in the 1930 season, he persuaded general manager Ed Barrow that it was worth taking a chance on the young pitcher. Bob Quinn, the owner of the Red Sox, was in debt and concerned that he might lose the team to foreclosure. A $50,000 infusion from Yankee owner Jacob Ruppert was an enticing offer. To sweeten the pot, the Yanks also sent along a journeyman outfielder by the name of Cedric Durst, who was playing the last season of a largely undistinguished career.

Shawkey, it turned out, knew exactly what he was doing. In addition to changing the motion with which he threw his fastball, Ruffing developed a sharp-breaking curve and what might have passed for a screwball or a fadeaway, a pitch that broke the other way. It was all done without much fanfare, as Ruffing was not given to ostentation; in fact, he was virtually the prototype of what was known then as "the strong, silent type." Ruffing at one point recounted a brief conversation he had with catcher Bill Dickey about his pitching repertoire: "One day, Bill Dickey said, 'You're pitching a slider,' and I said, 'It's all news to me.' I was holding the ball a little different. I have picked up the fadeaway, and I can throw a lot of other fancy stuff."

Whatever he was throwing, batters were having trouble hitting it. Rarely in the annals of baseball, or any other endeavor, has someone undergone so dramatic a change in fortune in so short a time. Before the trade, Ruffing had an 0–3 record with Boston. After coming to the Yankees, he won fifteen games while losing only five, and he went on from there to fashion a Hall-of-Fame career. He won twenty or more games in each of the Yankees' four straight championship seasons. For added measure, he possessed another asset that improved his team's prospects; he could hit. The ninth spot in the batting order was no automatic out when Ruffing was pitching. He hit better than .300 in eight seasons, with a lifetime average of .269. He also accounted for 36 home runs, 98 doubles, and 13 triples while winning 273 games. And he flourished in big-game situations. He had won his first World Series start in 1932 against the Cubs before losing to Carl Hubbell in 1936. He came back to beat the Giants 8–1 in 1937 and now was poised to open against the Cubs in 1938.

The Cubs countered Ruffing with twenty-two-game winner Bill Lee who pitched creditably but fell short. The Yankees scored twice in the second inning on singles by Bill Dickey and Joe Gordon sandwiched around an error by Chicago second baseman Billy Herman. The Cubs cut the lead in half in the third, but the Yanks tacked on an insurance run in the sixth to close out the opener, 3–1.

Game two matched Lefty Gomez against Dizzy Dean in what was nostalgically called "Ol' Diz's Last Stand." While not quite his last stand, Dean made it memorable, pitching three-hit ball and holding a 3–2 lead going into the top of the eighth. The Cubs had gone ahead 1–0 in their first at-bat on a sacrifice fly by center fielder Joe Marty, but the Yankees answered immediately with a pair of runs in the second when, with DiMaggio and Gehrig on base, Gordon sent them both home on a ground-ball double to left that was mishandled by Chicago's defense. The Cubs regained the lead in their next turn at bat on singles by Stan Hack and Billy Herman, a bunt sacrifice, and a two-run double to deep left by Joe Marty, who accounted for all of Chicago's runs that day.

Nursing a 3–2 lead, Dean was pitching as though the years had fallen away and he was back in full throttle. Except for giving up a single to Gehrig in the fourth, he set down the side in order in the third, fifth, sixth, and seventh innings, taking his one-run lead into the eighth with the bottom of the order coming up. But it was clear by then that Dean had tired. Selkirk reached him for a single. Gordon forced Selkirk; and Hoag, batting for Gomez, forced Gordon. That brought to the plate Frank Crosetti, not known for the long ball, but the light-hitting shortstop drove a limp pitch from Dean over the left-field ivy wall to give the Yanks a 4–3 edge. Dizzy then struck out Rolfe to end the inning. But it was already too late.

Murphy, in relief of Gomez, set down the Cubs in their half of the eighth, and the Yankees put the game away in the ninth. Henrich led off with a single, and DiMaggio followed Crosetti's example with a homer to the same precincts but a bit deeper into the seats. Larry French came on to finish the rest of the inning, but the Cubs went quietly in the bottom of the ninth, and the Yankees were on their way back to the Bronx with a two-game lead.

For game three, the Yanks gave the ball to Monte Pearson. Any notion that Pearson might reclaim the form he showed pitching his no-hitter at the Stadium a few weeks earlier was dispelled quickly when Joe Marty, who was on his way to a phenomenal Series, nudged an infield single to shortstop with one out in the first inning. Nonetheless, Pearson was not too far short of masterful, giving the Cubs only two runs, one of them unearned, and five hits on the way to 5–2 victory. Marty accounted for the Cubs' only earned run with a solo homer in the eighth, but by then the Yankees already had the game in hand, with home runs by Gordon and Dickey.

No team had ever come back from a three-game deficit, and the Cubs gave no sign of becoming the first. Game four was a rematch of game one—Ruffing against Bill Lee—and the Yanks opened up with a cluster of three unearned runs in the second inning, Crosetti accounting for the final two with a triple. To their credit, the Cubs did not surrender. They scored a run in the fourth and two more in the eighth on a home run by catcher Ken O'Dea. Henrich having homered in the sixth, the game was sitting at 4–3 entering the bottom half of the eighth. Manager Hartnett had not spared the horses. He used a total of six pitchers, three of them in the eighth when the Yanks were in the process of putting the game away. The last was Dizzy Dean who came on after two runs had already scored, with the bases loaded and two out. The batter was Crosetti, who was swinging a hot bat, and he greeted Diz with a drive to left field that brought home the final two runs. The score was 8–4, giving the Yankees a sweep of the Series and a record three straight world championships.

All told, it was New York's seventh world title and the fourth time they had swept the Series 4–0. Over that period, the opposing team had won only five games, giving the Yankees a winning margin of 28–5. The cry of "Break up the Yankees" was growing louder and more intense, but it would be, to the chagrin of the opposition, of no avail.

A footnote to the Series was the performance of Lou Gehrig. He had played a flawless game at first but had contributed only four singles and had not driven in a run. It was an ominous portent of what lay ahead. But the Yankees remained in focus, their sights set on a fourth straight championship, adding to a record that was already their own.

1939

The Yankees' conclude their four-year dynasty with what many consider to be the best single-season team of all time.

12

1939 Opens with Events that Will Mark Its Place in History

There is a certain allure attached to rooting for a loser. It is a no-risk proposition that offers immunity from the despair of defeat while extending the promise of unexpected triumph. For the underdog, every victory has a spiritual message; it speaks of the conquest of forces larger than itself. Winners and those who back them, by contrast, carry with them always the relentless burden of their own success. Winning is expected; it is in the natural order of things, and so losing brings with it the taint of disgrace. So it had become with the Yankees. The players, and even more so their followers, had begun treating winning as if it were the confirmation of a birthright. The occasional loss was deemed to be no more than a misstep, a subtle nod to the gods who oversee such things, acknowledging the mortality that sometimes gets lost in perception.

Nineteen-thirty-nine was a year that had its own distinct texture. It began with the death of one of the barons of baseball; then, the whole country watched while one of the game's towering figures wasted away before its eyes; and finally a World's Fair whose slogan was "Building the World of Tomorrow" opened in New York, while beyond its borders the world was being drawn slowly but inexorably toward the worst conflagration in its history. Through it all, the Yankees powered their way to a record fourth straight world championship.

The year was not yet two weeks old when Colonel Jacob Ruppert, owner of the Yankees since 1915, died at the age or seventy-one. In addition to his baseball connection, Ruppert was an American brewer, businessman, colonel in the Nation Guard, and United States Congressman who represented New York for four terms, from 1899 to 1907. As Marty Appel recounts his last moments:

> Ruppert, who had long been suffering from phlebitis along with other ailments, was in an oxygen tent in his luxury apartment at 1120 Fifth Avenue, between Ninety-third and Ninety-fourth Streets. The tent was removed briefly when Babe Ruth came to visit on the evening of January 12, 1939. Ruth held and patted Ruppert's hand.
>
> "'Colonel,'" he said, "'you're going to snap out of this and you and I are going to the opening game of the season.'
>
> That got a faint smile out of the old brewmaster, and as Ruth began to leave, the Colonel was heard to say, 'Babe . . .' and nothing more.
>
> Ruth left in tears. It was the only time the Colonel had called him that. Ruppert called everyone by their

last name, and in his German accent, Babe had always been 'Root.' That evening, Ruppert was given the Last Rites of the Catholic Church.

On Friday the thirteenth, Ruppert awoke, drank some orange juice, and fell into unconsciousness. . . He died at 10:28 a.m.

Although he is best remembered for his role as owner of the Yankees, Ruppert came to baseball through the back door. He had joined the family brewing business after attending Columbia Grammar School. In 1890, at the age of twenty-three, he was appointed the general manager of the brewery. He had been active in the New York National Guard since 1886, rising from the rank of private to the distinguished level of colonel. In 1899, he became the Tammany Hall Democratic candidate for the Fifteenth District. Although the district was largely Republican, Ruppert won the election by a comfortable majority of ten thousand votes. He maintained his interest in the brewery and invested lavishly and wisely in real estate. The *New York Times* reported that despite having to deal with the deprivations of the Depression and Prohibition, he had become one of the richest men in the world, estimating his estate at as much as $100 million. As for Prohibition, Ruppert noted that wherever it had been adopted, there ensued a state of disorder and an increase in the consumption of alcoholic beverages.

Ruppert's original interest in baseball was not so much about the game itself but as an investment outlet for his substantial wealth. According to the *Times*, he regarded baseball as a hobby, much the same as his interest in race horses, horse shows, and his kennel of St. Bernard dogs. He placed his stake on baseball in 1915 when he and Colonel Tillinghast L'Hommedieu (TL) Huston paid a total of $450,000 for a Yankee franchise that was struggling to survive and that showed few signs of improving. They had finished next to last in 1914 and were 32½ games behind Ruth's league-leading Red Sox in the year he purchased the team. The Yankees did not have a winning season until 1918, and then, of course, two years later, along came the Babe.

Ruppert never married. He lived alone in his lavish twelve-room apartment on Fifth Avenue along with a staff of servants that included a butler, maid, valet, cook, and laundress. Following his death on a Friday, funeral services were initially scheduled for Monday at St. Ignatius Loyola at Park Avenue and 84th Street but were moved to St. Patrick's Cathedral when it became clear that the smaller church would not be large enough to hold the throng of notables who would be attending. It was estimated that as many as fifteen thousand people gathered on Fifth Avenue and across the street into Rockefeller Center to observe the event. Among those from the world of baseball were Ruth, Gehrig, McCarthy, Honus Wagner, Clark Griffith of the Washington Senators, and Yankees general manager Ed Barrow, along with Horace Stoneham of the Giants and Marie Mulvey of the Dodgers. The political scene was represented by Mayor Fiorello LaGuardia; Al Smith, the Democratic presidential candidate in 1928; Senator Robert Wagner; and former Boston mayor John Fitzgerald. Also notably present was Bill "Bojangles" Robinson who often entertained the fans between innings at the Stadium by tap dancing atop the Yankees dugout. A fifty-car motorcade made the trip to Kensico Cemetery in Westchester County, about forty minutes from midtown Manhattan, where he was interred in the family mausoleum.

As spring training approached, there was guarded concern about the condition of the team captain and first baseman, Lou Gehrig. He had ended the 1938 season exhibiting signs of physical decline, and his performance had flagged noticeably. He was in the process of extending the all-time record of consecutive games played, his total at season's end standing at 2,122. Spring training was scheduled to open on March 6, with pitchers and catchers reporting about ten days earlier, as was the custom. This year, McCarthy had ordered two rookie outfielders—Charlie Keller and Joe Gallagher—to arrive with the early birds. Gehrig volunteered to join them. McCarthy had an ulterior motive for bringing Keller in early. He was highly touted, and rightly so, and the manager had notions that he might be ready to start in place of Henrich, allowing Henrich to be groomed to play first base in the event that Gehrig was unable to continue. There were other candidates to replace Gehrig if need be, foremost among them a sparingly used four-year veteran by the name of Babe Dahlgren, whom the Yankees obtained in 1937 from the Red Sox in a straight cash deal.

Reflections on Gehrig's future varied from hopeful to cautiously optimistic to realistically sober, often depending on who it was making the appraisal. There were reports that he was not quite himself during the off-season, that he had been diagnosed with a gallbladder condition, that he had taken an occasional flop when ice skating with his wife, Eleanor. But when he reported to camp on February 26, he was said to look fairly good for a thirty-five-year-old athlete who had not missed a single day's service in the past sixteen years. However, there were telltale signs that could not be missed. Once deceptively quick afoot, he was clearly a step or two slower. At the plate, even in batting practice, he was often late in getting to the fastball. In the field, he seemed uncertain of his movements, often late getting to the base on a ground ball. And on the bases, he chugged would-be triples into doubles. By the end of spring training, he had not hit a home run. Sports columnist Joe Williams, writing in the *New York World-Telegram,* put it bluntly:

> They watch him at bat and note that he isn't hitting the ball well; they watch him around the bag and it's plain he isn't getting the balls he used to get; they watch him run and they fancy they can hear his bones creak and his lungs wheeze as he labors his way around the bases. Every mental note they make contributes to the broad conviction of physical disintegration. On eyewitness testimony alone the verdict must be that of a battle-scarred veteran falling apart.

The gravity of Gehrig's condition would not be fully known or understood for several months. In the meantime, other concerns, on a far wider scale, were troubling the perceptions of the nation. With the start of the season just weeks away, President Roosevelt, who had taken delight in throwing out the first ball on every opening day since 1933, had other things on his mind. On April 2, he left the Little White House in Warm Springs, Georgia, and told his neighbors that he would return in the fall "if we don't have a war." His fears were not unfounded. A few weeks earlier, on March 15, Germany annexed what was left of Czechoslovakia, breaking the 1938 agreement that gave Germany the Sudetenland in exchange for its pledge to leave the rest of country intact. By all measure, Czechoslovakia now ceased to exist. At the same time, Hitler announced that his non-aggression pact with Poland was null and void. The infamous Munich Pact, as history remembers it, had been rendered meaningless. For all his tireless effort and good intentions, British Prime Minister Neville Chamberlain had failed to bring back what he had called "peace with honor," and the term "appeasement" was given new meaning.

While freedom was being suffocated in Europe, it was not faring much better in the United States. On April 9, Easter Sunday, the world-renowned opera singer, Marian Anderson, performed at an open-air concert at the Lincoln Memorial in Washington, DC. That was not where the concert was supposed to take place. It had originally been scheduled for Constitution Hall, but the Daughters of the American Revolution (DAR), which managed the concert hall, barred her from singing because Marian Anderson was black. The DAR is an organization whose founding was based on the principles that fueled the birth of American democracy. Its motto was and remains "God, Home, and Country." Its barring of the African American singer testified to the view that bigotry can have no more fertile breeding ground than the union of patriotism and religion dressed in the vestments of self-righteous moralism.

First Lady Eleanor Roosevelt was quick to step in. She resigned her membership in the organization in protest and, with the help of Secretary of the Interior Harold L. Ickes and the approval of her husband, arranged for the concert to be held, appropriately enough, at the foot of the Lincoln Memorial. Ickes introduced the singer to a crowd of 75,000 that stretched the considerable distance from the Lincoln Memorial to the Washington Monument. Members of the Supreme Court, the Cabinet, and the Congress sat up front. Thousands of others listened on the radio. Anderson opened her performance with a moving rendition of *My Country, 'Tis of Thee*, the last line of which is "Let freedom ring."

For Marian Anderson, it was just the first in a sequence of events that made her a notable figure in the country's grudging but steady progress toward civil rights. In 1955, she became the first African American to perform at New York's Metropolitan Opera House. Three years later, President Dwight D. Eisenhower made her an honorary delegate to the United Nations. In 1963, President John F. Kennedy awarded her the Presidential Medal of Freedom.

To its everlasting credit, the DAR later saw fit to apologize to Anderson and welcome her to Constitution Hall on several occasions. In 1942, she starred at a benefit concert for World War II relief. In 1964, the year the Civil Rights Act was passed, Anderson chose Constitution Hall as the venue to launch her farewell tour as she marked her retirement. In 1992, a year before her death at the age of ninety-five, the DAR awarded her its Centennial Medallion, which honors women who gave outstanding service to the nation. On January 27, 2005, the

DAR co-hosted with the US Postal Service the first "day of issue" dedication ceremony, at which the Marian Anderson commemorative stamp was introduced and Anderson's family was honored.

13

Quest for Fourth Title Begins with Gehrig Hurting

Opening Day, scheduled for Monday, April 17, in Washington, DC, was postponed because of rain. It was a hard April rain that was not ready to quit anytime soon. It continued to come down for two days, and the series with the Yankees was called off. The Senators opened at home three days later against the Athletics, and the Yanks took the train home to start their season against the Red Sox. The Sox, having made a wild charge to finish the 1938 season in second place, passing Cleveland on the way, were considered New York's chief threat, and with good cause. Their lineup, already of all-star caliber, was enhanced by the presence of the young outfielder, Ted Williams. A look at the opening day box score offered immediate notice that more than half the players in the starting lineups of both teams were headed to the Hall of Fame. For the Yankees, they included: Dickey, Gehrig, Gordon, DiMaggio, and Ruffing. Gomez, who would start the next day, gave the Yankees a total of six, seven if you counted manager McCarthy. Boston had five of its starters on the road to glory: Jimmy Foxx, Bobby Doerr, Joe Cronin, the rookie Williams, and Lefty Grove, whose matchup with Ruffing promised—and delivered—a sparkling pitchers' duel to get the season underway.

Ruffing was on his way to his fourth straight twenty-plus-win season. Grove, at age thirty-nine and nearing the end of his seventeen-year career, had statistics that few could match. While with the A's, he had won twenty or more games seven years in a row, from 1927 to 1933, including thirty-one in 1931. After being traded to Boston in 1934, a sore arm limited his contribution, and he closed the season with a record of 8–8. He returned to form the following year with a 20–12 mark. All told, over the course of his career, he led the league in wins four times, strikeouts seven years in a row, and he had the league's lowest earned run average a record nine times. In consecutive years, 1930 and '31, he won the pitching Triple Crown, leading the league in wins, strikeouts, and ERA. His record for those two seasons, which marked the second and third straight pennants in manager Connie Mack's championship run, was a stunning 59–9. In 1931, he tied the American record, winning sixteen straight games in a single season and was rewarded by being named the league's Most Valuable Player.

Although occasionally sharing notice with the Yankees' own fire-balling Lefty, Grove had little in common with Lefty Gomez. While Gomez's zaniness made him exceptionally popular among both players and fans, Grove was not much liked by either constituency. He was reputed to be a rather humorless man, of solemn disposition and given to world-class temper tantrums. He brought to the pitcher's mound a laser-like focus, but his fierce commitment to his work left room for little else.

Born in Lonaconing, Maryland, in 1900, Robert Moses Grove became a sandlot star in the Baltimore area during his teens. He broke into organized baseball in 1920, making his professional debut with the Martinsburg Mountaineers of the Class D Blue Ridge League. Featuring a blazing fastball, he appeared in just six games, giving up a miserly 30 hits in fifty-nine innings. His performance, though limited, was enough to catch the eye of Jack Dunn, Sr., the manager/owner of the Baltimore Orioles of the International League. Dunn's most notable discovery was, at the time, another left-hand pitcher by the name of Babe Ruth.

Ironically, Grove's overwhelming success delayed the start of his major-league career. Understandably reluctant to part with him, Dunn held him in tow for five years, during which Lefty posted a record of 108–36 and struck out a minor-league record of 1,108 batters. But the pressure on Dunn mounted as teams began offering sums that were difficult to ignore. In his fifth year with the Orioles, 1924, Grove went 26–6, striking out 231 batters in 236 innings. In exhibition games against major-league teams, he seemed to rise to even greater heights. As described by Jim Kaplan in an article for SABR, upon meeting Ruth on the exhibition circuit, Lefty told him, "I'm not afraid of you," and proceeded to strike out the Babe nine times in 11 at-bats. By the end of the 1924 season, the bids were flowing in. The Cubs and Dodgers each offered the princely sum of $100,000. But Dunn chose to sell Grove to an old friend of his, Connie Mack, for $100,600. The extra $600 made the sales price that much higher than the sum the Yankees had paid to the Red Sox for Ruth after the 1919 season, although other financial amenities were included in the Ruth deal.

With the Depression tightening its grip in the thirties, Mack began unloading some of the star talent that comprised his championship teams. Among those to go was Grove, who went to Boston along with pitcher Rube Walberg and second-baseman Max Bishop, in exchange for a pitcher and a utility infielder who were, and remained, largely unnoticed; a cash sum of $125,000 sweetened the pot. Upon Grove's departure, Mack apparently felt the need to justify the one-sided deal. With Lefty's fastball perhaps a mile or two slower as he moved through his thirties, Mack described his meal ticket as being chiefly a "thrower" who never really learned the art of pitching. Yankee shortstop Frank Crosetti did not disagree, but he put his own spin on Mack's depiction. "When planes take off from a ship," Crosetti said, "they say they catapult. That's what his fastball did halfway to the plate. He threw just plain fastballs—he didn't need anything else."

Nineteen-thirty-nine, during which Grove compiled a record of 15–4, with an ERA of 2.54, was his last good year. He slipped to 7–6 in 1940 and was seven wins short of the magic mark of 300 when the 1941 season opened. They did not come easily. He had just six wins, against four losses, by midseason. On July 25, with Cleveland visiting Fenway Park, Joe Cronin handed Grove the ball and told him there would be no relief available; one way or the other, he was in from start to finish. Grove struggled, but his team kept him in the game. The

Indians scored a run in the second and three in the third. The Sox responded with a pair of runs in both the fourth and fifth, and each team scored twice in the seventh. With the score tied at 6–6 going into the bottom of the eighth, the Bosox put the game away for their once-great pitcher. Jimmie Foxx tripled with two men on, and Jim Tabor followed with a homer. The final score was 10–6. Grove had his three hundredth win and a record of 7–4. He had become the game's twelfth three-hundred-game winner, the first since Grover Cleveland Alexander in 1926 and the last until Warren Spahn in 1961. As it turned out, the three hundredth was also the last victory of his career. He lost his final three starts. However, that hardly tarnished his achievement. His winning percentage of .680 (300–141) was the highest among three-hundred-game winners and, at the time, the eighth best overall.

Now, still at the top of his game as the 1939 season opened, Grove pitched well enough to win most games, but it was not quite good enough on this day. Dickey opened the second inning with a home run, and that was really all that was needed. The Yanks scored an unearned run in the fifth, rounding out the day's scoring. The Sox put runners on base in every inning, but Ruffing escaped unscathed each time to claim a 2–0 victory. A crowd of slightly more than 30,000 turned out, many of them drawn to get a first look at Boston's prized rookie. Williams, batting sixth, struck out in the second inning before getting his first major-league hit, a double into right-center field. Gehrig, batting fifth behind DiMaggio, went hitless in four times at bat, grounding weakly into double plays in the third and fifth innings. He also made an error, failing to hold on to a throw from Red Rolfe on a ground ball in the ninth.

The game was notable for two other reasons. A four-man umpiring crew was used on an experimental basis. Two-man teams had been the norm throughout the twenties and into the early thirties. Starting in 1933, three umpires were used routinely—one behind the plate and one at first base, while the third moved between third and second as circumstance dictated. The four-man umpiring crew did not become a staple until 1952, but it appeared, probably for the first time, in the 1939 Yankee-Red Sox opener. Interestingly, the third-base umpire was George Pipgras, who happened to be the starting pitcher for the Yankees in the 1929 opener. The opposing pitcher for the Red Sox was Red Ruffing.

Also of note was that the game was broadcast live on radio. The first radio broadcast of a baseball game dated back as early as 1921. Daily game broadcasts in Chicago began in 1924, and the practice spread throughout both leagues. The three New York teams were the last holdouts. They had entered into an agreement in 1934 that none of them would offer live broadcasts of their games. By 1938, they were the only major-league teams that maintained a blackout, the concern being that live descriptions of the game would cut into attendance, already suffering because of the Depression. However, Larry MacPhail, the new general manager of the Dodgers, was not the type to be hamstrung by tradition. He believed that radio broadcasts would help to popularize the game and, in the long run, increase attendance.

Having just left Cincinnati, where he was general manager, in favor of a similar position in Brooklyn, he announced that the Dodgers would not renew the agreement with the Yankees and Giants. By way of emphasis, he took with him from Cincinnati his radio broadcaster, the amiable Southern smoothie, Red Barber. Thus, New Yorkers were introduced to such down-home subtleties as the pitcher is "sittin' in the catbird seat" when things were going his way, and when circumstances were working against him, he had "his big toe caught in the pickle vat." And the Old Redhead, as he was affectionately known, was at his best when the Dodgers were "tearin' up the pea patch" at Ebbets Field with the runs pouring in and the bases loaded, or, as he would have it, the bases were "FOB—full of Brooklyns."

The Yankees and Giants grudgingly followed suit but in a circumspect manner. Counterintuitively, they chose to broadcast only home games. Since the two teams were never home at the same time, their games were broadcast on the same station, WABC, which was the flagship station for the CBS network, and by the same announcers, the veteran Arch McDonald and his young assistant, another southern gentleman by the name of Mel Allen. McDonald had already contributed to Yankee lore when, on March 3, he dubbed DiMaggio the "Yankee Clipper," named for the new Pan American trans-Atlantic airliner which, like the Yankee outfielder, was known for its speed and range.

The following year, McDonald moved to Washington and Melvin Allen Israel, at age twenty-six and out of Birmingham, Alabama, was on his way to becoming the Voice of the Yankees. He broadcast both Yankee and Giant home games until leaving for military service in 1941. When he returned in 1946, the Yanks and Giants each went their own way on the radio networks, broadcasting a full schedule of 154 games. Yankee games were aired on station WINS, and Allen was teamed with Russ Hodges. In 1949, Hodges became the number one broadcaster of Giants games, and he soon earned broadcasting immortality with his frantic call of "The Giants win the pennant, the Giants win the pennant," when Bobby Thomson hit his "Shot Heard 'Round the World" against the Dodgers in 1951.

Although Mel Allen, like Barber, was a product of the South, they appropriated very different broadcast styles. Barber, soft-spoken and understated, delivered his play-by-play with a direct, largely unbiased approach. Allen, by contrast, was a partisan, an unabashed cheerleader. After introducing himself as he came on the air with his patented, "Hello there, everybody, this is Mel Allen," he soon launched into an energy-driven play-by-play that would morph, when the occasion arose, into his rollicking home-run call of "Going, going, it is *gone.*" He was also an enthusiastic advocate for his beer and cigar sponsors, designating homers as a Ballantine Blast or a White Owl Wallop. While his home-favoring style made him a bona fide hero to his legions of Yankee fans, his partiality was detested by advocates of the other two New York teams.

Allen studied at the University of Alabama and graduated from its School of Law in 1937. In New York a year later, he won an audition with CBS to do the Yankee and Giant games. Between 1946 and 1964, he was as much a celebrity as many of the players. When television intercepted radio, he joined up with Barber when "the Old Redhead" left the Dodgers in a contract dispute, and they shared both the radio and television broadcasts on the Yankee network. Allen left the broadcast booth, some said not altogether voluntarily, after the 1964 season and became the first host of the television program *This Week in Baseball*. In 1998, the Yankees dedicated a plaque to his memory in the Stadium's Monument Park, where he joined the likes of Ruth, Gehrig, and DiMaggio. As Mel Allen himself would have said, "How about that?"

The day after their home opener, the Yankees moved back to Washington, where the rain had finally stopped. The Senators had opened their season in Philadelphia with a 2–0 loss to the A's. Now, initiating their home season, Vice President John Nance Garner threw out the first ball, substituting for President Roosevelt who was consumed with events that were heating up in Europe. With Gomez starting for the Yankees, DiMaggio gave him an early one-run lead with an RBI double in the first inning. The Senators responded in the second with three runs of their own on four straight hits, but the Yanks put the game away with a five-run fifth. All the runs came on home runs—a two-run shot by DiMaggio and an inside-the-park, three-run homer by the rookie Joe Gallagher, who was playing right field in a Yankee career that would be over before the season ended. Gehrig, having gotten on base on an infield single, scored one of the runs on Gallagher's home run. But he did not look well at the plate, and for the second straight day, he made an error, muffing a ground ball by Buddy Lewis in the seventh.

The Yankees' 2–0 start came to an abrupt end the following day when Washington's knuckle-balling ace, Dutch Leonard, outpitched the latest addition to New York's rotation, Oral

Hildebrand, 3–1. Hildebrand, acquired in the off-season from the St. Louis Browns, pitched a neat four-hitter over seven innings, but three of those hits came in the third, accounting for the Senators' total run production for the day. Hildebrand had arrived with solid credentials. He began his big-league career with Cleveland in 1933, going 16–11, leading the league in shutouts with six and being named to the All-Star team in his rookie season. He continued to pitch well for the Indians but was dealt to the Browns in 1937 in a blockbuster trade involving five other players before coming to New York. Although he lost his first two starts with the Yankees, he would go on to make a solid contribution to the team's quest for a fourth consecutive title. He lost only twice more during the season while winning ten times and finished with a career-low ERA of 3.06.

Heading into the season's fourth game, Gehrig, who had gone hitless in four at-bats in the loss to Washington, was one-for-ten in the first three games. His lone hit was an infield single. He had more errors than hits. Things did not improve. He went zero-for-four again on Sunday, April 23, while Steve Sundra was working his way to a 7–4 decision. Back at the Stadium the next day, Monte Pearson pitched a neat four-hitter, besting Philadelphia 2–1. The Yanks scored on a home run by Red Rolfe in the sixth and got an unearned run in the seventh. Gehrig again failed to hit in three chances. He was now one-for-eighteen in five games. He was batting .059. But the numbers did not tell the full story. He was clearly sluggish both at the plate and in the field. Even when he put the bat on the ball, it was not with authority. Several opposing pitchers noted that his reflexes appeared to be so slow that they were hesitant to pitch him inside fearful that he might not be able to get out of the way.

Finally, he came through with two hits at home against the Athletics in an 8–4 Yankee win. On one of those hits— a blooping Texas Leaguer just beyond the infield—he was thrown out trying to stretch it into a double. He never got close; he was tagged out at second before he had a chance to slide. He got his first RBI of the season on a ground-ball out in the fifth. On Saturday, April 29, he got another hit against the Senators. Despite the sanguine turn of events, there still appeared to be little room for optimism. All three of his hits were singles; his bat tended to be late on a fastball; his every movement was constrained, lacking the certainty of function that marked the unstudied style of an athlete.

McCarthy had dropped Gehrig from the cleanup spot he had held since the twenties, when he batted behind Ruth, to fifth in the order, hitting in back of DiMaggio. DiMaggio, off to a good start with a batting average approaching .400, had singled leading off the second inning of the April 29 game. But when he returned to the field, misfortune awaited. With the Senators ahead 3–1, Bobby Estalella lined a Gomez fastball into left-center field. DiMaggio ran to his right in an effort to cut off what would become a triple, but the April rains had left the field a bit soggy, and the cleats on his right shoe got caught in the muddy turf. DiMaggio went down hard and needed help getting up. He finally limped off the field aided by the trainer Doc Painter and team physician Dr. Robert Walsh. He was taken to Lenox Hill Hospital and initially diagnosed with torn muscles in his lower right leg. A few days later, he received the good news that the injury was not as serious as first suspected, and he was moved to St. Elizabeth Hospital for further treatment. All the same, it would be a month before Joe would return to the lineup. The 3–1 score stood up until game's end, and as the last day of April loomed, the Yankees had a record of 5–2 and held first place with a one-game lead over the Red Sox.

If New Yorkers were in need of a respite, a distraction from their early season woes—the physical erosion that was wearing away at Gehrig, the temporary but rather lengthy loss of DiMaggio—they received it in spades. On an unseasonably hot Sunday, the last day of April, the 1939 World's Fair opened in Flushing Meadows, Queens, in New York City. In typical New York fashion, it dwarfed most of the previous fairs, including the Chicago Fair in 1893 and the one in St. Louis in 1904, which is best remembered for its popularization of the ice cream cone. The fair had been promoted nationwide for more than a year. Howard Hughes, the celebrated film mogul, airplane pilot, and all-around tycoon, flew a special World's Fair flight around the globe to publicize its opening. Baseball also did its part. The three New York teams wore patches on the sleeves of their uniforms throughout the 1938 season featuring the Trylon and Perisphere and "1939." The Trylon and Perisphere were two monumental, modernistic structures that together were known as the Theme Center of the Fair. The Perisphere was a huge sphere, 180 feet in diameter connected to the 610-foot-high spire-shaped Trylon by what was then the world's longest escalator.

The opening was timed to mark the 150th anniversary of George Washington's first inauguration as president. More than 206,000 people heard President Roosevelt give the address on opening day, which had as its slogan "Dawn of a New Day." Reflecting a wide range of technological innovations on display at the fair, the president's speech was not only broadcast over the various radio networks, it was also carried on a new medium called television. An estimated one thousand viewers saw the telecast on some two hundred television sets scattered throughout the New York area. Albert Einstein also addressed the crowd, speaking on the existence of cosmic rays.

Spread across 1,216 acres, the fair was the first of its kind to focus entirely on the future. It offered an extravagant display featuring the imagined wonders of a new world yet to be discovered. It was bright and welcoming and full of hope. Seventy-nine countries were represented. Germany had signed on for a pavilion but it never came to pass as anti-Nazi groups throughout the country protested loudly and incessantly. New York's Mayor LaGuardia stated the case this way: "Brute force will not be featured at our fair at all." In the spring of 1938, the German government withdrew, citing what it said was a lack funds. The nation was perhaps financially stressed as its economy by now was devoted to turning out the tanks and planes necessary for its assault on the European continent. The fair, ironically enough, promised a world based on international cooperation; its theme was "Building the World of Tomorrow." The timing and chief purpose of the fair was to lift the spirits of the country during a dark period in its history. It attracted large throngs from all over the world in a year that was also notable for its many distinctions in the world of entertainment and the arts.

Popular music was at its peak. A young singer by the name of Frank Sinatra had joined the Harry James band and began attracting serious attention, particularly from an adoring group of female teenagers who became known as bobby-soxers. The Benny Goodman orchestra, which had brought the sound of "swing" to Carnegie Hall the previous year, was drawing large crowds all over the country. Two of the most popular movies of all time—*Gone with the Wind* and *The Wizard of Oz*—opened within months of one another, but neither won the Academy Award; that went to the Frank Capra film *You Can't Take It with You*, starring Jean Arthur, Lionel Barrymore, and an up-and-coming James Stewart. John Steinbeck's *The Grapes of Wrath* gripped the heart of America with its portrayal of the Joad family, devastated by the Oklahoma dust bowl travesty, making its way across the continent to the glittering but false hope of California. For those with a taste for more challenging reading, James Joyce provided the nearly impenetrable *Finnegan's Wake*, which made *Ulysses* read like a grade-school primer.

With it all, the vision of the World of Tomorrow, viewed from across the ocean, was growing bleaker by the day. While in America the bands were playing and the titles rolling, the world was drifting, slowly but inexorably, down a road which had no turning.

14

A Door Closes; the Beat Goes On

On the last day of April 1939, Lou Gehrig played in his 2,130th consecutive major-league game. It would be his last. Gehrig knew that something was wrong but was uncertain what it was. For a while he thought he might be able to work out the kinks and regain his previous form. But as the days passed and his performance failed to improve, the suspicion grew that the issue might be more serious. Then, on April 30, as the Yankees were losing to the Senators and Gehrig was again going hitless, a single play provided the impetus that decided matters for him. Johnny Murphy, in relief of Hildebrand, fielded a routine ground ball between the mound and first base, but he had to delay his throw while Gehrig labored to get to the bag. As they walked off the field, Murphy said, "Nice play, Lou." "I knew then," Gehrig later said, "that it was time to quit."

It appeared to all who covered the team that McCarthy would have benched him if it had been anyone but Lou Gehrig. With the team's record at 5–3 and DiMaggio out for the foreseeable future, the manager was aware that he needed to add some punch to the lineup. He was, however, understandably reluctant to make a move. He seemed to trust that Gehrig would soon comprehend the gravity of the situation and offer to step aside and end his playing streak. That day came in Detroit on the evening of Monday, May 1. Given the luxury of an off-day, McCarthy had stopped off for a brief visit to his home in Buffalo on his way to Detroit. When he arrived at the Book-Cadillac Hotel that night, he found coach Art Fletcher waiting for him in the lobby. Fletcher told McCarthy that Gehrig wanted to speak with him. The manager told him to send Gehrig up to his room. McCarthy had a sense of what was on his mind. He was not at all surprised when Gehrig asked to be removed from the lineup. He also made it clear that he did not want to be used as a pinch-hitter in order to preserve his streak; he believed his career was over. As prime evidence, he cited Murphy's remark and said it was clear that the other players thought he was hurting the team. After the starting lineup was announced with Gehrig's name missing, Lou explained the move to the sportswriters. As recounted by James P. Dawson in the *New York Times,* Gehrig said:

> I decided last Sunday night on this move. I haven't been a bit of good to the team since the season started. It would not be fair to the boys, to Joe, or to the baseball public for me to try going on. In fact, it would not be fair to myself, and I'm the last consideration.
>
> It's tough to see your mates on base, have a chance to win a ballgame, and not be able to do anything about

it. McCarthy has been swell about it all the time. He'd let me go until the cows came home, he is that considerate of my feelings but I knew in Sunday's game that I should get out of there.

I went up there four times with men on base. Once there were two there. A hit would have won the ball game for the Yankees, but I missed, leaving five stranded as the Yankees lost. Maybe a rest will do me some good. Maybe it won't. Who knows? Who can tell? I'm just hoping.

He later added that he was unsure what the problem was. "I just can't understand," he said, "I'm not sick." As team captain, Gehrig was sent out to hand the lineup card to the home plate umpire. The public address announcer informed the sparse crowd of just over 11,000 that Lou was ending his streak and suggested that he be given a big hand. The fans responded with a two-minute standing ovation that brought tears to Gehrig's eyes. He tipped his cap and returned to the dugout. The streak, which had begun in 1925 and earned him the designation of "The Iron Horse," was over. The previous consecutive game mark, 1,307, was held by Everett Scott who had played shortstop for the Red Sox and then for the Yankees from 1916 to 1925. Curiously, Gehrig's streak had begun the same year that Scott's ended. Scott, playing for the Yankees at the time, was replaced at shortstop by Pee Wee Wanninger in May 1925. Even more curious, Gehrig's streak started on June 1 when manager Miller Huggins sent him up to pinch-hit for Wanninger. The following day, the consecutive game run began in earnest when he replaced the veteran Wally Pipp at first base.

The story of Gehrig's replacing Pipp has, over the years, taken on the stuff of legend and myth. The story had been bruited that Pipp had complained of a headache and Huggins granted him a day off. Pipp, who had twice led the league in homers during the dead-ball era, was depicted as something of a wimp who begged off with a minor discomfort. The headache tale was replaced some years later with a more heroic account of Pipp's sitting out the game. The new narrative had it that Pipp had been beaned in batting practice, was helped off the field, and then hospitalized for two weeks. That story was true except for one detail: the beaning had actually taken place a month later, on July 2. That the June 2 story was apocryphal could be easily confirmed; Pipp had played an inning at first base the next day and had come to bat once.

The most likely truth is that Huggins was seeking to buttress a lineup that had his team in seventh place, thirteen-and-a-half games off the lead. Pipp was sporting a meager batting average of .244, well below his customary mark of around .280. Sitting on the bench was the promising kid from Columbia University who, in a total of 38 times at bat in 1923 and '24, had mustered 17 hits—including five doubles, a triple, and a home run, while driving in 14 runs—for a gaudy, if incipient, average of .447. In any event, the unbridled and relevant truth is that Gehrig had taken immediate advantage of the opportunity, getting three hits, including a double in an 8–5 win at Washington.

Gehrig, who would turn twenty-two on June 19, was a native New Yorker, born in the Yorkville section of Manhattan, the second of four children of German immigrants. His father, a sheet metal worker by trade, was often unemployed, largely the result of his addiction to alcohol. His brother had died in infancy and his two sisters at early ages due to the then-potent diseases of measles and whooping cough. Lou was obliged to grow up quickly. Hardworking and conscientious, he helped his mother, performing ordinary household chores and picking up supplies from local stores. When he was seven years old, his family had moved to the Washington Heights section in Upper Manhattan where he attended PS 132 before moving on to Commerce High School. It was there that he first attracted national attention for his baseball prowess. His Commerce team was playing a team from Chicago's Lane Tech High School at Cubs Park, later named Wrigley Field. There, before a crowd of more than 10,000 spectators, Lou hit a grand slam home run that left the ballpark and landed on Waveland Avenue, a prodigious drive for a seventeen-year-old, even one who stood at a sturdy six feet and weighed in at 200 pounds.

After graduating from Commerce, Gehrig went to Columbia University on a football scholarship, planning to study engineering. But fate intervened. Giants' manager John McGraw, who had seen him play baseball at Commerce, advised him to play professional baseball during the summer. Lou took his advice, playing a dozen games for the Hartford Senators under the assumed name of Henry Lewis. His brief stint as a professional cost him his college eligibility in his freshman year. But a year later, in 1922, he resumed his collegiate career, playing fullback for the football team and splitting time between first base and pitching during the baseball season. It was as a power-hitting first baseman that he would find his fortune.

On April 18, 1923, the same day that Babe Ruth baptized the opening of Yankee Stadium with a home run against the Red Sox, pitcher Lou Gehrig struck out seventeen Williams College batters at Columbia's South Field. The strikeouts were a team record, but that was not what attracted the attention of Yankee scout Paul Krichell, who was in attendance. Krichell had been following the left-hand hitting youngster for several days and was nothing less than awed at the prodigious drives that came off Gehrig's bat. He was perhaps envisioning the prospect of Lou batting behind Ruth and focusing on the Stadium's short right-field porch. Such musings were fed on April 28 by a 450-foot drive at Columbia's South Field that cleared the roof and finally fell to the pavement at Broadway and 116th Street. Two days later, Gehrig signed a contract with the Yankees. He received $2,000 for the balance of the 1923 season plus a signing bonus of $1,500. Then he returned to Hartford where he played parts of the 1923 and '24 seasons, batting a cumulative .344 and hitting 61 home runs in 193 games. During each of those two seasons, he auditioned briefly with the Yankees before taking over at first base in 1925.

His rookie season was promising though not spectacular. He batted .295 with 20 home runs and 68 RBIs. His numbers improved the following year, but it was in the legendary season of 1927 that Gehrig served notice on what the future held. He put together one of the best offensive seasons in baseball history: he hit .373, with 218 hits including 52 doubles, 18 triples, 47 home runs, a then-record 175 runs batted in, and a slugging percentage of .765. His 117 extra-base hits were second to Ruth's 119 compiled in 1921; and his 447 total bases were third all-time to Ruth's 457 in the same year and Rogers Hornsby's 450 in 1922. Despite Gehrig's extraordinary performance, which earned him the Most Valuable Player award, the 1927 season of Murderers' Row has always been remembered as the year of Ruth's 60 home runs, which set a record that would remain unequaled for thirty-four years until Roger Maris hit 61 in 1961. It was to be part of Gehrig's legacy to reside always in the shadow of the Bambino, whose shadow, after all, enshrouded all who came before and all who would come after.

Nineteen-twenty-seven proved to be no aberration; it was the beginning of a career during which Gehrig would be one of the most productive hitters of all time. He earned the MVP award again in 1934 when he won the Triple Crown with a batting average of .363, 49 home runs, and 165 RBIs. He also led the league in home runs in 1931 and '36 and was the RBI leader five times. He was the first batter ever to hit four home runs in one game, on June 3, 1932. An All-Star seven times, he played for six World Series champions during his 17-year career. Among the records he owned when he retired—in addition to his 2,130 consecutive games—were: most grand slam home runs, 23; most years with 300 or more total bases, 13; most years with 100 or more runs driven in, 13; and the American League record for most RBIs in one season, 184.

Now, on May 2, 1939, with Gehrig out of the lineup for the first time since 1925, the Yankees attacked the Tigers as if in tribute to their fallen hero. They opened up with six runs in the first inning, followed with two in the third and fifth, three in the sixth, and closed things out with a nine-run outburst in the seventh for a total of 22 runs while Ruffing held Detroit scoreless until he surrendered a pair of runs in the bottom of the seventh. Leading the assault was the Yanks' new left fielder, Charlie Keller. Starting for the first time, Keller went four-for-five with a home run, a triple, six RBIs, and four runs scored. Henrich and Selkirk also homered, and so did Babe Dahlgren who was inserted into the lineup, batting eighth and playing first base. It was Dahlgren whom McCarthy had chosen from among a bevy of other candidates—including the possibility of moving Henrich in from the outfield—to replace Gehrig.

A native of San Francisco, Ellsworth Tenney "Babe" Dahlgren broke into the major leagues with the Red Sox in 1935 at the age of twenty-two. He played in 149 games, hit a respectable .263, and drove in 63 runs. But his career with Boston was short-lived. The Sox obtained Jimmie Foxx from the A's in the off-season and Dahlgren was dispatched to the minor leagues where he performed well enough for the Yankees to purchase his contract in 1937. He played just one game that year and a handful of others in 1938 before assuming the full-time job when Gehrig stepped down. Growing up in San Francisco and watching the Seals, Dahlgren had been a devout Yankee fan, with a scrapbook filled with pictures of Ruth and Gehrig. So it was with mixed feelings that he played a part in ending the streak of his boyhood idol that day in early May. Years later, he recalled the moment, as described by Richard Goldstein in the *New York Times* on September 6, 1996, on the occasion of Dahlgren's death:

> I remember Lou taking the lineup card up to the plate that day. When he came back to the dugout he went over to the water fountain and took a drink. He started to cry. Lou stood there with a towel on his head, taking the longest drink I've ever seen anybody take.
>
> I hated to break his streak. But there was no special pressure. In fact, I almost hit four home runs the day I took his place. I hit one homer, a double off the fence, and two more balls were caught at the fence.

While his batting numbers for the season were in no way Gehrig-like, Dahlgren was reasonably productive, hitting .235 with 15 home runs and 89 runs batted in. He had one memorable day at the plate during a June 28 doubleheader at Philadelphia, when the Yankees swept the A's by the intimidating scores of 23–2 and 10–0. Dahlgren contributed with a combined seven hits in ten times at bat that included three home runs and seven RBIs. However, it was his fielding that was his chief stock in trade, and it supplied the credentials that kept him in the major leagues. He played first base with the grace and precision of a ballet dancer, often drawing comparisons to Prince Hal Chase who had been acclaimed the archetype of first baseman since his days with the Yankees when they were still known as the Highlanders. In 1940, Dahlgren played every game, hitting an honest .264 with 73 RBIs and four home runs. It was, as it turned out, a typical year for Dahlgren though it was his last with the Yankees. His tenure with the team was brief and ended abruptly in unfortunate circumstances.

Late in the season, with the Yankees battling the Indians and Tigers for first place, Dahlgren uncharacteristically mishandled a throw in a game against Cleveland that cost them the game and, McCarthy insisted, any chance for a fifth straight pennant. They finished the season in third place, two games behind Cleveland and one in back of Detroit. With no apparent justification, McCarthy claimed that Dahlgren had muffed the throw because he had been smoking marijuana, which dulled his reflexes. Specifically, he was quoted by *New York Times* sportswriter John Drebinger some years later as saying that "the Yankees would have won the pennant in 1940 had it not been for an error Dahlgren made against the Indians late in the season," adding, "Dahlgren doesn't screw up that play if he wasn't a marijuana smoker."

Dahlgren did not learn of the rumor until 1943, which was when he would become the first major league baseball player to take a test for a performance-enhancing drug. He took the test voluntarily, and the results were negative. The rumor was, and remained, unfounded and uncorroborated by anyone else. At the end of the 1940 season, Dahlgren was sold to the Boston Braves. He continued his major-league career in vagabond fashion until 1946, moving from the Braves to the Cubs to the St. Louis Browns, and from there to the Dodgers, the Phillies, the Pirates, and finally once more to the Browns. The rumor haunted Dahlgren throughout his career and beyond. In 2007,

eleven years after the player's death, his grandson, Matt Dahlgren, self-published a book entitled *Rumor in Town* in which
he maintained that McCarthy had initiated the story with no
evidence at all, and that it was also spread, for reasons un-
known, by Branch Rickey, then general manager of the Brooklyn Dodgers.

Discussing the book in the *Times*, Murray Chass wrote:
"The story of [Barry] Bonds or any other player doesn't approach the tale of Babe Dahlgren . . . whose career and life
were ruined by an unsubstantiated rumor that he smoked
marijuana . . . Dahlgren agreed to be tested and he underwent
a series of examinations by a doctor in Philadelphia to prove
he was not a user of marijuana."

With Gehrig now a spectator and Dahlgren installed at first
base, the Yankees went on a tear. It was as if they had banked
a store of resources, preserving it for a time when it might best
be put to use. Now that time had come. After the May 2 game,
the Yankees' record stood at 6–3 and they were tied with the
Red Sox for the league lead. They won four of their next five
games but remained tied with Boston. The Sox, of course, were
more dangerous this year than they had been in 1938. Now
hitting back-to-back, Ted Williams and Jimmie Foxx were on
their way to becoming a formidable duo, recalling the exploits
of Ruth and Gehrig, and Gehrig and DiMaggio.

Moving into May, Foxx was hitting .412 and Williams .333.
At season's end, they would be at .360 and .327, respectively.
Foxx would lead the league in homers with 35 while driving
in 105 runs. Williams, concluding his rookie season, led the

league in RBIs with 145, including 31 home runs. They were a perfect combination of seasoned veteran and newcomer. Foxx, at age thirty-one and in his fourth season with the Red Sox, still had five good years ahead of him, though not of the caliber of his production with the Athletics. With the A's, he had led the league in homers three years in a row, from 1932 to 1934 with 58, 48, and 44, and in RBIs in 1932 and 1933 with 169 and 163. In 1933, he also led in batting with an average of .356. He was named league MVP in both those seasons. Williams, for his part, was at the very start of a career that would include batting .406 in 1941. He was the last batter to hit better than .400 for at least the next seventy-five years, and he remains in the conversation as arguably the best hitter of all time.

Even so, the Bosox were no match for the Yankees. On May 9, the two teams were still in a virtual first-place tie that was not destined to last very long. On that date, the Yankees embarked on a twelve-game winning streak, launching them into first place where they would reside for the balance of the season. Following a loss to Detroit, they won another six in a row, making it 18–1 over the three-week period from May 9 to 29. By the end of the month, they led the Red Sox by six-and-a-half games. And they were not yet done. The six-game streak ended when they dropped the first game of a Memorial Day doubleheader with the Red Sox, but they won the second game, which was the start of yet another streak of five games. By then, June 4, the lead over Boston was eight-and-a-half lengths.

Most remarkable about the Yankees' early season dominance is that it was achieved with both Gehrig and DiMaggio out of the lineup. The slack was taken up by Bill Dickey, George Sel-kirk, Charlie Keller, Joe Gordon, and Tommy Henrich, who was patrolling center field in place of DiMaggio. Dickey, now thirty-two years old and in the early stages of what would be his last great season, was batting .354. Keller, by contrast, was in his rookie year as the regular left fielder and batting .316. Selkirk, the Yankees' right fielder since the departure of Ruth, had never received the acclaim he deserved and now, in the midst of perhaps his best season, he was sporting a batting average of .325; the ever-reliable Henrich was at .287, and Gordon, batting a commendable .289, was leading the team in home runs with six.

So offense was of no concern. The team had scored in double digits in nine of their twenty-nine games in May. It was pitching that caused McCarthy to ponder the prospects for the remainder of the season. Monte Pearson, suffering from a sore arm, missed two early season starts before returning on May 6 with a neat three-hit, 5–1 decision over Cleveland. Of more concern was the status of Lefty Gomez. Winner of eighteen games in 1938, Gomez injured his back on May 10 when he was knocked down while covering first base on a ground ball. The injury led him to alter his pitching motion, causing a strain on his arm from which he never fully recovered. After missing a few starts, he came back to win his next five decisions, but he was limited the rest of the way and would close the season with a modest record of 12–8.

A less consequential loss was the abysmal failure of Wes Ferrell, the late 1938 acquisition who McCarthy was hoping could deliver some needed innings while the rotation was still in flux. Ferrell, whose prospects were in any event questionable as he neared the close of a fine career, disappointed early and never recovered. He suffered two of the Yankees' total of four losses in May, including a 6–1 drubbing by Detroit, which ended the Yanks' twelve-game winning streak. It was to be his last appearance for New York. At season's end, he had pitched a meager nineteen-and-a-third innings in three games and resumed what was left of his career in Brooklyn in 1940.

McCarthy's chief consolation was that Ruffing, the bellwether of the staff, was at his best with a record of 7–1 at the end of May. The rest of the staff, makeshift though it was, was gradually rounding into shape. Pearson, his arm restored, was 5–0. In his second season with the club, Steve Sundra was 3–0, on his way to eleven straight wins. A newcomer by the name of Atley Donald was making his presence felt with four straight victories to open his career; he also was on the way to setting an American League record by winning his first twelve decisions as a rookie. Johnny Murphy had eight saves, a category in which he would lead the league with a total of 19, at the time the second highest number in history. Additional help was on the way at the start of June with the arrival of Marius Russo, a rookie southpaw who would end the season with an 8–3 record.

June started well enough for the Yankees. They won their first four games before dropping two in a row to Detroit. Their record at the time stood at 33–9, and they retained their reasonably secure lead over Boston. What was even more comforting was that DiMaggio was on the way back. He had been released from the hospital a month earlier and spent the next four weeks-plus rehabilitating his leg. Now he was fit and ready to take his position in center field and cleanup in the batting order. His batting average after the first seven games of the season stood at .435. For the Yankees, DiMaggio's return was like getting a tax refund the day after winning the lottery.

With their main man back in the lineup on June 7, the Yanks went four-for-four against Chicago and St. Louis. For his part, DiMaggio looked better than ever, going eight-for-fifteen and lifting his average to .487. His hits included three doubles, a triple, and a home run. Following a July 11 doubleheader sweep against the Browns, the Yankees' record stood at 37–9, a winning percentage of .804. They had a nine-game lead over the Red Sox. How could things be any better?

15

Baseball Hall of Fame Puts Cooperstown on the Map

Every sport has a past; only baseball has a history. The heroes of other sports strut their hour upon the stage, but their deeds tend to be devoured by the years. Few football fans can tell you how many touchdown passes Peyton Manning threw, and even fewer remember the exploits of Sammy Baugh or Sid Luckman, both star quarterbacks in the forties. But every serious baseball fan knows that Babe Ruth hit 60 home runs in 1927 or that Joe DiMaggio hit in fifty-six consecutive games in 1941. Baseball, whose numbers resonate from one era to the next, creates its own mythology. The past serves as a nutrient for what comes next, and long-ago events take on a greater dimension of reality as they recede deeper into the pockets of recollection. There are only two keepers of the past—time and place—and time has no memory.

The Baseball Hall of Fame was created in 1936 with the induction of five of the game's preeminent talents—Babe Ruth, Ty Cobb, Christy Mathewson, Honus Wagner, and

Walter Johnson—but it existed only in theory; it did not have a physical presence, where the artifacts of great deeds could be housed, until 1939 when the National Baseball Hall of Fame and Museum opened in Cooperstown, New York, a small village about two hundred miles northwest of New York City. The selection of so nondescript a location is a story worth noting, for it goes to the very heart of the roots and beginnings of the sport itself.

Every baseball fan of a certain age spent at least part of his youth believing that the game was invented in the summer of 1839 by a man named Abner Doubleday. The site of his birth was said to be Cooperstown, thus the siting of the game's shrine. Eventually, it was learned that the story was not true; not even remotely. Doubleday, who would become a general and a decorated hero during the Civil War, was still at West Point in 1839. What's more, he never claimed to have anything to do with the game called baseball. The bogus tale, as best it can be determined, was fashioned by one Abner Graves, a mining engineer and onetime resident of Cooperstown. In 1907, Graves presented what he said was an eyewitness account of the game's birth to the Mills Commission, a group created by the sporting goods magnate A. G. Spalding that was charged with determining whether baseball originated in the United States or was a variation of a game called rounders that was popular in Great Britain.

Most cultures have some form of stick-and-ball games, the best known being cricket, which dates back to the sixteenth century and is still a popular sport in England. One form or another of what we now call baseball was played in the larger cities of the United States throughout the early years of the nineteenth century. The rules varied from city to city until 1845 when a merchant seaman by the name of Alexander Cartwright took it upon himself to formalize the rules of the game. Cartwright, a volunteer firefighter who played bat-and-ball games on the streets of Manhattan with other volunteers, formed a team called the Knickerbocker Base Ball Club, and what is the first recorded baseball game was played in 1846 at the Elysian Fields in Hoboken, New Jersey. Cartwright was officially designated the father of the game of baseball by the United States Congress in 1953.

However, myths have a way of enduring despite all evidence to the contrary. Cooperstown businessmen knew a good deal when they saw one. They trumpeted the Doubleday story and used it to their advantage. Leading the drive was the owner of a local hotel, Stephen Carlton Clark. The Clark family was heir to a healthy slice of the Singer sewing machine fortune, and Stephen Clark was troubled by a downturn in business. The Depression had resulted in a dramatic decline in tourism that hurt the hotel business, and Prohibition had devastated the local hops industry. So the story of Abner Doubleday and Cooperstown was perpetuated, and Ford Frick, a former newspaperman who had become president of the National League, spearheaded the effort to enclose the Hall of Fame in a museum in time for the game's presumed centennial in 1939. It opened on June 12 and received its baptism with a choose-up game played on Doubleday Field, about two village blocks from the museum.

The induction class of 1939 included George Sisler, Eddie Collins, Wee Willie Keeler, and Lou Gehrig. Sisler,

Collins, and Keeler all received the required 75 percent of the vote among members of the Baseball Writers Association of America (BBWAA) in balloting that took place in 1938. Gehrig, though not yet officially retired, was ushered in in a special election. The four inductees joined the class of 1937 that featured players Napoleon Lajoie, Tris Speaker, and Cy Young; managers Connie Mack and John McGraw; and two executives—Morgan Bulkeley and Byron "Ban" Johnson, former presidents, respectively, of the National and American Leagues. Only Grover Cleveland Alexander made the cut in 1938.

All eleven surviving members of the Hall of Fame were on hand for the ceremonies, which had been designated the "Cavalcade of Baseball." A special two-car excursion train came chugging into Cooperstown carrying an exceptionally notable cargo. Exiting the train that morning were Babe Ruth, Connie Mack, Walter Johnson, Cy Young, Honus Wagner, Tris Speaker, Eddie Collins, Napoleon Lajoie, George Sisler, and Grover Cleveland Alexander. Ty Cobb would arrive later along with thirty-two major-league players who would play an exhibition game. To mark the occasion, every major-league ballpark closed for the day. NBC radio broadcasted the festivities nationally.

Following brief speeches by some of the dignitaries, the new Hall-of-Famers and the players who came to town for the exhibition game—two from each of the sixteen major-league teams—marched up Main Street to Doubleday Field, the mythical site of baseball's first game. There, Wagner and Collins chose sides. Wagner's team defeated Collins's team,

4–2, but the highlight of the day was a pinch-hit appearance by the Babe who, after a few Ruthian swings, popped out to the catcher.

While events at Cooperstown captured the nation's attention on that hot summer afternoon, another exhibition was taking place in the country's heartland. After completing a doubleheader sweep of the Browns in St. Louis on June 11, the Yankees made the short trip across the state of Missouri to Kansas City for a game against their American Association farm club, the Kansas City Blues. The game drew a record crowd of more than 23,000 at Ruppert Stadium. It offered a number of attractions, including the DiMaggio brothers, Joe and Vince, playing center field for their respective teams. Also in the lineup for the Blues, considered one of the best minor-league teams ever to take the field, were future Yankees Phil Rizzuto at shortstop, Gerry Priddy at second base, and Johnny Sturm who would play most of the game at first. But the real attraction was the man who started at first base for the Yankees. Lou Gehrig, still in uniform and traveling with the team, was making what truly would be his final appearance on a baseball field, playing three innings while in extraordinary pain. His abbreviated performance showed why he had called it a career. He grounded weakly to second base in his only time at bat and managed to get by in the field without an error, although he was not quite able to reach a ground ball by Kansas City pitcher Joe Vance that scored the only run of the game for the Blues.

Visibly exhausted, Gehrig left the field after the third inning, escorted by his road roommate and closest friend on the team, Bill Dickey. Dickey had, in essence, signed on as Gehrig's unofficial caretaker from the time Lou began showing signs of decay. They were an unlikely pair of bedfellows—Gehrig of German descent and a product of the streets of New York; Dickey, who was born in Louisiana but grew up in Arkansas, speaking with the soft locutions of the South on his tongue and in a manner that was as far removed from the Big City as one might have it. But the two men gravitated toward one another right upon meeting. Dickey explained: "Lou and I liked to do the same things. We liked movies, same foods, same hours. We liked to talk baseball, we had similar ideas, we looked at life in much the same ways."

Born in 1907, William Malcolm Dickey was four years Gehrig's junior. Baseball was in his blood from the very beginning. His father, a brakeman for the Missouri Pacific Railroad, had played semipro ball in Memphis, Tennessee. An older brother, Gus, was a second baseman and pitcher in the East Arkansas Semipro League, and a younger brother, George, made it to the majors as a part-time catcher for the Red Sox and White Sox after Bill had already earned fame as a Yankee.

Bill got his own start at Searcy High School in Arkansas where he played as a pitcher and second baseman. He played both baseball and football during a brief stay at Little Rock College, but he got his first break when he was called upon to substitute for a friend as the catcher on a semipro team in Hot Springs, Arkansas. Lena Blackburne, the manager of the Little Rock Travelers of the Class A Southern Association, was scouting an outfielder, but it was Dickey who attracted his attention. Blackburne was particularly impressed by the strength and accuracy of his throwing arm and made haste to sign him. Dickey made his professional debut in 1925 at the age of eighteen. Over the course of the next two seasons, he moved from Little Rock to Muskogee, Oklahoma, and then to Jackson, Mississippi, in the Cotton States League. It was there that Yankee scout Johnny Nee took notice and stamped him with a can't-miss label. At the end of the 1927 season, Nee wired general manager Ed Barrow and told him to sign Dickey immediately. He told Barrow he was prepared to stake his considerable reputation on the young catcher. "I will quit scouting," he said, "if this boy does not make good."

The Yankees purchased Dickey from Jackson for the bargain price of $12,500. He started the 1928 season back at Little Rock where, while hitting .300, he was promoted to the Buffalo Bisons of the Class AA International League. The Yankees, on their way to a third straight pennant, brought him up in mid-August. Catcher was the one position on the Murderers' Row team that needed a bit of help. Benny Bengough was the regular catcher but he shared time with both Johnny Grabowski and Pat Collins. Dickey got his first major-league hit, a triple off George Blaeholder of the St. Louis Browns, on August 24. He played in only ten games, getting three hits in fifteen times at bat.

Manager Miller Huggins sensed that Dickey was trying to fit the mold of the team's power hitters—Ruth, Gehrig, Lazzeri—and, batting from the left side, taking aim at the nearby right-field seats. Huggins offered some advice: "Stop unbuttoning your shirt on every pitch," he told him. "We pay one player here for hitting home runs and that's Babe Ruth. So choke up and drill the ball. That way, you'll be around here longer." Gehrig, who was the first player to embrace the rookie, had something more specific to offer. He told Dickey that he was uppercutting on the ball, perhaps trying to get more loft and greater distance on contact. He suggested that Dickey level off on his swing in an effort to make more contact. Dickey appreciated the attention Gehrig paid him as well as the instruction. "Well," he said, "that was my first introduction to what a great fellow Gehrig was, and later on we became roommates and very good buddies."

Dickey followed the advice of both his manager and his mentor with outstanding results. When Johnny Grabowski broke a finger early in the 1929 season, Dickey stepped in and never let go. In his first full year as Yankee catcher, he hit .324 with 10 home runs and 65 runs batted in. It was, by later standards, a modest beginning. He batted .339 in 1930 and .327 a year later. By this time, he had become a team leader, a more intense, fiery complement to Gehrig's restrained manner. Although he was easy-going and friendly off the field, an incident in 1932 defined Dickey's fierce competitiveness between the lines.

In the first game of a July 4 doubleheader, with the Yanks trailing the Senators 10–7, Washington right fielder Carl Reynolds broke from third base toward home on a suicide squeeze. The batter missed the bunt, and Dickey threw to third baseman Joe Sewell in an attempt to nail Reynolds heading back to the bag. Sewell muffed the throw, and Reynolds turned and streaked back toward the plate. There, he barreled hard into

Dickey who dropped Sewell's throw. Dickey thought Reynolds rammed him harder than was necessary, and when Sewell moved back to the plate to make sure he had touched it the first time, Dickey landed a solid punch, breaking Reynolds's jaw in two places. The punch cost Dickey a thousand-dollar fine and a thirty-day suspension. The Yankees filed a protest, but American League president Will Harridge upheld both the fine and the suspension. Washington owner Clark Griffith also protested, insisting that Dickey should be suspended for as long as Reynolds was unable to play. As it played out, Reynolds returned to action on August 13, nine days after Dickey was reinstated.

Dickey batted better than .300 every year until 1935 when he slumped to .279. But it was in a sense a transitional season, for another adjustment in his swing converted him from the contact hitter that Huggins wanted to a power hitter that more closely suited the rhythms of the new-born Yankee dynasty. In 1936, he had a breakout year. His batting average of .362 set a new record for a catcher that stood until Joe Mauer hit .365 for the Minnesota Twins in 2009, seventy-three years later. He added to his performance with 22 home runs and 107 RBIs, the first time he bettered the unofficial standards of 20 and 100. He exceeded those marks with 29 homers and 133 RBIs in 1937, and, through 1939, he made it four straight years with more than 20 homers and 100 runs batted in. Despite his proficiency at the plate, it was his performance behind it that earned Dickey mention as perhaps the best catcher in baseball history. He had a rifle-like arm that was as accurate as it was strong. He blocked the plate with the best of them, as Carl Reynolds would likely confirm. But it was his handling of pitchers that most distinguished him. Pitchers rarely shook him off and, as at least one noted, they let him call their game.

At age thirty-two, Dickey had his last great year in 1939, rounding out his dominant performance during the Yankees' four straight championship seasons. Starting in 1940, some of the juice was gone. During the early years of the forties, he was still among the best catchers in the league, but he was spelled regularly, first by Buddy Rosar and then by Rollie Helmsley. Rosar, who batted right-handed, often played for Dickey when the opposition started a left-handed pitcher. Still, Dickey remained the Yankees' regular catcher through 1943, when he left for military service after hitting the home run that clinched the World Series against the Cardinals. He wound up his career with a cameo role in 1946, playing in fifty-four games. But his career with the Yankees was far from over. With the Yanks floundering in the first post-war season despite the return from service of such pre-war eminences as DiMaggio, Gordon, Keller, Henrich, and Ruffing, McCarthy felt the heat and resigned. Dickey was chosen to replace him. Under his command, the team went 57–48, but the new owner, Larry MacPhail, would not commit to Dickey for the following year, and he resigned as manager with fourteen games left in the season. Dickey felt no resentment regarding their differences. "I have no hard feelings about not managing," he said. "I didn't enjoy it."

But he did enjoy remaining as part of the Yankees' future. MacPhail left the Yankees after they won the 1947 World Series, and George Weiss, the new general manager, wasted no time in inviting Dickey to return to the fold as the first-base coach and catching sage. His first assignment, beginning in spring training, was to refine the techniques of a promising young catcher. Or as Yogi Berra put it, Bill's job was to "teach me his experience."

A scarcely noted item in Dickey's resume was a brief Hollywood movie appearance. He played himself in the 1942 film *Pride of the Yankees*, a biopic on the life of Lou Gehrig. Gary Cooper starred as Gehrig and Teresa Wright played his wife, Eleanor. The film, which debuted a year after Gehrig's death, was a box-office success and has become something of a classic. It is shown regularly on television, chiefly around the Fourth of July, the date of Gehrig's farewell speech at Yankee Stadium. Dickey's role, not long enough to have required acting lessons, portrayed his devotion to Gehrig, particularly as his career, and his life, were winding down.

Following the exhibition game in Kansas City, Gehrig and the rest of the team went in opposite directions. At Kansas City's Union Station, the Yankees boarded a train to take them back to New York, and Gehrig headed north to the Mayo Clinic in Rochester, Minnesota. He was on his way to keeping a June 13 appointment for an examination that had been made by his wife. While at the station, he explained to members of the Kansas City press who covered the exhibition game why he was going to the clinic. According to a report in the *Kansas City Star*, Gehrig said:

> I guess everybody wonders where I'm going, but I can't help believe there is something wrong with me. It's not conceivable that I could go to pieces so suddenly.

I feel fine, feel strong and have the urge to play, but without warning this year I've appeared to collapse.

I'd like to play some more, and I want somebody to tell me what's wrong.

Six days later, on June 19, his thirty-sixth birthday, someone told him what was wrong. Gehrig had a rare kind of paralysis called amyotrophic lateral sclerosis (ALS). It is not clear how much detail he was given at the time, but he was aware that the prognosis was dire. The progression involved a rapidly increasing paralysis, difficulty in swallowing and speaking, and a life expectancy of fewer than three years. ALS is physically painless but brutally cruel in its effects. There would be no impairment of mental functions. While the motor activities of the central nervous system are gradually eroded, the mind remains fully aware of the deterioration of all bodily functions until the very end.

ALS was first diagnosed in 1874 but through the years continued to be little-known or understood. The ALS Association describes it as a "progressive neurodegenerative disease that affects nerve cells in the brain and the spinal cord. Motor neurons reach from the brain to the spinal cord and from the spinal cord to the muscles throughout the body. The progressive degeneration of the motor neurons in ALS eventually leads to their death. When the motor neurons die, the ability of the brain to initiate and control muscle movement is lost . . ." In a letter to Gehrig which was made public through the press, the Mayo Clinic wrote, "In lay terms [ALS is] a form of infantile paralysis." Infantile paralysis, commonly referred to as polio, was a disease well-known to the public at the time, for it was a scourge that attacked regularly and often critically, leaving its victims, chiefly youngsters through the years of their teens, paralyzed in varying degrees. Gehrig's affliction, which would soon bear his name, was popularly called "chronic polio" by the media.

After being released from the Mayo Clinic, Gehrig spent some time at his apartment in Larchmont, a suburb of New York, where he wrote letters to his doctors, trying to learn more about his condition and get a clearer reading on what might lie ahead. At the end of June, he rejoined the team briefly in Washington, DC. As the train pulled into Union Station, he was greeted warmly by a group of Boy Scouts offering their best wishes. Lou waved back, then turned to a companion, Rutherford "Rud" Rennie of the *New York Herald Tribune*, and said, "They're wishing me luck—and I'm dying."

16

The Luckiest Man on the Face of the Earth

On the day Lou Gehrig received his diagnosis, the Yankees defeated Detroit 8–5 at Yankee Stadium and took off on a five-game winning streak. The streak ran through June 24 with a 2–1 decision over the St. Louis Browns. At the close of day, the Yankees' record stood at 46–12, an incredible winning percentage of .793. They led the Red Sox by an imposing thirteen games. DiMaggio was batting .397; Dickey, Gordon, Selkirk, and Rolfe also were over .300, and Henrich was close at .296. For all intents and purposes, the race appeared to be over. The Yankees seemed unbeatable and were on a pace to break all kinds of records as the most dominant team of all time. But it didn't turn out that way. Tough times lay ahead.

The spell seemed to break, at least for a time, on Monday night, June 26, in Philadelphia. The Yanks lost to the A's, 3–2, playing the first night game in the team's history. The result no doubt offended Yankee general manager Ed Barrow, to whom night baseball had been anathema from its very inception. Although games had been played at night since late in the nineteenth century, the practice was still fairly new in the major leagues. It arrived on May 24, 1935, courtesy of the ever-inventive Larry MacPhail, who became acquainted with baseball-after-dark four years earlier when he was with the Columbus team of the American Association. On the occasion of the first major-league night game, some 25,000 spectators saw the Reds beat the Philadelphia Phillies 2–1. To celebrate the breakthrough, President Roosevelt symbolically pulled the switch that lit up Crosley Field from the nation's capital. That season, the Reds played each of the other National League teams one game under the lights. MacPhail took night baseball with him to Brooklyn in 1938, and it was there, under the cover of darkness, that Johnny Vander Meer threw the second of his consecutive no-hitters.

Despite its popularity, night baseball infiltrated the majors in slow motion. Perhaps it was the cost of installing the lights that caused owners to balk at making a move, although baseball, much to its credit, has always been reluctant to change what historically defined it. The Yankees did not adorn its fabled roof with lights until 1946. The Cubs maintained an exclusively day-time operation until 1988. By that time, night baseball was the norm rather than the exception. It was chiefly the endearing profit motive that accounted for the change. Sponsors loved the prime-time audiences that were available at night, and by the seventies, the nighttime schedule had begun to encroach upon World Series and playoff games.

It was perhaps symbolic that the Yankees' first night game initiated a period of several weeks in which they stumbled and frittered away most of the lead they had compiled in the first three months of the season. What was more than symbolic was the burdensome schedule that awaited them during the latter part of June and right through July and into the depths of summer. Much the same as the previous season, a store of doubleheaders awaited them. They would be obliged to play a pair of twin bills on successive days at the end of June and then, after a single game on the month's last day, two more just one day apart at the start of July. The pitching staff, despite McCarthy's early season concern, was holding up quite well, but with the grueling schedule just ahead, the Yanks, looking to add another strong arm, tapped their talent-laden Newark Bears team and brought up a gifted young left-hander by the name of Marius Russo.

Russo, the son of Italian immigrants, was a native New Yorker, born in Brooklyn and raised in Queens. He was right-handed in all things except throwing a baseball. Fans who sought his autograph often wondered why he signed with his right hand, and Russo would tell them, playfully, that he was resting his pitching arm. At Richmond Hill High School, he joined the baseball team as a lefty-throwing, right-hand hitting outfielder/first baseman. Upon graduation, he enrolled at Brooklyn College, and it was there that he turned his attention to pitching. The baseball coach, Pinky Match, took notice of the velocity with which Russo made his throws from the outfield and suggested a move to the pitcher's mound. His success was immediate. As recorded by Cort Vitty in an article for SABR: "Pinky started me against Panzer College, a small school in northern

New Jersey. I guess I didn't do anything but peg the ball to the catcher as fast as I could, it seemed to work; I struck out 16 and beat them."

Featuring a sidearm fastball that sank, Russo left Brooklyn College to go to Long Island University (LIU) on an athletic scholarship, starring in basketball as well as baseball. He was co-captain of the undefeated LIU basketball team coached by Claire Bee, which was invited to compete in the tryouts for the 1936 Olympics scheduled for Berlin. However, the players voted to decline the invitation because of Hitler's anti-Jewish policies. It was a decision that put Russo on a path to a career with the Yankees.

Instead of taking part in the Summer Olympics, Marius signed to play semipro baseball for the independent Brooklyn Bushwicks. Bushwicks coach Charlie Hargreaves, a former major-league catcher, recommended him to Yankee management. He was promptly signed and joined the staff of the 1937 Newark Bears, considered by many to have been the best minor-league team in baseball history. It was a view supported by their season record of 109–43, which placed them 25½ games ahead of the second-place Montreal Royals. Russo did not set the league on fire. Pitching mostly in relief, he finished with an 8–8 record and an ERA of 3.63. His performance improved in 1938. He posted a record of 17–8 with a 3.15 ERA. He opened the 1939 season with Newark where, despite a 5–4 record, his earned run average of 1.97 in 64 innings caught the attention of the parent club which was in need of a bit more depth in its staff.

Russo made his big-league debut in Detroit on June 6, pitching one-and-a-third innings in relief and allowing two hits in a 6–2 loss. In his next relief appearance, on June 14, he secured the last two outs in a 4–2 decision over Cleveland's Bob Feller. Two days later, he earned his first save, pitching an inning-and-a-third and yielding one hit in a 4–3 victory over the Indians.

He started for the first time on June 25 and distinguished himself, though in a losing cause. Pitching against St. Louis at Yankee Stadium, Russo held the Browns to two runs on six hits through seven-and-two-third innings, but all of the damage came in the top of the eighth. Ahead 1–0, he was pitching a three-hit shutout when he seemed to tire. He gave up three singles and a walk, which produced two runs and a 2–1 lead for St. Louis. Murphy was brought in to get the final out, and the Yanks took the lead in the bottom of the eighth on a home run by Dickey with DiMaggio on base. A one-run lead in the ninth was a scenario that seemed made to order for Murphy, but the relief artist had nothing that day. He was battered for five runs in the ninth, and the Yanks ended up losing the game 7–3.

For Russo, the game had its positive aspects. He established his credentials as a starter, demonstrating a new curve to go along with his steaming fastball and pinpoint control. He lost his first two decisions as a starter before registering a complete game win on July 16 against Cleveland. Then, after losing a relief appearance to Philadelphia on August 13, Russo staked his claim as part of the Yankees' future with a four-hit shutout against the White Sox. The win was only his second against three losses, but he would not suffer another defeat for the rest of the season. He won his next six starts, concluding his rookie season with a record of 8–3 and a team-best ERA of 2.41.

The balance of Russo's career with the Yankees was respectable but brief. He had modestly winning records in 1940 and '41 and won a game in each of the 1941 and '43 World Series. But plagued by arm troubles, he won only five games while losing ten in 1943, his last full season before leaving for military service. Despite his abbreviated tenure, his 1939 performance earned him a niche in Yankee lore. His arrival relieved the heavy burden on the rest of the staff and eased the trip through the rest of the season.

From the latter part of June and into July, the Yankees played back-and-fill baseball, looking like champions one day and performing as if in a state of slumber the next. After the night-game loss in Philadelphia, the team came back with a vengeance. Following a day's rest, on June 28 they exploded in both ends of a doubleheader, defeating the A's by the lopsided scores of 23–2 and 10–0. In the opener, they led 15–2 after four innings; in the nightcap, as if to offer assurance that the first game was no fluke, they opened up with five runs in the first, including home runs by Crosetti and Gordon. In the course of the two games, DiMaggio, Gordon, and Dahlgren each had three home runs; Dickey, Selkirk, Henrich, and Crosetti, one apiece. Pearson won the first game to put his record at 7–1; Gomez tossed a three-hitter in the nightcap, his sixth win against two defeats.

But the heroics did not last long. After taking two of three from Washington, the Yanks opened July by dropping two of three to Boston. The team's indifferent performance was offset by the fact that neither had the Red Sox been playing lights-out baseball. The overwhelming thirteen-game lead had shrunk by just a game-and-a-half. The Yanks still boasted what appeared to be a commanding position as the season headed into the Fourth of July, traditionally a date that foretells the pennant winner. While no student of the game would have been reckless enough to bet against the Yankees at that point, the Red Sox would soon find themselves very much back in contention.

In the meantime, a holiday doubleheader against the Senators was to be played at Yankee Stadium on July 4, but the games were not the principal attraction. What drew more than 61,000 to the ballpark that warm, sunny Tuesday afternoon was the between-games ceremony that would honor Lou Gehrig. The day had been designated Lou Gehrig Appreciation Day. His uniform No. 4 would be retired, there would be speeches praising his character and his deeds, and Gehrig himself would offer a speech that, more than seventy-five years later, would still be looked upon as baseball's equivalent of the Gettysburg Address.

While the celebration honoring Gehrig was the focus of the ceremonies, it was part of a double feature. The festivities began with a reunion of the 1927 Yankees, the Murderers' Row brigade that was considered the greatest of all baseball teams until rivaled by the current Yankee squad. The 1927 version of Yankee dominance had won a record 110 games while finishing nineteen games in front of Connie Mack's Philadelphia A's and sweeping Pittsburgh in the World Series. It was Ruth's 60–home run season; Gehrig had followed with 47.

Of course Ruth was on hand for the reunion, and the supporting cast had come from all over the country—Bob Meusel from California; Wally Pipp, the man Gehrig had replaced to start his consecutive game streak, was in from Michigan; shortstop Mark Koenig came from Idaho; Deacon Everett Scott, whose endurance record Gehrig had broken, from Indiana. The entourage edging out of the Yankee dugout included Tony Lazzeri and Joe Dugan; pitchers Waite Hoyt, Herb Pennock, and Bob Shawkey and catcher Wally Schang. Earle Combs, now a Yankee coach, was in uniform, as was Benny Bengough, a coach with the visiting Senators. George Pipgras was wearing an umpire's uniform and was, in fact, working the day's games.

Marching behind Captain Sutherland's Seventh Regiment Band, the old-timers strode to the centerfield flagpole where they raised the 1927 championship banner. Then, they marched back to the infield and stretched out in back of the pitchers' mound, facing home plate. The members of the current teams followed onto the field; the Yankees lined up on the third-base side, the Senators between the mound and first base.

Finally, Gehrig came forth to a thundering ovation and took his place before a microphone at home plate. Clearly uncertain on his feet, his once muscular frame shrunken, Gehrig stood with his head slightly bowed, his cap tucked under his right arm, his hands clasped in front of him as a series of notables took turns at the microphone while sportswriter Sid Mercer served as emcee. Ed Barrow, stepping onto the Yankee Stadium field for the first time in his nineteen-year tenure with the team, announced that Gehrig's No. 4 would never be worn by another player, marking the first time in baseball history that a uniform number had been retired. Mayor Fiorello

LaGuardia, speaking directly to the honoree, said, "You are the greatest prototype of good sportsmanship and citizenship. Lou, we're proud of you." Postmaster General James Farley closed his remarks by saying ". . . for generations to come, boys who play baseball will point with pride to your record." Babe Ruth also spoke briefly.

As Gehrig stood motionless, his face reflecting the solemnity of the occasion, he was presented with an array of gifts: a fruit bowl and candlestick from the New York Giants; a silver pitcher and two silver platters from the concessionaire Harry M. Stevens and his employees; a silver cup from the Yankees' office staff; a scroll from the Old Timers Association and another from the Senators with the words DON'T QUIT inscribed at the top; and a tobacco stand from the New York Chapter of the Baseball Writers Association of America.

The final gift was presented by a visibly emotional Joe McCarthy. It was from Lou's Yankee teammates—a silver trophy, more than a foot and a half high with a silver baseball on top and a silver eagle atop the baseball. The trophy sat on a box in the shape of home plate with twin silver plates on either side. The right-hand plate was engraved with the signatures of all of Gehrig's teammates topped by those of McCarthy and Ed Barrow. On the left side was inscribed a poem written by John Kieran of the *New York Times*:

TO LOU GEHRIG
We've been to the wars together,
We took our foes as they came,
And always you were the leader

And ever you played the game.
Idol of cheering millions,
Records are yours by the sheaves,
Iron of fame they hailed you.
Decked you with laurel leaves.

But higher than that we hold you,
We who have known you best,
Knowing the way you came through
Every human test.

Let this be a silent token
Of lasting friendship's gleam,
And all that we left unspoken,
Your pals of the Yankee team.

McCarthy handed the trophy to Gehrig. Its weight an obvious burden, Lou set it down on the ground. Now, it was Gehrig's turn to speak. McCarthy helped guide him to the microphone. The crowd was chanting, "We want Lou." For a time, it appeared uncertain that they were going to hear from him. He had a written speech prepared, but, overcome with emotion, he was hesitant. He prodded Mercer to offer his gratitude and apologies to the crowd. "Lou has asked me to thank all of you," Mercer began, but McCarthy intervened. He moved close to Lou and whispered something that *Times* sportswriter John Drebinger thought might have been akin to, "Come on, Lou, rap out another." Gehrig, as always the team player, followed orders. The stadium was engulfed in an expectant silence. It was one of those rare moments within a large throng when no one would think to so much as clear his throat. Gehrig held up his hand and then began to speak, slowly and evenly. In the stillness of the cavernous stadium, the public address system echoed his every word, vibrating and lingering briefly as if emanating from a long-ago time and addressing the ages:

> Fans, for the past two weeks you have been reading about a bad break I got. Yet today I consider myself the luckiest man on the face of the earth. I have been in ballparks for seventeen years and have never received anything but kindness and encouragement from you fans.
>
> Look at these grand men. Which of you wouldn't consider it the highlight of his career just to associate with them for even one day? Sure, I'm lucky. Who wouldn't consider it an honor to have known Jacob Ruppert? Also, the builder of baseball's greatest empire, Ed Barrow? To have spent six years with that wonderful little fellow, Miller Huggins? Then to have spent the next nine years with that outstanding leader, that smart student of psychology, the best manager in baseball today, Joe McCarthy? Sure, I'm lucky.
>
> When the New York Giants, a team you would give your right arm to beat, and vice versa, sends you a gift—that's something. When everybody down to the groundskeepers and those boys in white coats remember you with trophies—that's something. When you have a wonderful mother-in-law who takes sides with you in

squabbles with her own daughter—that's something. When you have a father and a mother who work all their lives so you can have an education and build your body—it's a blessing. When you have a wife who has been a tower of strength and shown more courage than you dream existed—that's the finest I know.

So I close in saying that I may have had a tough break, but I have an awful lot to live for. Thank you.

At the conclusion of Gehrig's remarks, the silence continued to enshroud the proceedings for the duration of a heartbeat—then the ballpark erupted in a long, standing ovation. Ruth, the ever imperious presence under whose shadow Gehrig had spent his entire career, came to the microphone and wrapped his arms around Gehrig, just above the shoulders, looking directly at him. For his part, Lou returned neither the gaze nor the embrace. He smiled straight ahead, his arms hanging limp at his side. The photo, replicated countless times over the years, has become part of the record of its time.

The ceremony, in all its emotion-flooded grandeur, was summed up by the *Washington Post's* legendary Shirley Povich: "I saw strong men weep this afternoon, expressionless umpires swallow hard, and emotion pump the hearts and glaze the eyes of 61,000 baseball fans in Yankee Stadium. Yes, the hard-boiled news photographers clicked their shutters with fingers that trembled a bit."

The Yankees earned a split in the doubleheader with an 11–1 victory in the nightcap after dropping the opener 3–2. When the day's proceedings were over, Gehrig walked across the field to the exit gate he favored, a hitch in his gait, with Bill Dickey at his side. He remained with the team through the rest of the season, making most of the road trips and still in uniform. When the season ended, he officially announced his retirement. He said, "Don't think I am depressed or pessimistic about my condition at present. I intend to hold on as long as possible and then if the inevitable comes, I will accept it philosophically and hope for the best. That's all we can do."

Immediately after announcing his retirement, Gehrig was offered a position as a New York City Parole Commissioner by Mayor LaGuardia; the post was for a ten-year term. Gehrig moved from Westchester County, just north of New York City, to the Riverdale section of the Bronx to satisfy the residency requirement. He was sworn in on January 2, 1940. It was not a token appointment. Lou had turned down a number of previous offers, including lucrative guest appearances and speaking invitations that would have produced considerably more income than the $5,700-a-year commissionership. He explained that he accepted the city post because it held out the opportunity to perform public service. To no one's surprise, he was diligent in carrying out the duties of the office. He visited the city's correctional facilities regularly but insisted that his visits not be covered by the media. He enlisted the help of his wife, Eleanor, who served as his enabler in such chores as steadying his hand when he had to sign official documents.

However, his physical condition continued to decline until he was no longer able to perform the functions required of him. He resigned from the job in the spring of 1941. On June 2, he died at his home at 5204 Delafield Avenue in Riverdale. Upon learning of his death, Babe Ruth and his wife, Claire, went to the Gehrig home to console Eleanor. Mayor LaGuardia ordered flags to be flown at half-staff throughout the city. Major-league ballparks throughout the country followed suit.

17

Yanks Stutter-Step on Way to Finish Line

While the Yankees were engaged in the solemn ceremonies honoring their past, the Red Sox were going about business in mechanical fashion. On July 4, trailing the Yanks by eleven-and-a-half games, they swept a doubleheader from the Athletics and made it three in a row the following day. Their next stop was Yankee Stadium for a five-game weekend series leading up to the All-Star break. The schedule called for a single game on Friday and doubleheaders on Saturday and Sunday. Boston won them all. The Yankees had fallen into a run-scoring drought. They managed to score only 12 runs in the series, an average of just over two runs a game. Yet all of the games were close—three lost by one run and the others by two—and all were lost in the late innings. In the series opener, the Sox scored a run in the eighth off Ruffing for a 4–3 decision. Saturday's twin bill was lost by scores of 3–1 and 3–2. Jimmie Foxx decided the nightcap in the ninth with his thirteenth home run of the season; it came off reliever Johnny

Murphy who had fallen victim to a mid-season slump. Sunday's games were dropped by scores of 4–3 and 5–3. In each game, the Red Sox scored two runs in the eighth inning for the margin of victory, first off Monte Pearson and then off Bump Hadley. Just like that, the Yankees' lead was shaved by five games, and the next day it was cut another game when the Yanks lost to Detroit while the Sox were beating Cleveland. The lead, which was 13½ at the end of June, was down to 5½ thirteen days into July.

The five-game sweep of the Yankees was just the beginning for Boston. They went on to win twelve in a row. The Yanks, by turn, had dropped nine of their last twelve and had cause for concern. At the end of their streak, the Red Sox had a winning percentage of .653, and their performance was no fluke. They had a powerhouse lineup with Foxx at first, Bobby Doerr at second, Jim Tabor at third, and Joe Cronin at shortstop. In the outfield were Ted Williams, Doc Cramer, and Joe Vosmik. Johnny Peacock was the catcher. At the All-Star break, those who were not hitting .300 or better were close. There were no rest stops in the Boston lineup. The All-Star break was from Monday, July 10, to Thursday, and given the events in the early part of the month, the Yankees welcomed the time off. The game itself was scheduled for Tuesday, July 11, at Yankee Stadium. The venue was fitting, as the Yankees dominated the proceedings as never before.

For the fifth straight year, the managers of the eight teams in each league selected the entire all-star squads. They voted for the top twenty-five players in their respective leagues, the only restriction being that every team was to be represented. In the first few years, fans chose the starting lineups by popular vote and the managers picked the substitutes to fill out the roster. But the managers soon took full control on the grounds that the fans tended to vote based on a player's past record rather than being guided by their current performance.

In an era when the All-Star Game was played with winning as its object rather than as a showcase in which every player had to make an appearance, the managers—Joe McCarthy for the American League, Gabby Hartnett for the Nationals—went full-tilt for the league leaders. The Yankees placed six players on the starting team and three more among the reserves. The starters were Red Rolfe, Joe DiMaggio, Bill Dickey, George Selkirk, Joe Gordon, and Red Ruffing; the reserves were Frank Crosetti, Lefty Gomez, and Johnny Murphy. The three starters from other clubs were Boston's Doc Cramer in right field and Joe Cronin at shortstop; and Detroit's Hank Greenberg at first base. The five starters from the Cincinnati Reds, who were running ahead of the Cardinals in the race for the pennant, were Lonny Frey, second base; Ival Goodman, right field; Frank McCormick, first base; catcher Ernie Lombardi; and Paul Derringer, pitching.

In accordance with winning being the priority, McCarthy remained true to form. Except for the pitchers, he stayed with his eight position starters for the full nine innings. Fourteen players, including such notables as Jimmie Foxx and Luke Appling, never made it off the bench. It was, after all, McCarthy's style. He rarely made a substitution during the course of the season. Despite the score of the game or the Yanks' position in the standings, his basic lineup remained unchanged. No one was given a rest, and if you were a bench player, you gathered splinters game after game. For the National League, nine reserves failed to see action.

The game, played before 62,892 fans in the shadow of the elevated subway line that ran along Jerome Avenue in the Bronx, was completed in a business-like one hour and fifty-five minutes. The near-capacity crowd turned out despite an increase in ticket prices. With the raise, a ticket in the lower grandstand went for $1.65. Fifty-five cents got you a bleacher seat. The top price for a field-level box was $2.20.

The American League won the game 3–1, giving them a 5–2 edge since the start of All-Star play in 1933. Ironically, the uncontested star of the game was neither a member of the Yankees nor the Reds. It was a young pitcher from the Cleveland Indians by the name of Bob Feller. The National League had drawn first blood in the top of the third when Lonny Frey doubled home Arky Vaughan, who had opened the inning with an infield single. The AL took the lead in the fourth against Bill Lee, in relief of Derringer. A walk to Dickey, singles by Selkirk and Greenberg, and an error by Vaughan on a Joe Gordon grounder accounted for two runs and a 2–1 lead for the home team. The scoring was rounded out in the next inning when DiMaggio lined a home run into the seats in left field.

But the game's drama developed in the top of the sixth. Tommy Bridges, who had pitched two scoreless innings after replacing Ruffing, got in serious trouble when the National League loaded the bases with one out. It was then that Feller, whose record at the time was a dazzling 14–3, was hailed from the bullpen. It did not take him long to quell the rally. He induced Vaughan to ground into a double play to end the threat and proceeded to pitch shutout ball for the next three innings. Mel Ott opened the ninth with a single, the only hit off Feller in the three-and-two-thirds innings he pitched. He retired the next three batters—Vaughan on a fly ball to DiMaggio before striking out Johnny Mize and Stan Hack to seal the victory. Feller's performance, remarkable though it was, was not surprising. In his fourth major-league season, at the still tender age of twenty, he was already being spoken of as one of the potentially great pitchers of his time, and it was not by chance that he had reached this plateau.

Born on November 2, 1918, in Van Meter, Iowa, Robert William Andrew Feller was groomed to be a major-league star from the time he was born. His father, a farmer, had made that decision and wasted no time in implementing it. His training began before little Bobby could walk. His father would roll a ball to him and have him return it by throwing it into a pillow. By the time he was four, the youngster and his father played catch as part of a daily routine. At the ripe age of nine, Bobby could throw a ball 270 feet, more than the distance from home plate to the right-field wall at New York's Polo Grounds. The harsh Iowa winters brought no respite. His father set up arc lights in the barn so he and his son could maintain their practice schedule.

Playing for the Van Meter High School team in 1935 when Bobby was just sixteen, he was said to have thrown five no-hitters. At the end of the season, he played semipro ball for the Farmers Union team in Des Moines. According to statistics compiled by his father and reported by C. Paul Rogers III for the Society for American Baseball Research, Bobby struck out 361 batters in 157 innings that summer, allowing a meager 42 hits and compiling an earned run average of under 1.00. His future was accounted for in early July. A Des Moines semipro umpire, who knew talent when he saw it, tipped off Cleveland Indian scout Cy Slapnicka. Slapnicka checked him out briefly and reported to management that he had found "the greatest pitcher in history." He was quick to sign the young phenom to a contract under the auspices of his father. Feller received a signing bonus of one dollar and a baseball autographed by the Cleveland baseball team.

At the end of the school year in 1936, Slapnicka, who had been promoted to the equivalent of general manager, brought Feller up to the Indians; he had never played an inning of minor-league baseball. He made his first major-league appearance at age seventeen in an exhibition game against the St. Louis Cardinals' Gas House Gang with unforgettable results. In three innings of work, he struck out eight batters, including Rip Collins, Pepper Martin, and Leo Durocher twice, using a blazing fastball that left Cardinal hitters stunned. After his second at-bat, Durocher turned to the umpire and said, "I feel like a clay pigeon in a shooting gallery." At the end of the game, a photographer asked the Cards' ace, Dizzy Dean, if he would pose for a photo with the promising youngster. "If it's all right with him, it's all right with me," Diz responded. "After what he did today, he's the guy to say."

He was put on the Indians' roster on July 14 and made his official big-league debut five days later in relief. It was not impressive. Coming to the mound in the eighth inning of a game with Cleveland trailing the Washington Senators 9–2, he walked two batters and hit a third before retiring the side. With manager Steve O'Neill using him only in relief, Feller produced two other sub-par performances in mop-up duty. On July 24, with the Tribe leading the A's 15–2, he pitched the eighth and ninth, giving up three hits and one run. Two days later, in the ninth inning of a 13–0 loss to the A's, he allowed three hits, a walk, and two runs. O'Neill continued to use him in relief, with indifferent results, until August 23 when he got his first start against the feeble St. Louis Browns. The Browns were in seventh place, 32 games under .500 and 34½ behind the league-leading Yankees. Feller took full advantage of the opportunity. Pitching in ninety-degree heat, he hurled a 4–1 complete-game victory, yielding only six hits and striking out fifteen batters, one shy of Rube Waddell's American League record.

He started seven more games during the rest of the 1936 season but tended to be erratic. He was plagued by control problems, which, to some degree, neutralized the strikeouts he piled up. The balance between the strikeouts and his lack of control was never in sharper contrast than on September 13 in a 5–2 decision over the Athletics. He allowed only two hits but walked nine and permitted seven stolen bases. In the process, he struck out seventeen batters, setting the American League record while tying Dizzy Dean's major-league mark. He concluded his rookie year with a record of 5–3. In 62 innings, he allowed 52 hits, while striking out 76 and issuing 47 walks.

In 1937, still in a part-time role, Feller produced nine wins against seven losses. He joined the starting rotation in 1938 under the tutelage of a new manager, Oscar Vitt, who tried to improve his control by shortening his excessively high leg kick. On April 20, Feller pitched the first of twelve one-hitters in his career, again victimizing the St. Louis Browns. At season's end, he led the league in strikeouts with 240 and in bases on balls with 208. He did the same in 1939, which was his breakout year as he led the league with 24 wins, 296.2 innings pitched, 246 strikeouts, and 24 complete games. In 1940, he won the pitching Triple Crown, leading the league in victories, earned run average, and strikeouts. He won twenty or more games every season through 1948, with time out for service in the US Navy from 1942 to '45. Over the course of his career, which ended in 1956, he led the league in wins six times and in strikeouts seven times, and he pitched three no-hitters to go along with the twelve one-hitters.

Two days after the All-Star break, the Yankees took off on an eight-game winning streak, which boosted their lead over the Red Sox to nine games. DiMaggio was leading the offense with a batting average of .410 and 45 RBIs. An oddity of the streak was that the first seven games were won by seven different pitchers. All season long, the pitching staff had been run by committee. Eight pitchers started between eleven and twenty-six games. Ruffing, the bellwether of the staff with a record of 13–3 at that juncture, won the first and last decisions of the seven-game run. The six games in between were won by Pearson, Gomez, Russo, Hadley, Hildebrand, and a rookie sensation by the name of Atley Donald.

Richard Atley Donald was the stereotype of the endearing Southern rube of pre-war vintage who went about business at an easy, methodical pace, doing what he had to do in a manner that attracted little notice. A lanky 6-foot-1, and weighing in at 186 pounds, Donald could have been portrayed by Gary Cooper in much the style he appropriated in the 1941 film *Sergeant York*. His ancestors had come to Mississippi in a covered wagon midway through the nineteenth century from Sumter, South Carolina, within striking distance of Fort Sumter where the first shots of the Civil War were fired. Donald was raised in rural Louisiana and walked an unforgiving distance each day to his country school in Downsville, a small Louisiana community. After graduating from high school, he went to Louisiana Tech, starring in basketball and football as well as baseball, pitching against mostly small college teams. His college coach wrote to Ed Barrow in 1933, commending Donald to his attention, but Barrow did not follow up.

In January 1934, his father, Hugh, a farmer, gave Atley twenty-five dollars so he could take the bus to St. Petersburg, Florida, where the Yankees would soon start spring training. Supporting himself by earning twelve dollars a week in a local grocery store, the twenty-three-year-old Donald looked up Richard Nee, the scout who covered the South for the Yankees. Nee had seen Donald pitch at Louisiana Tech and was impressed—but not enough to sign him. He was, however, sufficiently attracted to introduce him to Joe McCarthy. McCarthy gave him a uniform with No. 28 on the back and sent him to the mound to pitch to Ruth, Gehrig, Lazzeri, Dickey, and Earle Combs. The Yankee skipper liked what he saw, and Donald was signed to a minor-league contract and shipped to Wheeling, West Virginia, a Class C team. From there, he moved along the Yankees' minor-league chain until, in 1937, he reached the Newark Bears just in time to be part of that team's legendary season in which it won 109 games and then completed back-to-back sweeps of the Syracuse Chiefs and Baltimore Orioles to win the International League title. Then, in the Little World Series, Newark made more history by coming back from a three-game-to-zero deficit to win four straight and take the championship from the Columbus Red Birds of the American Association. Donald earned a trip to the majors that season by winning fourteen consecutive games while putting together a record of 19–2.

He made his major-league debut on April 21, 1938, starting at Fenway Park against the Red Sox and losing 3–2. He started again on April 29, giving up four runs in just over five innings to the Red Sox at Yankee Stadium. Murphy won the game 6–4 in relief, but Atley was shipped back to Newark where he spent the remainder of the season. In 1939, he returned, with eye-catching results. He won for the first time on May 9, pitching 5.1 innings in relief of Steve Sundra and getting the decision in an 8–6 win over the White Sox. Nine days later, he started and went the distance against the Browns, winning 8–1. He went on to win his next nine decisions and became the first rookie in American League history to start a season 12–0. The streak ended on August 2 when he lost 7–2 to Detroit. He finished the season at 13–3, leading the league with a winning percentage of .813 and carrying an ERA of 3.71.

Donald's chief weapon was a sizzling fastball that rivaled Bob Feller's; in fact, it might have surpassed Feller's if a "top gun" competition held in August was a true measure. In 1939, a crude Rube Goldberg contraption for measuring the velocity of flying objects was developed, and baseball officials were quick to set up a contest among major-league pitchers. Feller was the favorite, but Atley edged him out with a fastball timed at 94.7 miles an hour. However, it was difficult to get by in the majors with only one dominant pitch, and Donald was never able to master an effective curve or off-speed delivery. In six subsequent seasons, he fashioned modestly winning records but never recorded more than the thirteen victories he put together in 1939 and replicated during the war year of 1945.

Donald's twelfth consecutive victory was followed by three more Yankee wins, and July ended after a doubleheader split with the White Sox, with the team holding a nine-game advantage over Boston. As the dog days of August approached, the Yanks exuded subtle but unrestrained confidence. A year ago they had won twenty-eight games while losing only eight in August, and hopes were high that they could replicate that script. But things got off to an uneven start.

18

Yanks Full Speed Ahead as Destiny Awaits

August dawned on a world that was headed toward the apocalypse. Hitler's armies were poised on the eastern border of Poland. August would be the last month of peace the world would know before it tipped into a conflagration that would last for the next six years. Exactly a month later, on September 1 as German troops marched into Poland, World War II would be underway.

While the world waited, the month had begun with an event that was unnoted at the time and remained little more than a footnote to history but that was of critical importance to the future of the planet. On August 2, Albert Einstein wrote a letter to President Roosevelt warning him that Germany was trying to develop a bomb of unprecedented destructive power and suggested that the United States mount its own program to harness nuclear energy. The letter, signed by Einstein, was drafted principally by the Hungarian-born Leo Szilard, one of several European scientists who had fled to the United States in the 1930s to escape Nazi oppression. It was Szilard who, in 1933, conceived the nuclear chain reaction and patented the idea together with Enrico Fermi.

However, delivering the letter in person was no simple matter. According to historian Lynne Olson in her book *Those Angry Days*, Einstein's first choice to take the letter to the president was America's hero aviator Charles Lindbergh. Einstein had met him in New York a few years earlier but was not yet aware of Lindbergh's isolationist views or his neo-Nazi sympathies. Having received no response to his August note, Einstein sent Lindbergh a reminder on September 13, which again went unanswered. Finally, the letter was delivered by Alexander Sachs, a Wall Street economist and longtime friend and unofficial adviser to the president. The two met at the White House on October 11, and Sachs briefed Roosevelt on the main points contained in Einstein's letter. He stressed the risk of allowing Hitler to achieve unilateral possession of "extremely powerful bombs." Roosevelt at first was noncommittal, but at a second meeting over breakfast the next morning, he acknowledged the danger and decided to take action. Thus was born the Manhattan Project, which built the world's first atomic bomb.

If August had begun amid an atmosphere that promised somber days ahead, fans of the Yankees received no solace from their team's performance. The Yanks were playing in-and-out baseball, entirely uncharacteristic of the previous two seasons. On August 2, as Einstein was drafting his letter, they completed a three-game losing streak at home. They followed that with a three-game winning streak and then dropped another

three straight games. They were 4–6 to open the month, nursing a slim five-and-a-half-game lead over Boston. On August
11, it all changed. Their drowsy bats stirred with a 9–5 victory
at Philadelphia. They then proceeded to unload on the hapless
A's with an 18–4 victory the next day, and, after dropping a
12–9 decision in the opener of doubleheader on August 13,
they unleashed a deluge in the nightcap. The Yanks scored
five runs in the second and five more in the third. They added
two in the fourth, one in the fifth, five more in the sixth,
and wrapped it up with three in the eighth. The final score
was 21–0. DiMaggio and Dahlgren each hit a pair of two-
run homers. The beneficiary of the barrage was Ruffing who
pitched a three-hit shutout for his seventeenth win against
four losses.

As it turned out, the game was the beginning of the end
of the pennant race. During a brutal heat wave, the Yankees
were as hot as the weather. Their victory in the second game of
the Sunday doubleheader was the start of a five-game winning
streak that, after a 5–4 loss to the A's, was followed by a run of
ten more wins. The 15–1 outbreak swelled their lead over Boston to thirteen games and put the rest of the season on cruise
control. When the streak ended, with a 7–6 loss at Detroit on
August 29, the Yankees' record stood at 87–34, a winning percentage of .719. DiMaggio was leading the way with a batting
average of .405, along with 20 home runs and 101 RBIs. The
supporting cast—Dickey, Gordon, Rolfe, Dahlgren, and Selkirk—were also contributing in fine style. As for the pitching,
Ruffing was 20–4; Sundra was in the midst of his undefeated
stretch at 8–0; Donald was 13–2; Gomez 11–6; Pearson and

Hadley were each 10–5. Worthy of special notice was the batting numbers being put up by the rookie Charlie Keller. Keller had been playing sparingly after being brought up from Newark at the start of the season, but on August 2 he was installed in right field as a replacement for the slumping Tommy Henrich who was hitting a modest .273. Keller never left the starting lineup. During the course of the August blitzkrieg, he was neck-and-neck with DiMaggio in leading the charge. His batting average rose from .305 to .356, and his RBI total stood at 56.

Charles Ernest Keller, Jr., was born in Middleton, Maryland, in 1916. He grew up on a farm and attended the University of Maryland, where he majored in agricultural economics and played some football as well as baseball. His quest for a degree was interrupted in his senior year when Yankee scout Paul Krichell, of Lou Gehrig fame, spotted him and decided a left-handed power hitter was a commodity the Yanks could use. Keller was dispatched to Newark in 1937 where he led the International League in batting with an average of .353. He also led the league in hits and runs scored while hitting thirteen homers. He was named both the International League Rookie of the Year and Minor League Player of the Year. Despite his outstanding season, Keller was not invited to New York's spring training camp in 1938. He responded by improving on his 1937 stats. He upped his batting average to .365, which was second in the league, and his home run total to 22; he finished third in the voting for the league's MVP. Yankee management needed no further evidence. He began his distinguished big-league career in 1939.

Somewhere along the way, Keller was bequeathed a nickname that he did not appreciate but that nevertheless stuck with him. The name "King Kong" was taken from an eponymous film that was a major box-office attraction; it was the story of a huge but tender-hearted gorilla that escaped from captivity and crashed its way through Manhattan. The nickname was based on Keller's power as well as his physical build. At 5-foot-10 and 190 pounds, he projected the appearance of a much larger presence. As described by the sportswriter Milton Gross, Keller "looked massive. His black beetle-browed eyes, his muscled blacksmith arms, his thick neck and hogshead of a chest were of wrestler's proportions."

Keller broke into the Yankees lineup on April 29 when DiMaggio was forced to leave the game after injuring his foot. McCarthy moved Powell from left field to center and inserted Keller in left. He started for the first time on May 2 at Detroit in a game the Yanks won by the lopsided score of 22–2. Batting fifth, Charlie marked his arrival with a home run, a triple, and six runs batted in. He remained in the starting lineup for the next thirty-four games, batting .319 with 24 RBIs. Still, when DiMaggio returned to the lineup on June 7, Keller found himself back on the bench. He remained there for most of June and July. When he took over right field in August, he was instrumental in driving the team to its near-record finish. Playing in 111 games throughout the season, he batted .334, fifth in the league, and drove in 83 runs. He was primed for a memorable performance in the World Series.

All the same, though he played a starring role for the next four years until leaving for service in the US Merchant Marine in 1944, he never again batted .300 over the course of a full season. When they signed him, the Yankees were hoping they had found a power-hitting, left-handed pull hitter who would earn his keep by driving the ball into the Stadium's beckoning right-field seats. However, Keller, though he had power to spare, was not that type of hitter. His natural tendency was to hit the ball where it was pitched, driving doubles and triples into left field or the gap between left and center. Herb Pennock, former Yankee Hall of Fame pitcher and a Red Sox scout at the time, said that Keller hit the ball harder to left field than any left-handed batter he had ever seen with the exception of Babe Ruth.

Although Keller resisted altering his swing, McCarthy prevailed. He got him to switch from a 43- to a 39-ounce bat, adding quickness to his swing, and persuaded him to take aim at the low fence in right field that stood a friendly 296 feet from home plate. The result was a drop in his batting average but a sharp rise in his home run and RBI production. From 1940 through 1943, playing an average of 143 games a year, Keller batted .287 and hit 111 home runs (approximately 28 a year) while averaging 102 RBIs and 107 bases on balls in the course of the four seasons.

After serving in the military during 1944 and '45, Keller returned after the war and played just one more year as a regular. In 1946, he hit .275, with 30 home runs and 101 runs batted in. A ruptured disc in his back essentially ended his career as a starter. He played part-time from 1947 to '49. Released by the Yankees in 1950, he signed a two-year contract with Detroit, serving chiefly as a pinch-hitter. In September 1952, he re-signed with the Yankees, played in only two games, and called it a career.

On September 25, 1948, he was honored at a Charlie Keller Day before more than 65,000 fans at Yankee Stadium. A Maryland delegation was on hand, led by Senator Millard Tydings. Keller was presented with a set of golf clubs, a watch, and a variety of monetary gifts. He used the money he received to start a scholarship at the University of Maryland. All these years later, he is remembered best as the power-hitting left fielder who filled out the meat of the batting order in the all-star outfield of Henrich, DiMaggio, and Keller. Not many recall him as the hit-to-all-fields rookie who helped revitalize the Yankees during the heat-ridden days of August 1939, when the team turned on the juice and coasted to its fourth straight championship.

As August ended, any hopes of peace in Europe went with it. On Friday, September 1, without declaring war, Germany invaded Poland with a coordinated air-and-land attack so brutal that it made the term "blitzkrieg" an official part of the lexicon. Honoring their treaty with Poland, Great Britain and France declared war on Germany. Australia and New Zealand did the same. On September 5, the United States declared its neutrality. Following the First World War, isolationism had become the prevailing mood of the country. A series of Neutrality Acts, passed throughout the thirties, barred the United States from giving aid of any kind to adversaries in a war. No distinction was made between aggressor and victim. President Roosevelt offered the only acknowledgment of Europe's plight by declaring a limited state of emergency. The start of World War II, as it was, had no effect on baseball in America. The games went on. The day after war broke out, the Yankees rolled into Fenway Park in Boston for a three-game, weekend series.

With the New Yorkers holding a 13½-game lead and only a month remaining in the season, the series could have been expected to be routine. It was not. It was, instead, an exercise in wonder when circumstance suggested nothing more than the mundane. The Red Sox won Saturday's game 12–7, shelling Ruffing and handing him his fifth defeat of the season to go with his twenty victories. What was remarkable about the game was that McCarthy allowed his ace to pitch all nine innings, while giving up 19 hits, in a game that was virtually meaningless. He treated starting pitcher Steve Sundra kindlier in the first game of Sunday's doubleheader, which was another loss, this time by the score of 12–11. After four-plus innings, Sundra was followed to the mound by Chandler and then Murphy, neither of whom was any more effective. Murphy had come in with an 11–9 lead and blew the save, yielding the tying runs in the seventh and the deciding run, unearned though it was, in the eighth.

However, it was the second game of the twin bill that captured the attention of baseball fans, players, umpires, and the American League president with a debacle that played out over a period of nearly two weeks. Joe Gordon had tied the game at 5–5 with a home run in the top of the seventh. An inning later, the Yankees struck with a late-game surge that had become known as five-o'clock lightning. Keller, DiMaggio, Dickey, and Gordon accounted for two runs crossing the plate for a

7–5 Yankee lead. But the hour now was past six, and Boston's Sunday curfew of 6:30 was close approaching. In order for the game to be considered complete, the Red Sox would have to have their turn at bat in the bottom of the eighth. With less than ten minutes remaining until curfew time, the Yanks knew they had to move things along briskly in their half of the inning. At bat, Dahlgren did his part by striking out on pitches that were clearly out of his reach. Selkirk, who was on third, came jogging home in a feigned attempt to steal and was tagged out by catcher Johnny Peacock. Gordon, now on third base, followed suit, bringing an abrupt end to the Yankee eighth with time still remaining for the Sox to bat, which would make the result, a Yankee victory, official.

But Boston fans seemed to be more aware of what was going on than the players. For example, Peacock could have permitted both runners to score rather than tag them out, which would have moved the clock closer to 6:30. Now the fans, 27,000 in number, took matters into their own hands. They bombarded the field with debris of all varieties. Umpire crew chief Cal Hubbard, aware that the field could not be cleared in time to resume play, declared the game a forfeit and awarded the Yankees a 9–0 decision, the default score of a forfeited game. Some two weeks later, league president Will Harridge reversed Hubbard's ruling. He held that no blame could be placed on the players or officials of the Boston club and that the demonstration of the fans was beyond the club's control. Therefore, he ruled the game a tie and ordered that it be replayed from the start later in the season, if necessary. As a footnote to the proceedings, Harridge, terming the behavior of Dahlgren, Selkirk, and Gordon "reprehensible," fined them each a modest sum.

The following day, the Yankees found themselves in Philadelphia for another doubleheader. They won both ends, 7–6 and 2–0. Chandler, in relief of Donald in the opener, picked up only his second win of the season; and Russo went all the way in the nightcap to bring his record to 5–3. The sweep was the start of an eight-game winning streak during which seven pitchers earned victories, with Russo winning twice.

When, following a day off, the Yanks returned home for the start of a seventeen-game home stand, beginning with a three-game set with the Red Sox, they were greeted by a sparse turnout of 11,715. It was not unusual. Attendance had been lagging all year. Most of the games on the home stand were attended by fewer than 10,000 fans. Total attendance for the season would be a slender 859,785, the fifth lowest since the opening of Yankee Stadium in 1923. The Yanks had drawn more than one million that year as they continued to do in all but one season until 1930 when the Depression doubtless took its toll. Still, it was difficult to account for the drop from the previous three seasons.

Low attendance notwithstanding, the empty seats did not slow the Yankees juggernaut that was steaming full speed ahead. They opened the home stand against the Red Sox and wasted no time in extending their lead. The first of a three-game set with Boston was a classic pitchers' duel between the Leftys Gomez and Grove, whose respective records at the time were 11–6 and 13–3. Each team scored a run in the third inning, and then the pitchers took control over the next four. The scoreless string ended when DiMaggio led off the bottom of the eighth with his

27th homer of the season and his 119th RBI. His batting average at day's end stood at .407. Two days later, on September 9, it reached a peak of .409 as the Yanks took the third straight from the Sox by a score of 4–1.

The winning streak continued with a three-game sweep of Washington, which boosted their first-place margin to 17½ games. DiMaggio, who had missed more than a month of the season in May and early June, had been flirting with the elusive .400 mark since his return. No one had achieved that milestone since the Giants' Bill Terry who hit .401 in 1930. No American Leaguer had done it since 1923 when Harry Heilmann batted .403 for Detroit. But whatever hopes DiMaggio might have harbored to reach that plateau were soon dashed. After going three-for-four on September 9, he proceeded to go hitless in his next thirteen times at bat.

He struck out in the opener of a September 10 doubleheader against Washington, an item that was noteworthy for few players other than DiMaggio; he would strike out only 21 times during the length of the season. Remarkably, over the course of his career, Joe D., as he was often called, had only eight more strikeouts than he had home runs—369 to 361. By way of comparison, Ruth had 1,330 strikeouts to go with his 714 homers, a difference of 616. Half a century later, another Yankee power hitter, Reggie Jackson, managed to strike out more than four times for every home run he hit—2,597 strikeouts against 563 round-trippers. DiMaggio's slump, such as it was, continued for the duration of the season, but he still led the league with an average of .381, twenty-one points higher than runner-up Jimmie Foxx.

Two weeks into September, the Yankees found themselves at the threshold of their fourth straight pennant. They wrapped it up on September 15 with a 10–3 decision over Detroit while Cleveland was getting the better of the Red Sox. It was Sundra's tenth win without a defeat. With the title in hand, the last two weeks of the season should have been a walk in the park, but McCarthy would have none of it. No rest was forthcoming, neither for the regular position players nor for the pitching staff. It was the heart of McCarthy's doctrine that rest dulls a player's skills; you needed to keep playing to stay sharp, and so far as he was concerned, the league championship was nothing more than the penultimate step toward his hallowed mission in October.

So the Yankees spent the rest of the month taking dead aim on the final phase of their journey. They embarked on another winning streak of eight in a row. On September 20, Sundra won his eleventh straight game. The following day, Russo registered his seventh consecutive win to bring his record to 8–3. The Yanks concluded their seventeen-game home stand with a mark of 12–5 and a seventeen-game margin over Boston. The season ended on September 30 with a doubleheader split with the Red Sox at the Stadium. In the second game, Sundra saw his perfect season spoiled, dropping a 4–2 decision, and he had to settle for a record of 11–1. He was one of seven pitchers to win ten or more games on the year, the first team to accomplish that feat since the 1914 Philadelphia Athletics. Ruffing led with twenty-one; Donald had thirteen; Gomez, Hadley, and Pearson, twelve each; and Hildebrand chalked up ten. Together, they won a total of ninety-one games, an average of thirteen apiece. Relief artist Murphy contributed by leading the league with nineteen saves. All told, the Yankees won 106 games against 45 losses, a winning percentage of .702.

The offense of course was spearheaded by DiMaggio. While leading the league in batting, his home run total of 30 trailed Foxx who had 35, Greenberg with 33, and the rookie Ted Williams with 31. His 126 RBIs were exceeded only by Williams's 145. His home run and RBI numbers were even more impressive considering that he was out of action for more than thirty games. Still, he was hardly without help. Four of the other starters—Red Rolfe, Charlie Keller, Bill Dickey, and George Selkirk—all hit over .300. So did Ruffing, perhaps baseball's best hitting pitcher, who batted .307 in 114 times at bat and drove in 20 runs in the process. Everyone in the starting lineup hit more than 10 home runs; Dickey, Selkirk, and Gordon all had more than 20.

Now, looking ahead, they were ready to take on a Cincinnati Reds team that had not a single .300 hitter in its lineup. But with a pitching staff that had three starters with ERAs under 3.00, they figured to keep the games close. The Yankees, by all accounts, were poised to begin their quest for a fourth consecutive World Series title. They carried with them, for all to see, the conviction that October was their private property. Look closely, and you would see "New York Yankees" stenciled across its face.

19

Fourth Straight Title Marks the End of the Beginning

One could hardly conjure two franchises that were less alike. The magisterial Yankees over the last two decades had acquired the patina of royalty. The Cincinnati Reds, by contrast, had fashioned the image of a work-a-day conglomerate with an undistinguished past and a future lacking in promise. Yet, a random sequence of events had forged a subtle bond between the two teams. As they prepared to meet for the world title, the Yankees had won ten pennants and seven World Series' over the past twenty-three years. The Reds laid claim to a single world championship that was, and forever will be, memorably tainted. In 1919, the Reds won the National League pennant by nine games over John McGraw's New York Giants and proceeded to win the World Series from the Chicago White Sox five games to three. But it soon came to light that the heavily favored White Sox had thrown the Series. Eight of their players were charged with taking bribes to lose games intentionally. The only championship that the Reds won has been remembered through the ages as having been the product of the Black Sox scandal.

The indelible stain on baseball's reputation led obliquely to the Yankees' rise to prominence. In an attempt to stimulate fan interest in a sport whose every nuance would now be viewed as suspect, management decided to alter the baseball. The dead-ball era would give way to the new, lively ball at the start of the 1920 season. Coincidentally, Babe Ruth, who had set a season home run record of 29 with the Red Sox in 1919, was traded to the Yankees in the off-season. The confluence of the lively ball and the Bambino playing for the Yankees transformed the game dramatically. From his 29 homers in 1919, Ruth broke his own record with 54 in 1920 and again with 59 the following year. However, the change to a new ball offered little help for the Reds. They struggled throughout the twenties and resided in the second division during the first eight years of the thirties. Their fortunes turned in 1938 when they finished fourth, mostly on the strength of the arms of Paul Derringer and Bucky Walters and the bats of Ernie Lombardi and Frank McCormick, all of whom would be in action for the upcoming World Series. But they had traveled a difficult road to get there.

The Cincinnati franchise had fallen on hard times with the start of the Depression. The stock market crash devastated the team's owner, Sidney Weil, and buried the Reds in the second division. Having suffered severe financial losses, Weil sold the team in 1933 to Lowell Crosley, the local appliance and auto-mobile magnate. After christening the stadium in his honor—changing its name from League Park to Crosley Field—the new owner made the critical move of bringing in Larry MacPhail as general manager. MacPhail came with the recommendation of Branch Rickey, one of baseball's legendary pioneers. MacPhail, Rickey said, was "a wild man at times, but he'll do the job." And, indeed, he did. Ever the innovator, MacPhail introduced season-ticket sales, night baseball, and radio broadcasts of games. The moves did not immediately turn the Reds into a winner, but they attracted fans at an accelerated rate, and the renaissance would continue.

MacPhail left for Brooklyn after the 1937 season, but Crosley compensated by making his next critical move. Warren Giles was chosen to replace MacPhail, and Giles hired Bill McKechnie as manager for the 1938 season. Under their new manager, the Reds finally breathed the air of the first division, moving from eighth to fourth place. McKechnie, who had had at best a brief journeyman's playing career, mainly as an infielder with Pittsburgh, found far greater success as a manager. He won pennants with the Pirates and the Cardinals and improved the chronically indifferent performance of the Boston Bees/Braves.

In 1938, the Reds moved into mildly serious contention, finishing in fourth place, six games behind the pennant-winning Cubs. Their record improved from 56–98 in 1937 to 82–68 in 1938, a margin of twenty-six games. The difference was largely due to the development of first-baseman McCormick, now turned twenty-five, who had played a total of only thirty-six games in the two previous seasons, along with the addition of Walters to the pitching staff. McCormick responded to his role as a starter by batting .327, leading the league in hits with 209 and driving in 106 runs. He would improve on those numbers in 1939, hitting .332 and again leading the league with an identical 209 hits, while his RBI total of 128 also was best in the league.

Walters came to the Reds in mid-season of 1938 in a trade with the Phillies. McKechnie, who had the team playing at around a .500 clip by early June, knew that he needed another starting pitcher to go along with Derringer and Johnny Vander Meer. He took the advice of one of his coaches Jimmie Wilson, who, as former manager of the Phillies, recognized Walters's potential. Wilson urged Giles to acquire the young pitcher. It took some persuasion to sell the idea, for Walters had not necessarily distinguished himself in the early years of his career.

Walters had started out as a third baseman for the Boston Braves in 1931. Seeing limited action, he batted .211 and .187 in his first two seasons. He did better during a short stay in the Pacific Coast League and was picked up by the Red Sox in 1933. His pitching career began when he was sold to the Phillies the following year. The conversion was not an immediate success. Walters compiled a record of 38–53 during his four-plus seasons with Philadelphia. In 1936, he lost twenty-one games, more than anyone else in the league. But those losing seasons might have been looked upon as an investment because it was during that time that he developed a lethal sinkerball, which eventually became his signature pitch. He arrived in Cincinnati in June 1938 with a record of 4–8 but went 11–6 the rest of the way, finishing the season with a winning mark of 15–14.

It all came together for Walters in 1939. He led the league with twenty-seven wins and an ERA of 2.29. He also helped himself at the plate, batting .325 with eight doubles, a triple, and a homer while driving in sixteen runs. More notably, he teamed with Derringer, who was 25–7, to win a combined fifty-two games, more than half the team's total of ninety-seven. They were the first duo to win more than fifty games between them since 1916 when Grover Cleveland Alexander and Eppa Rixey won fifty-five for the Phillies. No two pitchers on the same team have turned the trick at least through the next seventy-eight years. At season's end, Walters was named the National League's Most Valuable Player. The same award had been won the previous year by his battery mate, Ernie Lombardi.

Over the course of his seventeen-year career, Lombardi was one of the best players in the game but never seemed to be fully appreciated, largely because of a conflation of physical attributes and mannerisms that captured the attention of observers. He had joined the majors with the Brooklyn Robins (later the Dodgers) in 1931 and batted .297 in seventy-three games. He was traded to the Reds before the start of spring training in 1932 and flourished immediately. He reached his peak starting in 1935 when he hit .343, but he was shunned in the balloting for the All-Star team. He made the team with room to spare in the next three years with batting averages of .333, .334, and .342. In 1938, he also hit 19 home runs, drove in 95 runs, and was named MVP. But despite his on-field excellence, Lombardi's renown was bestowed on him for other reasons. He was, in the literal sense of the term, one-of-a-kind. The National Baseball Hall of Fame, to which he was elected in 1986 after being inexplicably and unjustly ignored for nearly four decades, describes him this way on its website:

Everything about the longtime Reds star seemed larger than life. He had one of the best arms in baseball, the kind of arm that tempted scouts at times to make him a pitcher. He had hands that seemed to almost make a catcher's mitt superfluous. He swung a 42-ounce bat that made everyone else's bats look like a toothpick, thanks to massive wrists and forearms.

There was his nose, a massive protuberance that earned him the almost inevitable nickname of "Schnozz," and there was his lack of speed. More than anything, Lombardi was one of the biggest, and best, hitters the game has seen.

. . .

Nothing about Lombardi was conventional, from his lack of speed, to his prominent nose, to his batting grip: He held the baseball bat like a golf club, interlocking his hands. There was no real reason to ever change to a more conventional grip, because Lombardi was able to rip line drives like few before or since.

Lombardi hit .306 for his career even though infielders played him deeper than usual because of his lack of speed. He hit better than .300 in ten seasons and won batting titles in 1938 and 1942. He was the last catcher to win a batting title until Joe Mauer did it for the Minnesota Twins in 2006. Lombardi was named National League MVP in 1938.

So it was on the "core four" of Walters and Derringer, McCormick and Lombardi that the Reds staked their hopes in trying to unseat the three-time champion Yankees in the upcoming World Series. They had, after all, prevailed in a season-long struggle with the St. Louis Cardinals. The Cards, with fragments of the storied Gas House Gang still remaining, had hung on relentlessly throughout the season after it appeared that the Reds were about to run away with the pennant in hand. On May 16, the Reds' record stood at 12–10 and they trailed the Cards by a game-and-a-half. But on that very day, Cincinnati launched a twelve-game winning streak which earned them no more than a first-place tie. For, on May 18, the Cards embarked on a seven-game run of their own, and the two teams remained tied until May 26 when they met for a four-game series at St. Louis. Cincinnati won three of the four and took a two-game lead, which they never relinquished. But the Cards did not go easily. They persisted through the heat of summer, and matters were not decided until September 28. With three games left in the season, Derringer won his tenth straight, defeating the Cards 5–3 in Cincinnati for the pennant clincher. Now, the Reds were on their way to the Bronx to take on the Yankees.

The Series opened at the Stadium on Wednesday, October 4, before a near-capacity crowd of 58,541. McKechnie elected to go with Derringer, the eleven-year veteran, against Ruffing for the Yankees. The game was everything it was expected to be, a tense duel between twenty-game winners, played in a crisp one hour and thirty-three minutes. After both teams went down in order in the first inning, McCormick opened the second with a single to left, but Lombardi hit a routine ground ball to third base that Red Rolfe turned into a double play. An inning later, shortstop Billy Myers's single to center was nullified as Derringer hit one off Ruffing's glove that kicked over to shortstop Crosetti who started another twin killing.

The Reds got the early advantage in the fourth. With two out, right fielder Ival Goodman drew a base on balls, stole second, and came home on McCormick's second hit of the game. The Yanks, who had only two hits going into the fifth, evened the score on a single by Joe Gordon and a double to left by Babe Dahlgren. Both sides went down harmlessly in the next three innings, leaving matters in the hands of the Yankees in the bottom of the ninth, and five-o'clock lightning struck. With one out, Charlie Keller drove Derringer's second pitch to the edge of the right-center-field bleachers where Goodman, known for his speed, ran the ball down and got his glove on it but failed to hold on, allowing Keller to make it to third. DiMaggio was intentionally walked, and Bill Dickey gave the Yanks an opening-game 2–1 victory with a line drive single to center.

The Reds tried, unsuccessfully, to even things the next day, with Walters going against Monte Pearson. At first glance, the pitching edge seemed to favor Cincinnati. MVP Walters, in addition to leading the league in wins and ERA, also led in games started, complete games, innings pitched, and strikeouts. Pearson, a respectable 12–5 on the season, pitched to an inflated ERA of 4.49. In his eight-year career, Pearson had never won twenty games. He had, however, virtually unnoticed, developed into a big-game pitcher, thriving especially in October. He had defeated the Giants 5–2 in game four of the

1936 World Series. He beat them again, 5–1, in the third game the following year. In 1938, he experienced arm problems but still managed to defeat the Cubs 5–2. His arm woes flared up again during the 1939 season, and he started only twenty games. McCarthy hesitated to put him on the post-season roster but decided to take his chances and start him in game two. It was a sound decision.

Pearson retired the side in order in the first three innings. Third baseman Bill Werber broke the string with a base on balls leading off the fourth, but he was not on base very long. He was thrown out trying to steal as second baseman Lonnie Frey struck out and Pearson set down the next twelve batters without incident, giving him a no-hitter through seven-and-a-third innings. Lombardi ended the no-hit bid with a single to center. Then, with two out in the ninth, Werber got the second and final hit of the game for Cincinnati with a single to left.

Walters, for his part, did not pitch poorly. He had only one bad inning. After blanking the Yanks in the first two frames, he faltered in the third. Dahlgren led off with a double, took third on a sacrifice bunt by Pearson, and scored the game's first run when Rolfe singled to right. Then the dam broke. Keller doubled to left, DiMaggio beat out a grounder to third, Dickey singled to right, and the Yankees had three runs. Dalhgren added a solo homer in the fourth, providing the Yanks with a 4–0 lead, and that was the way the game ended. Walters and Pearson both pitched shutout ball from the fifth inning on, and the Yanks left the Stadium leading the Series 2–0.

Game two had been a classic of economy. It was completed in one hour and twenty-seven minutes, six minutes shorter than game one. The first two games had taken a total of only three hours, with each pitcher going the distance. Pitch counts were not a relevant statistic in those days, but for those who were counting, Pearson threw a total of 103 pitches and Walters threw 94 in his eight innings of work. Now, with a day off for travel, it was on to Cincinnati, which would be host to a World Series game for the first time since 1919.

For the second straight game, McCarthy's pitching selection was made reluctantly. Lefty Gomez had torn a muscle in his back on September 24 while pitching against the Senators at Yankee Stadium and found himself in the hospital nine days before the Series was about to start. He had not won a game since September 6 when he bested Lefty Grove and the Red Sox. He lost his next two starts on September 12 and 17. McCarthy was prepared to start Oral Hildebrand in game three, but the irrepressible Gomez convinced him otherwise on the overnight train ride to Cincinnati. It did not go well.

The Yankees wasted no time in jumping on Cincinnati starter Gene Thompson when the game got underway. Crosetti drew a lead-off walk and Keller drove Thompson's first pitch into the right-field bleachers for a two-run Yankee lead. Gomez, who was 6–0 in World Series play coming into the game, ran into trouble quickly. After getting the first two outs, he was reached for successive singles by Goodman, McCormick, and Lombardi to cut the lead in half. That was not all that went wrong for Gomez. He had strained a muscle reaching for Goodman's ground ball, and when McCarthy noticed him wince while striking out in the top of the second, he called Bump Hadley to the mound to start the home half of the inning. It took Hadley a while to settle in. Singles by Myers, Thompson, Werber, and Goodman brought in two runs, and, at 3–2, Cincinnati had its first lead of the Series.

It did not last long. With two out in the third, Keller walked and DiMaggio, who had only two infield singles in seven times up in the first two games, homered deep into the center field seats to put the Yanks ahead 4–3. That, as it turned out, was all Hadley needed. He pitched unevenly the rest of the way, yielding a total of seven hits and three walks over his eight innings of work, but he kept the Reds off the board. The Yankees had given him an added three-run cushion in the fifth when Keller hit his second home run of the game with Rolfe on first, and Dickey hit a solo shot to make the final margin 7–3.

The future looked dim for Cincinnati. They came on as if history's message did not apply to them. Game four would be one of the most memorable of all World Series games. McKechnie, with no margin for error, went with Derringer, his opening game pitcher. McCarthy had the luxury of giving his own ace, Ruffing, an added day's rest and going with Hildebrand who had originally been scheduled to start game three.

Derringer was as good as McKechnie's best hope. He went through the Yankees' order effortlessly, retiring the side in order until Selkirk doubled with two out in the fifth. Hildebrand was almost as good. He yielded only two hits—a double by McCormick in the second and a single by Derringer in the third. But his day's work was brief. After setting down the side in the fourth on three ground balls, he felt a sharp pain in his side and gave way to Sundra to start the fifth. Sundra surrendered a two-out triple to Myers but then retired Derringer on a foul pop to end the inning.

The game remained scoreless until Keller opened the seventh with a home run, his third of the Series. After DiMaggio flied out deep to left, Dickey followed with another homer, and the Yankees led 2–0. With Sundra pitching well, all indications were that the Yanks would wrap things up with room to spare, but the Reds were determined to make it a game. Leading off the bottom of the seventh, McCormick reached base on an error by Rolfe, and after Lombardi struck out, future Hall of Fame outfielder Al Simmons stepped to the plate. Simmons, thirty-seven years old and in his sixteenth season, had come to Cincinnati from the Boston Bees at the end of August and was making his first appearance of the Series. He had long ago earned his place in baseball's pantheon. Beginning in his rookie season, 1924, Simmons had driven in 100 runs or more in his first eleven seasons.

Now clearly in the shadows of his brilliant career and trying to reclaim a touch of the old magic, he doubled to center, sending McCormick to third from where he scored Cincinnati's first run on a groundout by outfielder Wally Berger. The fire apparently lit, the Reds added two more runs. Myers walked and Willard Hershberger, the backup catcher, pinch-hit for Derringer and delivered a single to left, scoring Simmons. Another single, by Werber, scored Myers. That was all for Sundra. Murphy came in and ended the inning by striking out Frey, but Cincinnati had a 3–2 lead heading into the eighth. The fireworks were still to come.

With no room for error, McKechnie brought in Walters, who retired the side in order. The Reds added to their lead in the home half of the eighth when Lombardi singled, driving in Goodman, who had opened the inning with a double. Now, trailing 4–2, the Yankees were down to their final three outs facing the league's top winner and Most Valuable Player. It was no matter. Keller, who was having a lifetime's worth of success in a four-game series, started things off with a single to center. He scored the Yankees' third run when DiMaggio singled to left after Dickey reached first on a fielder's-choice error by Myers. The next batter, Gordon, grounded deep to third base, and Werber threw home trying to head off the tying run. DiMaggio beat the throw, sliding in hard and jarring Lombardi in what turned out to be a preview of what was yet to come. Knotted at 4–4, the game headed into extra innings.

Crosetti walked to open the tenth and advanced to second on a sacrifice bunt by Rolfe. Keller hit a hard ground ball to short that Myers bobbled, putting runners on the corners with one out. DiMaggio broke the tie with an opposite-field single, but it is what happened next that defined the game and the Series. DiMaggio's hit glanced off Goodman's glove and the ball rolled past him. The ever-alert Keller turned third and headed for home. Goodman's throw arrived ahead of the runner, but Keller crashed into Lombardi at full force; the ball came loose, and Lombardi fell to the ground as Keller crossed the plate. DiMaggio, who never slowed down, kept on coming and slid home safely as Lombardi lay prone, stunned and motionless, the ball resting about four feet away toward the third-base side of the plate.

Derisively and unfairly, the play entered the annals of base-ball lore known as "Lombardi's Snooze." But the truth emerged some time later, told to author Bill Gilbert by Johnny Vander Meer: "The throw from the outfield came in on a short hop and hit Lom in the [protective] cup. You just don't get up too quick. Somebody put out the word that Lombardi went to sleep, took a snooze. But he was paralyzed! He couldn't move. With anybody but Lombardi, they'd have to carry him off the field."

Keller has long been celebrated for his fearless collision with Lombardi at home plate. But he was by every other measure the hero of the Series. Still a rookie, he put up numbers that could stand on their own. In his sixteen times at bat, he had seven hits for an average of .438. Five of his seven hits were for extra bases—three home runs, a double, and a triple, good for six runs batted in. Although there was no such award at the time, he was clearly the Series' most valuable player.

With the crowd still buzzing about the play at the plate, Cincinnati, trailing 7–4, still had a glimmer of life remaining. Walters retired Dickey and Selkirk to close out the Yankees' tenth. The Reds kept hopes alive when Goodman and McCormick opened the bottom of the inning with singles, but Murphy secured the next three outs, and the Yankees were ready to celebrate their fourth straight championship. No other team had ever accomplished that feat.

Yet, what was most remarkable was the dominant manner in which the Yankees had prevailed. They won their four American League pennants by an average of nearly fifteen games. In the four World Series, they bested their opponents by a total of 16–3; outscored them by a margin of 113–52;

outhomered them 23–7; and compiled an overall ERA of 2.32. By any measure, the 1936–39 Yankees had staked their claim as baseball's greatest dynasty.

In many respects, however, it was not the end of an era, just the end of the beginning. The Yankees were about to enter upon a decades-long run of success that is unrivaled by any other team in any other sport. In the process, they would usher in an epoch during which the game of baseball would be transformed in much the same way as the world it reflected. Time would assert its inevitability, and the future would bond with a past that it barely resembled.

Epilogue
Baseball's Greatest Dynasty

Dynasties are measured chiefly by their duration. World dynasties such as the Roman and Ottoman Empires endured for centuries. Those in sports are by their nature abbreviated; there are other standards by which their prominence is gauged: How dominant was the reign? Was it continuous or interrupted by an occasional stumble? Did the team win the sport's championship—the World Series, for example—or did it falter in its quest for the title after winning its league's pennant? Of paramount importance, but often overlooked, is the margin by which the team dominated the opposition. Did it have to scrape and scratch its way to the top or did it demolish whatever stood in its way?

In the early years of baseball, there were a number of dynastic candidates in rapid succession. The Chicago Cubs of "Tinker to Evers to Chance" renown won the National League pennant in 1906 and the World Series in '07 and '08. Two years later, Connie Mack's Philadelphia Athletics won world championships in 1910 and '11 and again in 1913 after losing to the Boston Red Sox in 1912. The Sox, as it turned out, were just gearing up. They drew a deep breath and won the Series in 1915, '16, and '18, having finished second to the White Sox in 1917. The Yankees' intra-city rivals, the New York Giants, under John McGraw, were the first team to win four straight pennants, from 1921 to '24, but they won only the first two World Series, losing in '23 to the Yankees and in '24 to the Washington Senators. The Babe Ruth–led Yankees had been the default choice as greatest dynasty—winning American League pennants in 1921, '22, and '26 and the World Series in '23, '27, and '28—until a decade later when the DiMaggio-Gehrig team arrived on the scene. If sheer, un-relenting dominance was the measure, that team was without equal. But looking ahead, it was really just the beginning.

The end of the Yankees' four-year dynasty would prove to be little more than an interruption in a prolonged siege that, for decades to come, would inflict a benign abuse on all who opposed them. There were occasional blips in their domination of the game, periods during which they appeared to be out of sync, strangers in a world that was changing in ways they did not comprehend. Of course, the structure around which the sport operated had indeed changed vastly, particularly in the sixties and seventies when the leagues were expanding, franchises were moving, and players were no longer bound to the teams with which they started. Free agency and the player draft stole some of the Yankees' magic, but while they stumbled a bit, they even-tually steadied themselves and found their way back to the top.

Ninety-forty proved to be a one-year intermission in their long-range dominion. They broke poorly from the starting gate, unable to put together a succession of wins as the days passed and April eased into May. It was as if they had become aliens to their own past, imposters who donned the pinstripes but had forgotten what they stood for. Starting on May 4, they dropped eight straight decisions and were buried in last place, nine-and-a-half games behind Boston, with Cleveland and Detroit also far ahead. Their record stood at 6–14; their bats had gone dead. Dickey was hitting .159, Rolfe .198, Gordon .257, and Keller .240. Even DiMaggio's .316 was well below his standard. They began to pick up near the end of May, winning ten of eleven games beginning on May 26 and creeping back into the race. On June 3, they were in fourth place, four-and-a-half games in back of the Red Sox, still trailing the Indians and the Tigers.

As the season moved past the All-Star break and deep into July and August, Boston began to fade; Cleveland and Detroit were in a bitter battle for the lead, and the Yankees were inching closer behind them. Late in August, they mounted another eight-game winning streak and found themselves just one game behind on September 7. Their season would be decided in the week ahead when they would be on the road playing two games in Boston and Cleveland, then three in Detroit.

They took two straight at Fenway but gained no ground. The doubleheader at Cleveland, on September 11, was next. They were in third place, one game behind first-place Detroit, which led Cleveland by a half-game. If the Yanks could sweep the twin bill, they would move into first place for the first time in the season. They didn't. They beat Feller, who was 24–8, in the opener, but Ruffing, not having his best year at 13–10, dropped the nightcap 5–3. On to Detroit, they lost two of three and fell back to a three-game deficit. Their season was effectively over. The pennant was decided in Detroit's favor on the last weekend of the season when a pitcher by the name of Floyd Giebel, making only his second major-league start in a career that would be short and of little note, bested Bob Feller, who was 27–10 entering the game, with a 2–0 three-hitter.

The Yankees indeed had suffered an off year. DiMaggio, whose .352 batting average led the league for the second straight year, was the only regular to hit over .300. Henrich, who shared left field with Selkirk, finished at .307. The pitching also was off-pace. Ruffing, 15–12, and Russo, 14–8, were the only pitchers to win in double digits.

It was in a way fitting that after four years as preemptive champions, the Yankees were unseated by the team that had beaten them out the two seasons prior to the start of their run. It was fitting too that in Detroit's two championship seasons that sandwiched the Yankees' four-year run, Hank Greenberg was voted the league's Most Valuable Player. The Tigers' first baseman enjoyed a monumental season in 1940. He led the league in home runs with 41 and RBIs with 150 while batting .340. Two years earlier, Greenberg had drawn the nation's attention as he pursued Babe Ruth's home run record of 60, finishing with 58.

From the very start of his career in 1933, Greenberg had earned a special kind of renown as baseball's first Jewish superstar; both his parents were immigrants from Romania. He grew up in the Bronx where he was a multi-sport star at James

Monroe High School. His best sport, not surprisingly, given his height at something more than 6-foot-3, was basketball. He also excelled at soccer and track-and-field, and though he did not particularly care for football, he played a bit at end and caught a touchdown pass in a season-ending game. However, his future clearly was tuned to baseball. Basketball was a minor sport in the late twenties, and it was Greenberg's bat that attracted the attention of baseball's top scouts, including the omnipresent Paul Krichell, always on the prowl for new talent that would fit the Yankees' mold. Krichell perhaps made a critical mistake when he took his prize prospect to a game at Yankee Stadium in 1929. Greenberg watched Gehrig and concluded that as long as the Iron Horse was around, he himself would have no immediate future in Yankee pinstripes. Instead, Detroit scout Jean Dubuc signed the promising youngster to a contract, and four years later, at the age of twenty-two, Greenberg was posting big numbers for the Yankees' chief rival.

Greenberg was welcomed with open arms in Detroit, and he developed a wide following among Jewish fans in other big-league cities, most notably his native New York whose population at the time was nearly one-quarter Jewish. However, Jews were often an object of derision in the 1930s, particularly with Hitler on the rise in Germany, and in the fall of 1934, Greenberg found himself confronted with a dilemma. Though not a fully observant practitioner of his faith, like many other contemporary Jews, Greenberg made it a practice to comply with his religion's rituals on the High Holy Days of Rosh Hashanah and Yom Kippur.

In 1933, he had abstained from playing on either holiday. But a year later, the Tigers were in the midst of a tight pennant race, clinging to first place while the Yanks were breathing down their necks. After consulting with a rabbi, Greenberg decided to play on Rosh Hashanah, and he celebrated by hitting two home runs to account for all the scoring in a 2–0 win over the Red Sox that boosted Detroit's lead over the Yankees to four-and-a-half games. But nine days later, Greenberg declined to play on Yom Kippur, the holiest day on the Jewish calendar. His decision to sit the game out was not looked upon kindly by much of the Detroit press. One critic noted that Yom Kippur comes every year but the Tigers hadn't won a pennant since 1909. Resentment among Detroit fans grew even deeper when the Tigers lost to the Yankees 5–2. But Jews in large measure hailed Greenberg as a hero both off the field and on. He was greeted with a standing ovation when he entered the Shaarey Zedek synagogue on the Day of Atonement and was memorialized by the nationally syndicated poet Edgar A. Guest in a poem carried in daily newspapers on the morning of the game. It ended in the lines:

> We shall miss him on the infield and shall miss him at bat
> But he's true to his religion—and I honor him for that.

Of course, all was forgiven when Detroit won its first pennant in twenty-five years as Greenberg led the league with 36 home runs and 170 RBIs. In his twelve years with Detroit, Greenberg hit over .300 eight times, led the league in homers four times, and set the American League record for RBIs in a single season by a right-hand batter with 183 in 1937. Following Detroit's 1940 world's title, Greenberg played in nineteen games in 1941 before enlisting in the Army as the war in Europe began to heat up. He marked his last game before donning an army uniform on May 6 by belting two home runs in a 7–4 victory over the Yankees. Nearing the end of the year, Congress passed a law exempting men over the age of twenty-eight from being drafted, and on December 5, Sergeant Greenberg was given his discharge. But his return to civilian life did not last long. Two days later, when the Japanese attacked Pearl Harbor, Greenberg, now thirty years old, re-enlisted, this time in the Air Corps. He explained his decision this way: "We are in trouble, and there is only one thing to do—return to service. I have not been called back. I am going back of my own accord. Baseball is out the window as far as I'm concerned. I don't know if I'll ever return to baseball."

He did. When the war ended in 1945, Greenberg resumed his career late in the season. In his last year with Detroit, 1946, he led the league in home runs with 44 and RBIs with 127, splitting his time between first base and the outfield. With his career approaching its end, he was sold to Pittsburgh for the 1947 season where he put up respectable numbers before retiring at the end of the season.

The year 1941 opened on a world that was unlike any other before or since. What had been referred to as the "phony war" in the fall of 1940 was about to explode across the European continent and finally engulf the entire globe. It would soon involve the United States and leave its mark on every aspect of American life, baseball being no exception. The Neutrality Acts, which had prevented the United States from intervening in any way, were nullified in March. At the same time, a program called lend-lease was enacted under which the United States would supply the United Kingdom, Free France, the Republic of China, and later the Soviet Union and other Allied nations with food, oil, and war supplies. With the United States becoming increasingly involved and full participation clearly on the way, the United States brought back conscription, which had ended with the World War I armistice. It was the first peacetime draft in the nation's history. All men between the ages of twenty-one and thirty-five were required to register for one year of service with selection based on a national lottery. The term of service was extended to two years in August. Finally, after December 7, the draft would include men from age eighteen to sixty-four and the term of service would be for the duration of the conflict.

The effect of the draft on baseball was immediate, though gradual. The first ballplayer drafted, on March 8, was Phillies' pitcher Hugh Mulcahy. Greenberg returned to service two months later. But once the United States entered the war, the flow into the armed forces increased, with many men enlisting before they were given notice. Bob Feller was among the first to enroll, joining the Navy soon after hearing of the attack.

Despite the draft, most teams' rosters had remained intact for the 1941 season, and order of a sort seemed to be restored when the Yankees won the pennant by seventeen games over the Red Sox and then defeated the Brooklyn Dodgers in a five-game World Series. The last peacetime season was made memorable by DiMaggio's fifty-six-game hitting streak and Ted Williams batting .406, breaking the .400 mark for the first time since Bill Terry did it in 1930 and the last time—for at least the next three-quarters of a century.

The Yanks repeated as pennant-winners the next two seasons, splitting World Series titles with the Cardinals. They had now won seven pennants and six World Series in eight years, making the 1940 season appear as little more than a pause in a continuing dynasty. But the team had begun undergoing a change in personnel in 1941 that would become significant in the next two years. Crosetti had been replaced by Phil Rizzuto at shortstop; Henrich had largely usurped the outfield position of Selkirk; Dickey was sharing catching duties with Buddy Rosar. By 1943, the team that won the World Series was vastly different from those that preceded it. By contrast, with the exception of Gordon replacing Lazzeri at second base and the loss of Gehrig at first, the 1936 team underwent little change over the next three seasons. It was, by any reasonable measure, its own discrete dynasty, and despite several more such runs in the decades ahead, it retained the mark of its own distinction.

With the end of World War II and the return of players who had served in the armed forces, the Yankees put together a succession of independent dynasties that turned the franchise into what might have passed for an empire. In the sixteen years between 1949 and 1964, they won fourteen pennants and nine World Series. Only in 1954 and 1959 did they fail to win the league championship. From 1949 to 1953, they won five straight World Series, surpassing the string of four compiled by the thirties team. However, they did not come close to the domination

that the thirties team imposed on the opposition.   T h e i r
margin over the runners-up was barely an average of four games.
They swept only one World Series while losing a total of eight
October contests. During that span, no Yankee led the league in
any offensive department. Depending largely on the wizardry
of manager Casey Stengel, they found ways to win games in
which they were clearly inferior to their rivals. They rarely beat
themselves either in the field or at bat. They bunted, they played
hit-and-run, and they fielded and ran the bases with a precision
that regularly turned events in their favor. Most significantly, the
personnel underwent a major transformation over the course of
the five years. Only Phil Rizzuto and Yogi Berra were full-time
regulars in both 1949 and 1953. In fact, the cloak of leadership
was passed halfway through their run when, in 1951, Mickey
Mantle arrived and DiMaggio departed at season's end.

With Mantle becoming the face of the team, the Yankees
again won five straight pennants, from 1960 to '64, but they
lost the World Series to Pittsburgh in 1960, were swept by the
Los Angeles Dodgers in 1963, and were beaten by the Cardinals in 1964. Then, over the next three decades, the empire,
such as it was, went into something of a retreat, marked only
by a brief three-year revival between 1976–78.

It was in the mid-nineties that they bestirred themselves
under the guidance of their new manager, Joe Torre. Now, led
not by a single superstar such as DiMaggio or Mantle, but by
the "core four" of Derek Jeter, Jorge Posada, Andy Pettite, and
Mariano Rivera—as well as the veteran Bernie Williams—they
surprised in 1996 by winning their first pennant in fifteen years
and then taking four straight from the Atlanta Braves after

dropping the first two games of the World Series. After losing out to Cleveland in the 1997 playoffs, the Yanks began their most recent successful championship streak in 1998. During their string of four pennants and three World Series, they swept San Diego and Atlanta before losing just one game to the Mets in 2000; they then succumbed to the Braves in a seven-game series in 2001. Still, when viewed as a dynasty, the Yankees of the nineties fell one year short of the thirties team, and their winning percentage fell off sharply after 1998. Despite a 162-game schedule, they never won 100 or more games after 1998.

However, the 1998 team merits consideration—along with the 1939 and 1927 Yankees—as the best single-season team of all time. The numbers speak for themselves. They compiled a record of 114–48, a winning percentage of .704, two points better than the 1939 team but ten points shy of the 1927 squad, which won 110 games in the old 154-game schedule. Those three are the only teams ever to finish the regular season with a winning percentage of over .700, while also leading the league in runs scored and fewest runs allowed, and going on to sweep the World Series. The '39 Yankees hold the record for outscoring their opponents over the course of the regular season, 967–556; no other team ever outscored their rivals by more than four hundred runs.

Measuring the relative quality of teams of different eras has long been the nutrient of hot-stove league dialogues and disputations, none of which ever seems to reach a consensus. Rating systems that have been used over the decades invariably come to different conclusions. One of the more recent entries in the field is the Elo Rating System, named for its creator, Arpad

Elo, a Hungarian-born American physics professor. Professor Elo originally devised the system in 1961 as a way to measure the relative skills of chess masters. However, over the years it has been adapted to apply to athletes, teams, and those engaged in other endeavors.

The system was refined chiefly by the analyst Nate Silver and incorporated in a program that is called FiveThirtyEight. Sometimes identified by its numerals, 538 is a website that takes its name from the number of electors in the United States Electoral College. Founded in March 2008, it became a licensed feature of *The New York Times* online two years later. In 2013, ESPN became the owner of the site, and it was officially named *FiveThirtyEight: Nate Silver's Political Calculus.* In addition to politics, it can be applied to sports, science, economics, and popular culture. The system is driven by an intricately complex computer analysis which has been used to rate sports teams in general as well as in specific sports.

Its conclusions are particularly interesting in referencing the Yankees' dynasty of the thirties. It rates the 1939 Yankees as the greatest sports team of all time, followed by the 1906 Chicago Cubs. It states that those two teams "are in a league of their own, more than ten Elo points ahead of the other franchises." The third, fourth, and fifth teams are from football and basketball and are of more recent vintage: the 2007 New England Patriots, 2017 Golden State Warriors, and the 1996 Chicago Bulls. Three other Yankee teams—of 1927, 1998, and 1932— are included in the top ten. Rating baseball teams exclusively, the Yankees dominate the list, placing six teams among the top twelve—the '27 team is third; the '98 team is fifth, just in back of the 1909 Pittsburgh Pirates; and the '32 team is sixth. The 1937 and '38 Yanks are eleventh and twelfth. So, in rating the dynasty of the thirties, three of the four championship teams finish among the dozen best of all time.

It is worthy of note that the highest ranked teams in football and basketball are mostly contemporary, while the best-rated baseball teams range back to the early years of the twentieth century. Astonishingly, of Elo's top twenty-five baseball teams, twenty-one pre-date the post-WWII era beginning in 1946. Of later vintage, only the 1998 Yankees, the 1970 Baltimore Orioles, the 1976 Cincinnati Reds, and the 1954 Cleveland Indians make the cut, and only the 1998 Yankee team is in the top eighteen. Of course, physical attributes account for part of the difference. The increasing size and strength of the players is not nearly as critical in baseball as it is in the other sports. Talking basketball, one might question whether Bob Cousy or Bill Russell would be able to keep pace with the game as it is played today. Could Sammy Baugh or Steve Van Buren set passing and rushing records on current NFL gridirons? Yet no one would hesitate to place Ruth or Gehrig or DiMaggio at the very pinnacle of the baseball teams of any age.

But the athletes themselves do not account for the complete difference. The nature of the games also feeds the distinction. It is easier to compare baseball teams of different eras because baseball has remained largely immune to change in a way that other team sports have not. The playing field has not been altered, nor has the means of scoring. It is still ninety feet between bases and sixty feet, six inches from the pitcher's mound to home plate; the foul lanes haven't been widened nor the goal posts moved. Scoring is still achieved one run at a time, as each runner touches home plate; there is no three-point shot or two-point conversion.

Baseball has long been celebrated as the only team sport that is not governed by the clock. In the world of baseball, time stands still. The game is much the same now as it was one hundred and more years ago. The years fall away, but they never disappear. The past fuses with the present. Allowing imagination its due, one can sit in the upper deck at Yankee Stadium and still see the Great DiMaggio gliding poetically across the boundless stretch of outfield grass as time and space fuse in the vast banks of memory. As William Faulkner wrote in *Requiem for a Nun*: "The past is never dead. It's not even past."

End

Postscript

Are We Witnessing the Birth of a New Yankee Dynasty?

Some eighty years after the dynasty of the thirties, Faulkner's profound insight resonated throughout the 2017 season. The past seemed to be shadowing the present as the Yankees moved into an early lead and led their division as late as July 31. Then, they lost four straight games and fell behind Boston. They spent the remainder of the season in pursuit of the Red Sox, falling just two games short, on the strength of a blazing finish in September. They were not expected to be that good. They had not made the playoffs the previous season. They had not won a playoff game since 2012.

At the end of the 2016 season, following a fourth-place finish and just six games over .500, Yankee management decided to stake its claim on the future. They shed some of their aging veterans and instituted a youth movement. Their farm system was loaded with talent, and they determined that that was where their future resided. The core-three of outfielder Aaron Judge, catcher Gary Sánchez, and first baseman Greg Bird was brought up near the end of the season, and their cumulative performance, though far from flawless, pointed to a promising future. The fledgling group was christened the Baby Bombers, on their way, presumably, to qualifying as the reincarnation of the Bronx Bombers, and it did not take them long to earn the designation.

The 2017 season had barely started when the Yankees took off on an eight-game winning streak that propelled them to the top of their division, largely on the broad back of Aaron Judge. Judge started right off as if he might be the second coming of Joe DiMaggio. By the All-Star break, about the midway point of the season, he was hitting .329, with 30 home runs and 66 runs batted in. Still, there were vast differences between him and DiMaggio. Judge, a mountain of a man at 6-foot-7 and 282 pounds, had enormous power, his home runs often traveling close to five hundred feet. He hit 52 of them during the season, a total DiMaggio never approached. But entirely unlike the Yankee Clipper, he was prone to striking out at a record clip. DiMaggio struck out only 29 times in his rookie season while batting .323, with 29 homers and 125 RBIs. By way of contrast, Judge whiffed 208 times in 542 at-bats. His post-season figures were even more frustrating. In thirteen playoff games, he struck out 27 times in 48 at-bats. But despite his tendency to strike out, Judge often carried the team for long periods during the season. He hit a respectable .284 with 114 RBIs, performed well in the field, and ran the bases with conviction. At season's end, he was the unanimous choice for Rookie of the Year and runner-up for MVP honors.

All things considered, Judge showed himself to be a force around which a championship team could be built. The same could be said of Sánchez and Bird. Sánchez, who missed the first month of the season with an injury to his right biceps, still contributed 33 homers and 90 RBIs. Bird, hobbled by a bone defect in his right ankle, was out most of the season, but on his return, he left little doubt that stardom lay ahead with his picture-perfect left-handed swing taking aim at the beckoning right-field seats at the Stadium. There were other newcomers who fueled the surprising emergence of a team that was expected to be rebuilding in 2017 rather than contending for a championship: outfielder Aaron Hicks, pitchers Jordan Montgomery, Sonny Gray, Tommy Kahnle, and David Robertson, and third baseman Todd Frazier.

As it was, the Yankees came within one game of reaching the World Series while performing in heroic fashion. After dropping the first two divisional series games at Cleveland to a team that compiled a regular season record of 102–60, eleven games better than their own mark, the Yankees took three in a row to move into the championship round against the Houston Astros. Again, after losing the first two games on the road, the Yanks swept all three games at home before losing the final two at Houston.

Looking ahead to the 2018 season, their youthful band of warriors, now with a season's worth of experience under their belts and led by a new, equally youthful manager, the Yankees seem poised to embrace the prospect of postseason glories. Their already formidable lineup was buttressed just a few weeks before Christmas with the addition of Giancarlo Stanton, the

National League's 2017 MVP, who powered a staggering total of 59 home runs for the Miami Marlins. Paired with Judge, who hit just seven fewer, and perhaps bracketed in the batting order by Gary Sánchez and Greg Bird, a new Yankee dynasty does not seem to be out of the question.

Dynasties, even those of abbreviated duration, appear to have been lost to the ages. No team has repeated as World Series champions since the Yankees of 1998 to 2000. But as the 2018 season moves forward, there is the sense that the Yankees could be on the cusp of reclaiming a bit of history, Faulkner's projection ready for a new test. It might be time to see just how much of the past remains embedded in the Yankees' future.

President Franklin Delano Roosevelt throws out the traditional first ball in Washington, DC, to open the 1937 season on April 14 in a game between the Senators and the Yankees. From left: Roosevelt's son Elliott; Betsy Cushing Roosevelt, wife of FDR's eldest son, James; the president; Yankees manager Joe McCarthy; and Senators manager Bucky Harris. The Senators won the game, beating Lefty Gomez 1–0. *Credit: Associated Press*

Second-baseman Tony Lazzeri, who starred for the Yankees from 1926 to 1937, spanning the Murderers' Row team of Babe Ruth and the start of the Gehrig-DiMaggio era. *Credit: Associated Press*

Joe Gordon who was called up from the Yankees' Newark farm team to replace Tony Lazzeri at second base for the start of the 1938 season. *Credit: Associated Press*

A bird's-eye view of Bill Dickey's swing in spring training, 1937. *Credit: Associated Press*

Johnny Murphy, the Yankees' ace relief pitcher and one of the first relief specialists in baseball, getting ready for the 1939 season at spring training in St. Petersburg, Florida. *Credit: Associated Press*

Third baseman Red Rolfe slides safely into third base in game six of the 1936 World Series. Giant's third baseman Travis Jackson awaits the throw from outfielder Jo-Jo Moore. The Yanks won the game 13–5 to clinch the Series. *Credit: Associated Press*

Red Ruffing, with a season's record of 20–7, limbering up and looking forward to opening the 1938 World Series against the Chicago Cubs. The Yanks won the opener 3–1 and swept the Series 4–0. *Credit: Associated Press*

New York City Mayor Fiorello H. LaGuardia showing his batting grip to Lefty Gomez, left, and Bill Dickey after the 1938 World Series opener in Chicago. *Credit: Associated Press*

An aerial view of Yankees Stadium in the Bronx, 1937. *Credit: Associated Press*

Members of the 1937 American League All-Star team lined up at Griffith Stadium in Washington, from left: Lou Gehrig, Yankees; Joe Cronin, Red Sox; Bill Dickey, Yankees; Joe DiMaggio, Yankees; Charlie Gehringer, Tigers; Jimmy Foxx, Red Sox; and Hank Greenberg, Tigers. *Credit: Associated Press*

The Yankees pose for team photo before the opening of the 1939 World Series at Yankee Stadium. *Credit: Associated Press*

About the Author

Stanley Cohen is a veteran award-winning journalist who worked for many years as an editor, writer, and reporter for newspapers, magazines, and an international news service. He also taught writing, journalism, and philosophy at Hunter College and New York University. He is a member of the Hunter College Alumni Hall of Fame.

He is the author of eleven previous books, including *The Game They Played*, which was ranked among the Top 100 Sports Books of All Time by the editors of *Sports Illustrated*, and *Convicting the Innocent*, which dealt with the scourge of capital punishment and America's broken system of justice. Cohen also served as the program consultant for the award-winning television documentary *City Dump*, which was based on *The Game They Played*.

He resides in Tomkins Cove, New York, with his wife, Betty. Their two children and four grandchildren also live in the New York Metropolitan area.

Note on References

The information contained in this book was derived from a great many sources—Internet web sites, news media, and a number of books. In several instances where I quoted extensively, I cited the source and the author within the text. A full bibliography is listed at the back. The others, as complete as I can manage, are listed below. I apologize for any inadvertent omissions.

Web Sites

Of the many websites I explored, there are a few that provided an imposing volume of facts and observations and therefore deserve special notice.

Baseball-Reference.com was relied on heavily as it offered extensive details including the scores, box scores, and play-by-play accounts of every game, along with background details.

Wikipedia, the free encyclopedia, is a treasure trove of well-documented information, offering not only statistics but sidebar-type material and biographies of players.

The Society for American Baseball Research (SABR) provides lengthy, by-lined biographies of players. Among those I consulted were written by Laurence Baldassano, John

McMurray, David E. Skelton, Jim Kaplan, Bill Nowlin, Curt Vitty, Paul Rogers III, and Nelson "Chip" Green.

Baseball Almanac is a valuable site for rosters and statistics as well as human-interest offerings.

Thisgreatgame.com has well-written, splendidly complete summaries of the various seasons from the start through the World Series, complete with individual and team highlights.

Other useful sites were:

RetroSimba
yankeeanalysts.com
thebaseballpage.com
ballparksofbaseball.com
historicalbaseball
Retrosheet
MLB.com
Jewish Buffalo on the Web
ThePeopleHistory.com
TakeHimDowntown.com
Thehardballtimes.com
World Heritage Encyclopedia
nfoplease.com
espn.com
Boxing History: Louis Crushes Schmeling—Robert Ecksel
Bleacherreport.com
Alsa.org
Ask History—reddit
Sean Lahman's Baseball Database
This Day in History

The National Archives
The Constitution Daily
FiveThirtyEight
SportsEncyclopedia.com

News Media
The New York Times
The Kansas City Star
The Eagle Tribune—Massachusetts and New Hampshire
Liberty Magazine
The Associated Press

Source Notes

Chapter 1

Zach Schonbrun, "The Batter's Box Gets a Little Boring," *New York Times*, July 21, 2016. Accessed January 7, 2018. http://www.nytimes.com/2016/07/24/sports/baseball/the-batters-box-gets-a-little-boring.html.

Chapter 2

James P. Dawson, "Cards Halt Yanks as Frisch Excels; Manager Gets Four of Team's 14 Hits in 8 to 7 Victory—Broaca, Pearson Pounded. DiMaggio Has Great Day His Four Safeties Include a Triple in First Interclub Game—Ruffing in Stands," *New York Times*, March 18, 1936, 36

Tom Clavin, *The DiMaggios: Three Brothers, Their Passion for Baseball, Their Pursuit of the American Dream* (New York: HarperCollins Publishers, 2013).

Joe DiMaggio, *Baseball for everyone: a treasury of baseball lore and instruction for fans and players* (New York: McGraw-Hill, 1948).

Larry Schwartz, "Joltin' Joe was a Hit for All Reasons," ESPN.com, accessed January 7, 2018, http://www.espn.com/sportscentury/features/00014162.html.

Jim Murray, "His Dignity and Style Add to the Legend," *LA Times*, July 7, 1994, http://articles.latimes.com/1994-07-07/sports/sp-12911_1_joe-dimaggio.

Chapter 3

Lew Freedman, *DiMaggio's Yankees: A History of the 1936–1944 Dynasty* (Jefferson, NC: McFarland & Company, 2011).

Chris Lamb, "Public Slur in 1938 Laid Bare a Game's Racism," *New York Times*, July 27, 2008. Accessed January 7, 2018. http://www.nytimes.com/2008/07/27/sports/baseball/27powell.html.

Westbrook Pegler, "We Need Pictures Like These to Make Us Realize," *Athens Messenger*, August 5, 1938, 4.

Ray Robinson, "Jackie Robinson and a Barrier Unbroken," *New York Times*, May 18, 2013. Accessed January 7, 2018. http://www.nytimes.com/2013/05/19/sports/baseball/jackie-robinson-and-a-barrier-unbroken.html.

Chapter 4

David Halberstam, *Summer of '49* (New York: Perennial Classics, 2002), 56.

Lawrence Baldassaro, *Beyond DiMaggio: Italian Americans in Baseball* (Lincoln, NE: University of Nebraska Press, 2011), 84.

Chapter 6

Joseph Durso, "Joe McCarthy, Yanks' Ex-Manager, Dies at 90," *New York Times*, January 14, 1978, 24. http://www.nytimes.com

/1978/01/14/archives/joe-mccarthy-yanks-exmanager-dies-at
-90-a-conservative-manager-a.html.

Chapter 7

Cort Vitty, "Red Rolfe," Society for American Baseball Research. Accessed January 8, 2018. https://sabr.org/bioproj/person/f388510d.

Bill Burt, "The Tragic Story of Johnny Broaca," *Lawerence Eagle-Tribune*, May 16, 2010. Accessed January 8, 2018. http://www.eagletribune.com/news/the-tragic-story-of-johnny-broaca/article_7253d2d1-f6e8-5ad0-b717-0105ddd168a0.html.

Chapter 9

Joe DiMaggio, "1938's Baseball Surprises," *Liberty*, April 23, 1938, 14–15.

Joseph Durso, *DiMaggio: The Last American Knight* (New York: Little Brown & Co., 1995).

Dan Daniel, "Daniel's Dope," *New York World-Telegram*, September 20, 1938.

Chapter 11

Ben Walker, "'Old Reliable' Henrich Dies at 96," *Rutland Herald*, December 2, 2009. Accessed January 9, 2018. http://www.rutlandherald.com/articles/old-reliable-henrich-dies-at-96/.

Frank Graham, *The New York Yankees: An Informal History* (New York: G.P. Putnam's Sons, 1946).

Chapter 12

Marty Appel, *Pinstripe Empire: The New York Yankees from Before the Babe to After the Boss* (New York: Bloomsbury, 2014), 200–01.

Geoffry C. Ward and Ken Burns, *Baseball: An Illustrated History* (New York: Alfred A. Knopf Inc., 1996), 51.

Chapter 14

James P. Dawson, "Gehrig Voluntarily Ends Streak at 2,130 Games," *New York Times*, May 3, 1939.

Richard Goldstein, "Babe Dahlgren, 84, Successor to Gehrig When Streak Ended," *New York Times*, September 6, 1996. Accessed January 9, 2018. http://www.nytimes.com/1996/09/06/sports/babe-dahlgren-84-successor-to-gehrig-when-streak-ended.html.

Matt Dahlgren, *Rumor in Town: A Grandson's Promise to Right A Wrong* (California: Woodlyn Lane, 2007), 115.

Murray Chass, "Rumors of Drug Use Have Damaged for Decades," *New York Times*, November 18, 2007. http://www.nytimes.com/2007/11/18/sports/baseball/18chass.html.

Chapter 15

Vahe Gregorian, "On Gehrig Anniversary, George Brett, Tom Watson, John Dorsey Share Sorrows of ALS," *Kansas City Star*, June 6, 2018. Accessed January 8, 2018. http://www.kansascity.com/sports/spt-columns-blogs/vahe-gregorian/article497802/On-Gehrig-anniversary-George-Brett-Tom-Watson-John-Dorsey-share-sorrows-of-ALS.html.

Falon Wagner, "An Icy Challenge That Brings Awareness to ALS," *Claresholm Local Press*, September 10, 2014.

Chapter 16
Cort Vitty, "Marius Russo," Society for American Baseball Research. Accessed January 8, 2018. https://sabr.org/bioproj /person/f12997d8.
"Luckiest Man," National Baseball Hall of Fame. Accessed January 9, 2018. https://baseballhall.org/discover/lou-gehrig -luckiest-man.
Shirley Povich, "This Morning With Shirley Povich: 'Iron Horse' Breaks as Athletic Greats Meet in His Honor," *Washington Post*, July 4, 1939.

Chapter 18
Lynne Olson, *Those Angry Days: Roosevelt, Lindbergh, and America's Fight over World War II, 1939–1941* (New York: Random House, 2013).
Milton Gross, "Charlie Keller's Comeback," Sportfolio, September 1948.

Chapter 19
"Ernie Lombardi," National Baseball Hall of Fame. Accessed January 9, 2018. https://baseballhall.org/hof/lombardi-ernie.
Marty Appel, *Pinstripe Empire: The New York Yankees from Before the Babe to After the Boss* (New York: Bloomsbury, 2014), 215.

Epilogue

Hank Greenberg with Ira Berkow, *The Story of My Life* (Chicago: Ivan Dee Publishers, 2001), 58.

Other Bibliography

Anderson, Dave, ed. *New York Times Story of the Yankees: 382 Articles, Profiles and Essays from 1903 to Present*. New York: Black Dog & Leventhal Publishers, 2012.

Charyn, Jerome. *Joe DiMaggio: The Long Vigil*. New Haven & London: Yale University Press, 2011.

Hubler, David E. and Joshua H. Drazen. *The Nats and the Grays: How Baseball in the Nation's Capital Survived WWII and Changed the Game Forever*. Lanham, MD: Rowman & Littlefield, 2015.

Reichler, Joseph L., ed. *The Baseball Encyclopedia*. New York: Macmillan Publishing Company, New York, 1985.

Tofel, Richard J. *A Legend in the Making: The New York Yankees in 1939*. Chicago: Ivan R. Dee, 2002.

A Note of Appreciation

My friend Rich Warous proofread the manuscript chapter-by-chapter with care and discernment.

Herman Graf, my long-ago classmate and publisher of my most recent books, kept tabs on my progress and offered some welcome and useful advice as I proceeded.

Kimberley Lim, assistant editor at Skyhorse, line edited the manuscript with customary insight and precision.

Sean Sabo proofread the manuscript with great care and discernment.